TEACHING BODIES

Teaching Bodies

Moral Formation in the *Summa* of Thomas Aquinas

Mark D. Jordan

FORDHAM UNIVERSITY PRESS

New York 2017

Fordham University Press has no responsibility for the
persistence or accuracy of URLs for external or third-party
Internet websites referred to in this publication and does
not guarantee that any content on such websites is, or will
remain, accurate or appropriate.

Fordham University Press also publishes its books in a
variety of electronic formats. Some content that appears in
print may not be available in electronic books.
Visit us online at www.fordhampress.com.

Library of Congress Cataloging-in-Publication Data
Names: Jordan, Mark D., author.
Title: Teaching bodies : moral formation in the Summa of Thomas Aquinas
/ Mark D. Jordan.
Description: First edition. | New York, NY : Fordham University Press, 2017.
| Includes bibliographical references and index.
Identifiers: LCCN 2016015037 | ISBN 9780823273782 (cloth : alk. paper) | ISBN
9780823273799 (pbk. : alk. paper)
Subjects: LCSH: Thomas, Aquinas, Saint, 1225?–1274. Summa theologica. |
Ethics, Medieval.
Classification: LCC B765.T53 S8165 2017 | DDC 230/.2—dc23
LC record available at https://lccn.loc.gov/2016015037

Printed in the United States of America
19 18 17   5 4 3 2 1
First edition

CONTENTS

PREFACE

I may have read a few words from the *Summa of Theology* for the first time in middle school. They were a quotation, in English, from the "five ways," the rational ascents to God that help to begin Thomas's book—and that become for some its only memorable passage. I was writing a wistful term paper on medieval religious orders and found the quotation (or was it only a paraphrase?) in a popular panorama of medieval history. A few years later, when I was fifteen or sixteen and deliberating conversion, I began to study Jacques Maritain and Etienne Gilson, champions of paired Thomisms from the last century. Only in college was I encouraged to read as much Thomas as I could. I even took my first steps into his Latin, guided by the Blackfriars edition that put the comfort of the English on facing pages. Two years later, I went off to graduate school in philosophy to become a licensed teacher of Thomas because it seemed the only practical way to buy more time for reading him. Perhaps I also wanted for a while to become a Dominican—or at least a Jesuit. Clearly, I had already absorbed some of the old rivalries among Thomas's interpreters.

All of this took place decades ago. I tell it now on the way to asking what it means to read and reread the *Summa* for a long time—the time of a moral formation, a mortal life, or an interpretive tradition. These questions can be put to any book read over decades, but they apply especially to the *Summa* since they are also its central concerns. From the book's prologue forward, Thomas urges readers to consider moral reading as moral shaping. His insistence raises many questions. Which dispositions does the *Summa* suppose in those who would read it seriously? How does it understand its own role in eliciting or fostering those dispositions? What changes does it hope to encourage over a properly long reading? These questions are topics for the *Summa* itself. They animate its plan and determine its topics. They reveal the unity in the *Summa* of form and content, purpose and procedure.

Pursuing these questions, I will sometimes contend with what I judge to be misreadings. The word "misreading" may itself mislead. My concern is not so much with mistakes in construing terms, syntax, images, or arguments. The mistakes that matter most are distorted relations to Thomas's whole effort of teaching. They often result from approaching the text with the wrong assumptions about how and what it teaches. For example, many contemporary readers twist their relation to the *Summa* by failing to negotiate the ways in which it is official, antiquated, and demanding.

During centuries, the *Summa* has been *official*. For some contemporary readers, Thomas Aquinas defines correct Christianity—nothing less but also nothing more. This conviction leads some readers to follow Thomas only so long as he agrees with their formulas for orthodoxy or their programs for the Church. Yet, one imperative for establishing a pedagogical relation with the *Summa* is to disentangle it from both its official uses and current doctrinal quarrels.

Disentangling Thomas from his official exponents or advocates is not easy. Generations of authorized interpreters have promoted expectations about what his books must mean. Thomas has now got assigned roles to play in cultural histories inside and outside Christian churches. He is the great synthesizer who reconciled reason with faith—or at least Aristotle with Augustine. He is the grand architect of the culminating hierarchy of all arts and sciences—at least those known to the Latin-speaking Middle Ages. He is chief among the Scholastics but therefore also the leading Inquisitor. The *Summa* is, Lacordaire once said, a "masterpiece that everyone talks about, even those who do not read it, just as everyone talks about the Egyptian pyramids, which almost no one has seen."[1] A book that many "know" and few read is hard to approach with fresh attention.

The official appropriations of Thomas and the cultural narratives about him can conceal a second distortion of relation to the text: Thomas's texts are now *antiquated*. The *Summa* is separated from contemporary readers by a long series of cultural dislocations. Many pages are studded with unfamiliar terms and outdated sciences. On other pages, there are now obnoxious prejudices about social groups or political arrangements. More pervasively, if more subtly, Thomas practices forms of reasoning that contemporary readers have been taught to distrust.

During the last century and a half (to go no further back), the official appropriation of Thomas was countered by an emphasis on his historical distance—on his antiquity. The emphasis sponsored programs of historical recovery on every textual level. Uncertain lines of textual transmission were retraced in order to establish a better sense of the words that Thomas might actually have written. His sources were recovered and reconstituted. His interlocutors and successors were brought forward to speak again. Instead of presenting Thomas in a false present, every effort was made to underline his historical otherness. His texts were scoured of encrustations to produce the shock of the old.

Like many readers of Thomas now alive, I depend on these efforts at historical recovery. I also notice how quickly they can generate another sort of distortion. They can make it seem that the *Summa* was written in order to yield historical knowledge. Wanting to fit the book back into "its time" (as if there had been only one), historically minded readers often assume that it was at home there. They presume, for example, that the *Summa* would have been immediately recognizable to Thomas's contemporaries. This understates the book's novelty. It also misses the demands that the book places on readers in any age. In many ways, the *Summa* stands against whatever might be called "its time," not least because it wants to indict and then reform its readers' moral education.[2] The book's first audiences were certainly better placed than contemporary readers are to handle its technical terminologies, to recognize its sources, and to move within its genres. For that very reason early audiences found it hard to accept Thomas's boldest innovations. There is abundant evidence that the *Summa* was misread and rejected from the beginning by expert readers—indeed, by its main addressees.[3] They, too, faltered before the third cause of distorted relation: The *Summa* is a *demanding* text. Its main hope is to make moral demands on its readers.

The *Summa* is official, antiquated, and demanding. Reading it responsibly requires ongoing negotiations between its pedagogical hopes and our diverse dispositions. Because our dispositions *are* diverse, the negotiations will issue in different results. To complain of distorted relations to the text is not to imply that there is only one correct relation leading to one result. To speak of moral education is not to predict a single progress in it. I assume that engaged readers may well disagree about what the *Summa* says just as they disagree about the application to an actual case of natural law or scriptural precedent or prudential judgment. I further admit that a long and fully attentive reading of the *Summa* may issue in a negative judgment. A reader may refuse the moral teaching that Thomas offers. She may even be repulsed by it.[4] Engaged readings that end with rejection seem to me greatly preferable to readings that treat the *Summa* only as a source of "information." Thomas's book most wants to lead its reader to a way of life more articulate about its movement toward God. That relation of reading will thus be as personal as any vocation.

I can illustrate the point exegetically in a final recollection. When, as a college sophomore, I was trying so eagerly to make myself all at once the best possible reader of Thomas Aquinas, I wrote a letter to Bernard Lonergan. I did not know him, of course. My only claim to a connection was that I had stumbled upon his collected articles on Thomas's doctrine of the inner word or *verbum*.[5] I doubt that I understood a twentieth of what Lonergan wrote, and I shudder to think what confusions I may have typed out. With a generosity that astonishes me more each year, Lonergan took time to answer me. On a single-spaced page, he gave advice about reading Thomas. The advice condensed his actual reading practice in the *verbum* articles and other interpretive works. Having recommended that I gather passages from various texts by Thomas around several topics, he counseled: "List such passages. Read them. Determine what they say. Compare them."[6]

In the years following, I tried to follow Lonergan's advice. I grew to appreciate the subtlety of his emphasis on the mirroring processes in Thomas's writing and in any serious reading (as Lonergan would go on to show throughout *Method in Theology*).[7] Thomas's texts are not calcified monuments to some accomplished system. They are repeated efforts to write out an inquiry at the edge of human language and the center of human desire. Readers will see that I still cling to this part of Lonergan's advice. But I have also come to appreciate that it is possible to respect or even revere another reader of Thomas without wanting to imitate exactly. So, in recent years—and especially in this book—I relapse to my original desire in reading Thomas. I do *not* want to understand the mutations in Thomas's writing on a single topic over time. My desire is the opposite. I want to understand his writing of singular texts—and most of all the *Summa*.

Introduction. The *Summa*'s Origins: Three Fables and a Candid Counterproposal

Some readers begin to negotiate with a text by reflecting on what can be known of its origins. I agree with them this far: Fables about the origin of the *Summa* can indeed allow us to expand our imagination of the book's purposes. They help us to take up a useful relation to it—to practice undistorted attention.

I call them "fables" to emphasize that even the most plausible historical account depends on both factual suppositions and the formulas for a good story. They are fables in the plural because they are stories about three different origins for the *Summa*. They situate the book within Thomas's biographical and institutional circumstances, the series of his compositional experiments leading up to it, and the textual elements out of which he chose to compose it. After retelling these fables about the *Summa*'s origin, I will propose an unusual order for reading it now.

A First Fable: The Summa's Circumstances

Thomas opens the *Summa* with the briefest of prologues on the obligations of the Christian teacher (1 pro).[1] The teacher is obliged to provide not only for the accomplished but also for those just beginning. So the intention of the *Summa* is to "deliver what belongs to the Christian religion (*Christiana religio*) in the way that befits the teaching of beginners (*incipientes*)." Readers and commentators sometimes suppose that "religion" means doctrine and that the "beginners" have undertaken to study it academically. They hear Thomas promising a survey of academic theology for university students. In Thomas, the key words have other meanings.[2] Later in the *Summa*, Thomas will use "religion" to name both a virtue of devotion to God and the vowed ways of life, the "religious orders" as they are still called (2-2.81–91, 2-2.186–189). Using "religion" in the preface to the *Summa*, he also recalls the prologue to the earliest Dominican constitutions.[3] "Beginners" might then refer to those in early stages of religious formation—to "novices," as Thomas will call his intended readers a few lines later. Such beginners need teaching that offers effective truth about their divine destination but also for their ministries. So Thomas's prologue continues with criticism of theological books that fail to offer it. They multiply "useless questions, articles, and arguments."[4] They do not proceed according to an appropriate order of study. They produce both "distaste and confusion" through pointless repetition. The *Summa*, by contrast, promises to teach "briefly and clearly" only what is useful, according to an appropriate order, and without frustrating duplication.[5] It will include only what is pedagogically needful to beginners in Christian religion—or so the prologue promises.

The promise is not a dull cliché. When he undertakes to teach beginners only what they need, Thomas endorses a pedagogical style that is at once diagnosis and prescription. Let me call it "minimalist," though I immediately acknowledge that the word is alien to Thomas.[6] Thomas's minimalist pedagogy produces stylistic effects by repeated selection, by deliberate omission and rearrangement. When Thomas assumes this style as an obligation for teaching, he sets it before the reader as an ideal of learning. The reader should find in the *Summa*'s selection means for moving beyond "useless questions, articles, and arguments." In this book, brevity and clarity are not the assurance of positivist intuition. They are ways of opening an uncluttered path so that the reader can hasten toward what cannot yet be seen or spoken.

The deliberateness of what I am calling Thomas's minimalism can be verified in the discoverable circumstances of the *Summa*'s composition. Here is one fable to be told from the evidence. In 1265, around the age of forty, Thomas was assigned by his province of the Dominicans to open a house of studies in Rome—perhaps at his own suggestion.[7] The assignment was not abrupt: He had already been teaching for six years in Dominican houses throughout central Italy. Now he was asked to open his own school as a sort of bridge between ordinary pastoral training and advanced academic study. During his first year at Rome, Thomas tried to redo his commentary on the *Sentences* of Peter Lombard. As part of his own licensing as a teacher of theology, he had already commented in Paris on this recently prescribed text. He had used that earlier occasion, as most did, to present impressive solutions to inherited technical problems. At Rome, he proceeded more simply, excluding both his own elaborations and many advanced topics. Still, after revisiting parts of the Lombard's first book, Thomas turned to something simpler still—to the book that would become the *Summa*. His decision is surprising. Besides being a set university text, Peter Lombard's order of topics was recognizably a variation on the structure of the Nicene Creed, that venerable form for Christian catechesis. Why not prepare beginners by taking them through the creedal pattern as reflected in a standard textbook?

In the *Summa*'s prologue, Thomas faults theologians who follow the sequence required by the exposition of an authoritative text without consulting the needs of beginners. The complaint only makes sense if the sequence of the underlying text is in fact unsuitable for them. It is not hard to fill in the implied judgment about Peter Lombard. The Nicene Creed contains no moral code and little sacramental prescription. While those omissions are justified by the creed's original uses, they become significant defects when its pattern is adopted as a comprehensive organization of theological topics. Peter Lombard tries to overcome the defects by distributing moral topics over the creedal pattern. He cuts up teaching on human action and detaches the incarnation from the sacraments of Christian life.

Thomas rejects the Lombard's compromise when he invents the *Summa*. He begins by dividing his new work into three parts. The first treats God's essence and the distinction of persons in the Trinity, God as exemplar, and the creatures that proceed from God. The second part considers "the motion of the rational creature towards God" (1.2 pro). It is further divided into two sections. The first of them presents moral matter generally or "universally": the end of human life, the elements of properly human action, and the intrinsic or extrinsic principles of human acts. The second section surveys moral questions compendiously under the headings of the main virtues before integrating them into ways of life. *Summa* 3 presents Christ as the way by which the rational creature can reach God. The portion of this last part that Thomas finished teaches the appropriateness of divine incarnation, the lessons of Christ's earthly life, and the efficacy of his sacraments as extensions of his saving work. Thomas broke off writing at 3.90.4, in the middle of the discussion of the sacrament of penance. He had promised to proceed from it to the sacraments of orders and matrimony before ending with immortal life. His own death intervened.

Even in such bald summary, the structure of the *Summa* evidently improves on Lombard's *Sentences*—especially for the formation of preachers and confessors. First, Thomas's pattern unifies the treatment of moral matter, while distinguishing more cogently between elements or principles (2-1) and composite actions (2-2). Second, it brings together incarnation and sacraments in a continuous divine communication (3). Third, the *Summa* shows the usefulness of the whole of theology to the soul's motion toward God. The intended reader of the *Summa* is not a remote spectator so much as a participant in salvation history already underway.

The *Summa* reorients the received topics of theology toward the predicament of human souls. Even in the first part, there are more questions about creatures than about God, more about human beings than about the Trinity. The entire second part is a moral consideration of human life. In the third part, the *Summa* then devotes as many questions to a moralized retelling of gospel events as to the metaphysics of the incarnation, and it gives more questions still to the sacraments as extensions of Christ's saving work (incomplete as that section remains). Evidently the beginners who are Thomas's intended readers most need from theology what it can teach them about their return to God. Their need justifies the very existence of the body of knowledge called "theology." Human beings must be instructed by divine revelation about how to reach their end "more appropriately and certainly" (1.1.1).[8]

I keep punning, as Thomas does, on "beginners." The word refers to a class of Dominican learners. It also names the condition of all human beings before divine teaching. To say that the *Summa* was aimed at a pedagogical challenge for Dominicans in the thirteenth century is not to say that it was a temporary solution to a local problem. The largest quandaries of human learning present themselves time after time in particular classrooms or lives. Augustine's *Confessions* is not useful only for Carthaginian rhetoricians who convert after their mothers have forced them onto the marriage market. So, too, the specificity of the *Summa*'s original circumstances, like the historical particularity of divine incarnation, limits neither its address nor its effects.

Emphasizing the *Summa*'s pedagogy, I do not settle its relation to Thomas's classroom teaching. It is not clear how exactly he intended to use the text once completed. The abandoned exposition of the Lombard's *Sentences* in Rome looks to be a register of classroom teaching. Is that also true for the parts of the *Summa* he composed there? If so, then Thomas had already displaced Peter Lombard from his classroom, since the *Summa* is not a good supplement to the *Sentences*. Did Thomas intend the once completed *Summa* as a self-contained text that could be reviewed as a complete curriculum? This is in fact what happened some centuries on but only after many other changes in the conception of theology—and of Thomas. Or did Thomas see the *Summa* as a sort of outline, a skeleton, to be filled in with other authorities, arguments, and cases? The fable of circumstances does not settle these questions.

A Second Fable: Thomas's Experiments in Writing Theology

If a work of theology responds to the needs of a particular audience, it is also an episode in a theologian's efforts to write the unwritable. The *Summa* has a second origin in the succession of Thomas's compositions. He wrote it after trying four other experiments with curricula for the whole of theology.

The first form that Thomas used for gathering and arranging theological speech was his required commentary on the *Sentences* of Peter Lombard. Thomas's *Scriptum* or "writing" on the *Sentences* is his first experiment with a pattern both for organizing and for producing theological speech. It remains the axis or standard against which he thinks the problem of theological curriculum. Following his academic predecessors, Thomas's *Scriptum* accepts the Lombard's basic pattern while interrupting it at almost every point with new topics, controversies, and authorities. Still the pattern remains as a buried outline—like the *cantus firmus* of a chant under its polyphonic elaboration.

The second pattern Thomas tested was the corpus of Boethius. For medieval theologians, Boethius was not only or chiefly the author of the *Consolation of Philosophy* and some commentaries on Aristotle. His name was attached to a group of short theological treatises. In what might seem an excess of charitable reading, Thomas takes these treatises as a pattern for the whole of theology, divided into three movements.[9] The first movement of Boethian theology treats the Trinity as unity and as three persons. The second movement considers the procession of good creatures from the good God. The third movement traces the reparation of creatures in Christ. Having found this pattern in the treatises and commented on (parts of) two of them, Thomas abandoned the project of a Boethian theology. I suspect that his reason was the still obvious one. While the compiled treatises join saving faith to the means of incarnation, they make no room for an account of moral life or moral education by sacraments.

Thomas's third experiment in theological order turned to the corpus of Ps-Dionysius the Areopagite. In his commentary on the *Divine Names*, he explains how to read the corpus as a complete model for theology.[10] His explanation repeats Dionysius' own account in *Mystical Theology* 3 of the relation between four books, two of them missing, that recapitulate all the names of God only to deny them in reverse. (Thomas does not include in his enumeration the books on the celestial or ecclesiastical hierarchies, though he certainly knew them.) Thomas's commentary on Dionysius begins with the *Divine Names*, but it becomes increasingly perfunctory after the early chapters. He does not proceed to comment on *Mystical Theology*. Perhaps he was stopped by the missing books—the phantom books. It is hard to use the Dionysian corpus as a pattern for theological writing without filling them in. It is impossible to use the Dionysian corpus to teach theology to Dominicans without getting to the celestial and ecclesiastical hierarchies on the other side of the gaps.

Thomas's fourth experiment with the arrangement of theological speech was more striking, though it might be read as a distant variation on Anselm's project in the *Monologion*. The work is traditionally called the *Summa against the Gentiles*, though its original title was probably something more like *On the Truth of the Catholic Faith*. In it, Thomas proposes to present first the truths that can be explored by reason and only then those that require revelation. Thomas disagrees with Anselm about where to draw that line. For Thomas, Trinity, incarnation, sacraments, and the final events of history (or beyond it) require divine revelation in order to be known. They are put into Book 4. The preceding books move through all the other topics as far as reason can reach them. The originality of this division suggests that Thomas had already decided to rearrange the inherited creedal patterns. He had also decided to gather moral material into a single treatment, Book 3, which begins with the human end and culminates in ways of life under divine grace. Still the plan of the *Against the Gentiles* is unstable. The blurring of the work's basic distinction between reason and revelation in Book 3 shows that it is impossible to treat human life fully without revelation. Indeed, in *Against the Gentiles* Thomas risks promulgating another version of the Lombard's separation of morals from Incarnation and sacraments. Certainly he did not regard it as his final effort to write theology at large scale. Sent to Rome only a year or two later, he began the teaching that would lead him to the *Summa of Theology*. At least that is the title we think he gave it.[11]

Does the title tell us anything about what his new plan added to his earlier experiments? It would be tidy to think that the *Summa against the Gentiles* was somehow perfected as a *Summa of Theology*. Unfortunately, there is good reason to suspect the first title, and even some reason to doubt the second. If *Summa of Theology* is in fact the title that Thomas preferred, little can be learned from it. *Summa* is hardly a precise genre-term.

Thomas typically uses *summa* and related terms as adjectives to mean highest or best. As nouns applied to segments of text, they usually name the result of condensing. Sometimes in Thomas a *summa* is a summary solution or conclusion.[12] At other times, it is gathered out of particulars or specifics.[13] In a related sense, it can be what is essential in the Scriptures, a sacrament, a creed, or a prayer.[14] A *summa* can also be an outline or overview of something complicated. In these cases, the word is roughly synonymous with *capitulatim*, which means rehearsing chapters-headings without going into details.[15] There is only a short step to using *summa* to express brevity, at times even the false brevity that omits actually indispensable elements.[16] Indeed, Thomas sometimes contrasts the abbreviated discourse of a *summa* for advanced students with the slower, more discursive instruction needed by beginners—roughly the opposite of what this *Summa*'s prologue promises.[17] At other times, the compression of teaching in a *summa* is so great that it becomes opaque or oracular.[18] Adopted as a title, then, a *summa* for Thomas might promise a set of conclusions or of generalities; it might refer to a statement of the essential; it might introduce an outline or a brief summary or even a partial overview. If we put this title into the sequence of Thomas's compositions, we could perhaps say this much: the *Summa of Theology* concerns the whole of theology, simplified for beginners without too much compression. Or we might say that it is a work about how to foresee the wholeness of theology near its beginning—which is where every mortal reader stands.

The *Summa of Theology* does share some of these features with the *Summa against the Gentiles*. What is more important, Thomas's last two experiments in theological writing agree in a fundamental compositional choice. They do not follow the order of any existing text—not Boethius, not Ps-Dionysius, and not Peter Lombard. They choose instead to trace a new curriculum for the reader. In the *Summa against the Gentiles*, the curriculum moves by persuasive stages from the truths that embodied reason can reach to those that it must receive in revelation.[19] In its successor, the *Summa of Theology*, the textual curriculum retraces the creedal pattern now opened to an exploration of moral matters that the creeds seem to presuppose without enumerating. The arc of Thomas's experiments begins with the Lombard's creedal patterns to end with their thorough reworking.

The originality of the *Summa* can be highlighted by comparisons with other authors. For example, it can be helpful to juxtapose the *Summa* to other grand works of Dominican learning, like the scriptural annotations, emendations, and concordances of Hugh of St. Cher; the encyclopedic *Mirror* of Vincent of Beauvais; the *Summas of Vices and Virtues* by William Peraldus; or the digest of decretals and *Summa of Cases* by Raymond of Peñafort. Among other things, this series of comparisons shows that Thomas's *Summa* is not (or not only) a reference work. More interesting comparisons are possible with experiments by other authors eager to integrate morals into theological teaching. The years during which Thomas conceived and wrote the *Summa* also yielded Roger Bacon's *Greater Work* (*Opus majus*, 1267–68) and Bonaventure's university conferences that culminated in the *Collations on the Six Days of Creation* (*Collationes in Hexaëmeron*, 1273–74). While these works also situate morals within a larger wisdom that is not ordered by the creedal pattern, they differ significantly from the *Summa* in sources, structures, and scale.

A Third Fable: The Summa's Choice of Textual Elements

The fables about the *Summa*'s circumstances and its place in the sequence of Thomas's compositional experiments correct some common assumptions about it. They draw attention to its insistent concern with moral and pastoral matters. They point to its improvisations in response to pedagogical needs. They direct a reader to selection and sequence. Still, the fables can also mislead a reader into thinking that the questions about the *Summa* are solved by looking outside it. Even if we knew the circumstances of the work's composition better than we do, even if we understood much more about Thomas's compositional choices, we would still have to ask how the pedagogical intentions of the *Summa* operate through its text. We need a third fable—corresponding to a third meaning of textual origin: the elements out which a text is composed. What are the textual units with which Thomas makes the *Summa*?

Some Thomistic commentators like to praise the *Summa*'s orderliness. One can start with the prologue to the second question in the first part, they claim, and then proceed through all the subsequent divisions without a slip or stutter. In fact, there are a few difficulties of consistency. Some questions appear in transposed order.[20] In a few other places, questions are inserted without explicit justification.[21] What is much more important, heuristic structures are rearranged without comment depending on cases. The relation between the consideration of virtues and their opposed vices changes markedly depending on the number and kind of the virtue's parts. The opposed vices are mentioned in the main enumeration of topics under faith, hope, and prudence (respectively. 2-2.1 pro, 17 pro, and 47 pro). They are not mentioned for charity, justice, fortitude, or temperance (2-2.23 pro, 57 pro, 123 pro, 141 pro). To do so would be unwieldy: the last four are also the longest treatments in *Summa* 2-2.

These can be regarded as slips, I suppose, and then excused by saying that even Thomas nods. Of course, there would be no need for excuses if we abandoned the notion that the *Summa* is a uniform deductive system. This notion is favored especially by commentators who want to identify Thomas with Aristotle and then reduce Aristotelian "method" to some remarks on demonstration in the logical works. It is notoriously true that Aristotle himself hardly followed the model of deduction when he (or his students) wrote his masterworks. How much less likely is it that Thomas, who was writing a *summa* of theology encompassing dozens of forms of argument, would confine himself to a philosophical idealization of the syllogism? His *Summa* is not a demonstrative system meant to transport the reader from beginning to end by irresistible deduction.[22] If there are many deductions in it, they do not form a single system. More: They are not the text's main motive. Readers move from the beginning of the *Summa* to its end by rational desire rather than deduction.

Another misunderstanding lurks here, in a familiar suggestion about the text's teleology. At least from the late 1930s on, Marie-Dominique Chenu argued that the *Summa* followed the great arc of *exitus* and *reditus*, the transit of all creatures from a divine origin back to a divine end.[23] As Chenu understood perfectly well, this arc is hardly unique to the *Summa*. Thomas himself explicitly invokes *exitus/reditus* to explain the division into four books of Peter Lombard's *Sentences*.[24] The pattern was a commonplace of theological composition. Adopting it, Thomas affirmed the traditional notion that a work of theology ought to narrate a redemptive history, not least as an ideal curriculum for its readers. Unfortunately, some readers go much further. They take Chenu as suggesting both that Thomas invented the *exitus/reditus* pattern and that it works as the *Summa*'s only structuring rationale. The difficulty here is that Thomas refers only rarely to the commonplace.[25] It applies to his text only abstractly, in summaries. The actual pedagogy must be worked out from page to page, as readers learn their way from one article to another.[26] A reader is drawn through the *Summa* dialectically, by a series of rational persuasions that address a changeable series of doubts and questions. This dialectical motion is written into every level of the *Summa*'s structure, from the smallest to the largest.[27]

The articles in the *Summa* abbreviate a standard pattern of medieval teaching, the public dispute. In Thomas's universities, disputation was instruction spoken to be heard. (Considered in this way, his articles share more with the Platonic dialogues or the discourses of Epictetus than with the modern treatise or textbook.) Whether performed *viva voce* or imitated in writing, a dispute is a device for arranging and judging contrary precedents on a controverted issue. It is a scene of instruction in which the contradictions or confusions of traditions are laid before a teacher for public resolution. Common across medieval disciplines, this form of teaching is obvious for an intellectual community that learns from authoritative texts.[28] (It has more affinities with the Talmud or with Aristotelian dialectic than with strict demonstration.) By Thomas's time at Paris, the form for disputing had been ritualized and expanded. A full-scale dispute took two days and assigned participants to distinct roles, all presided over by the *magister regens*, the master who would settle the controversy. One privilege conferred by the license to teach theology that Thomas earned at Paris was this power to preside.

Thomas did indeed lead several series of public disputes that he then edited for publication. They explore knotted controversies, with inherited arguments for and against each point often running into the dozens. For the *Summa*, Thomas reduces controversy to its schematic minimum— most often three or four "arguments" (or "objections") against the view he will sustain, one argument for it ("on the contrary"), a very short determination of the issue, and then succinct replies to the opening arguments.[29] This is the most obvious application of Thomas's promise of pedagogical minimalism.

The arguments typically represent different points of view, and they often rely on authorities that are not consistent except in their conclusion. Thomas often selects these views and authorities from previous works of theology, but he insists on giving a good sample of possible arguments around a point. He counters these authorities with his own selection to the contrary, which he may also have inherited along with the topic. I stress the inheritance of language in topics, authorities, and argument because it is the underlying motive for the article form.[30] Indeed, it is worth recalling the obvious: the "body" of every article begins with the phrase, "I answer that it should be said that . . . " The magisterial determination that follows resolves a conflict of authorities by proposing a way to speak amid inherited vocabularies. It is a prudential judgment upon contending grammars.

Each article moves from the arguments through the reasoning "On the contrary" to the determination of the "I answer that . . . " Some readers forget that the comments on the objections are an indispensable next step. In the replies, Thomas qualifies or applies principles that he has enunciated. He does the same over a sequence of articles. No article is meant to stand on its own. A group of articles is carefully composed into a question.[31] Within a single question, there is often an important progression through the articles. Simple distinctions or models proposed in early articles are amended in later ones. The same is true from one question to the next. Later questions in a sequence can qualify or correct initial views of the topic. So, for example, the description of the New Law stretches and in some ways undoes the overly neat definition of law proposed fifteen questions earlier (compare 2-1.106–108 with 2-1.90).

In other writing, Thomas sometimes abandons the question form altogether, as he had done successfully in *Against the Gentiles* and as he would do again in the *Compendium of Theology*. Why does he keep the form of dispute in the *Summa*? Perhaps he wanted to accustom his readers to the argumentative procedures prevailing in academic theology. He may also have judged that even a simplified imitation of living dispute is the safest form for theological reflection on inherited texts. The dialectical play of the articles within a question mirrors the motion of learning that Thomas constructs at much larger scale across the *Summa*. Later readers began to separate groups of questions into "treatises" so that they could separately expound (or elaborate) a "treatise on law" or a "treatise on the sacraments." Not only does this add a layer of textual organization that Thomas refused, it can disrupt his dialectic by cutting between topics. Thomas reduces textual units to propel the reader through the dialectic of the whole.[32] This is another application of his minimalist promise to give the reader only the needful.

In sum, the teaching of the *Summa* traces a narrative arc, a progressive pedagogy. It is not a string of discrete articles alphabetized in an encyclopedia. It is not a series of steps in a system of deductions. It is a curriculum that encourages and represents learning across time—the time of present reasoning about authorities from various times past. In the *Summa*, the standard structure of the individual scene of dispute is reduced in order to accelerate motion along the larger arc. The shape of that arc marks time for a reader. Of course, some readers may need to enter the *Summa* from a very different time.

A Candid Counterproposal: The Varied Times of Embodied Readers

My three fables about the origins of the *Summa* converge on a single conclusion. The circumstances of the work's composition suggest that its structure was a teacher's invention at once particular and general. The place of the *Summa* in the sequence of Thomas's experiments with theological writing at large scale argues the originality and importance of its unified structure of rational persuasion. Thomas's choice of textual elements shows his concern for continuous dialectical sequence. On all three accounts, the signal achievement of the *Summa* is its pedagogy.

The book is teaching for Dominicans but thus for human beings. It aims to form future teachers of moral maturity. Its order of topics must situate practices of caring for souls within traditional professions of Christian faith. Thomas anchors the moral matter of his middle part between two doctrines. He secures it on one side to the creation of human beings as embodied minds. He attaches it on the other side to divine incarnation, the life of Christ, and Christ's legacy of bodily sacraments. This pattern is meant to remind human beings—embodied intelligences with a traumatic history of violent sin—about deeds undertaken in the flesh for their rescue.

The *Summa*'s moral part is framed by expositions of creation and redemption, but it also directs the pedagogy in them. By medieval standards, no single part of the *Summa* is a self-contained treatise of human nature. Indeed, the *Summa* omits a number of topics that medieval readers would have expected, including basic physiology and an account of the senses, outer and inner. As Thomas explains, the theologian studies the details of the human body only so far as it has bearing on the soul, and within the soul attends only to intellect and appetite, for which all other powers are "preambles" (1.75 pro, 78 pro, 84 pro).[33] Thomas divides the properly theological concerns with human nature between the first and second parts of the *Summa* in order to treat them quite differently. He presents the intellect quickly in *Summa* 1. Then, after a cursory introduction to sensory appetite, will, and free choice, Thomas postpones any discussion of their acts into the moral consideration of *Summa* 2-1 (1.84 pro). If the postponement seems awkward, it means to focus the reader's attention on a single point in the first part: The human being is distinguished from other creatures as an intellect that learns through the body. A woman or a man is not an intuitive intellect trapped somehow in soiled flesh from which it should strive to escape. Human beings have abstractive intellects that infer their relation to God from sensory experience (1.85.1). Thomas's selective teaching about human beings emphasizes the cognitive consequences of their embodiment.

The *Summa*'s moral teaching culminates in another embodiment—in the divine incarnation. The most famous objection against the structure of Thomas's *Summa* is that it postpones the appearance of Christ into the third part. How can any properly Christian theology delay so in announcing Christ? A quick reply to the objection is that Christ, his deeds, and his teachings actually appear throughout the *Summa*. He is mentioned in the prologue to the work and then regularly from its first question on.[34] A more extended reply might begin in this way: So far as the *Summa* is preoccupied with the learning of embodied minds, it prepares for Christ's appearance from the doctrine of divine creation onward. Still Thomas must wait until the end of the moral part before he can justify the incarnation most convincingly. It makes no sense for him to assert that God becomes incarnate for the sake of teaching human beings their salvation until it is somewhat clear why human beings require to be saved, from what moral condition and by which moral means.

There is another reply to the objection, perhaps a better one. It lies both inside and outside the text, at the book's expected intersection with readers. The presence of Christ was assured for the *Summa*'s immediate readers by their membership in churches and vowed communities of Christian life. The Christ who is present from hour to hour in liturgical prayer, in the virtues of common life, in mutual acts of charity, in preaching and hearing confessions—that Christ is a constant companion to the reader of the *Summa*.[35] So, in the earlier parts of the *Summa*, Thomas can speak Christ as it were softly—both elliptically and allusively. He builds textual anticipation for the divine response of an incarnation because he can trust that his first readers are reminded in the shape of their daily lives of a God who has already taken flesh and whose flesh becomes present again with each Eucharist.

The *Summa* traces a sequence from the embodiment of human creation through bodily history to divine incarnation. The book further supposes that its readers will be living in bodies sanctified by sacramental grace and tutored by ecclesial formation. The fact that a contemporary reader can describe these expectations in the text does not mean that she can meet them. To recall a pedagogy by means of historical scholarship is not to undergo it. Indeed, insofar as modern historiography descends from the European Enlightenment, historical reconstruction of a theological pedagogy may actually work against any experience of it. As Karl Barth remarked when introducing his reiterated reading of Romans, a critical reconstruction is at best only a preparation for reading an old text—especially a text that makes moral demands on its readers.[36]

Historical distance—the distance of critical historiography—is not erased by the claims of faith. Whatever the continuities of Christian community, they do not make cultural differences disappear. Even if a contemporary reader considers herself a Christian and belongs to a sacramental community—even if she claims to belong to the very same Church that counted Thomas a servant and then a saint—she will inhabit a significantly different Christianity. When she receives the same sacraments, she understands and lives them otherwise.

How then is a contemporary reader to enter into the *Summa*'s pedagogy? This is a question about the relation between the moral curriculum of an old text and the dispositions of contemporary readers. My point is not to solve the question theoretically (whatever that would mean). I hope to address it with a practical counterproposal about how to use a reader's time. I propose to read the parts of the *Summa* backward. The proposal may seem perverse. Having spent so much time arguing the importance of pedagogical sequence in the *Summa*, I now suggest reversing it. Let me offer some preliminary justifications for the counterproposal, while recognizing that any satisfying justification can only come in performing the reading.[37]

A familiar Thomistic maxim advises that you should think an action backward from its end—from the purpose revealed in its completion. The maxim holds for the human activities of teaching and writing. We can understand a pedagogical or compositional sequence only after we reach the end. This is certainly true for any pedagogy as intricate as that of the *Summa of Theology*. But the Thomistic maxim poses a sharp challenge to contemporary readers. We inhabit communities of interpretation quite different from the ones Thomas expects. We are liable to have other notions both of ethics and of the human end. We are not Thomas's beginners; we cannot begin just where his text does. For many of us, if not for all, any beginning must make clear not only the end towards which the teaching of the *Summa* aims but the grounds of bodily teaching on which it proceeds. We urgently require a methodological correction—a pedagogical jolt—in order to enter into the teaching sequences of the *Summa*. One way to jolt our expectations is to begin with Thomas's third part.

If you read the *Summa* beginning with its last part, you begin with the incarnation, the life of Christ, and the Christian sacraments as continuations of that life. For Thomas, moral formation ultimately depends on these scenes of embodied instruction—not on assent to abstract "principles" from which one attempts to make binding deductions. We learn the best way to teach human beings by watching how God taught us. God did not send down a numbered list of moral axioms or a crisply formulated universal imperative. God took flesh. Embodied souls learn through bodies and from bodies. They learn from particular scenes enacted in time. Given the effects of sin in human hearts and human history, these scenes must be both urgent and memorable. Sacraments, too, must both represent and effect new patterns (characters, narratives) for the confused bodies that will share in them. Only when a reader appreciates such a pedagogy can she rightly assemble the elements of the moral account that make up the middle of the *Summa*. Without a vivid reminder of the moral teaching in incarnation and sacraments, the "moral part" of the *Summa* cannot achieve its distinctive effects.

Does this mean that a reader who ignores or rejects the incarnation cannot benefit from reading the *secunda pars*? No. Readers' responses are unpredictable, deeper ones especially so. A reader who disdains the Gospel might turn to Thomas for "purely philosophical" arguments and so begin a conversion. Still, I do argue that the moral part of the *Summa* does not offer a self-contained moral teaching, much less a complete formation. The second part leads to the third: Thomas's rational persuasion to right action is not complete without incarnation and sacraments.

This book has no intention of replacing the *Summa*. I reject the notion that books of moral teaching have contents that can be conveyed, like real estate, by proper documents. The most important content of the *Summa* can only be reproduced in a reader's embodied life. So I hope to help others in their rereading. My best offer of help is a selective study of parts of the *Summa* in an order meant to resist the intellectual prejudices most likely to afflict us. (I apply a similar selectivity with regard to secondary sources, which I treat almost entirely in notes.)[38] If this book works, it will perform an adjustment of expectations—a tuning of readers' ears—after which it ought to be possible to read the *Summa* right through. Or at least to foresee better what such a reading might yield.

Just here we need a little pedagogical candor. In decades of studying Thomas, I have met only few people who claim to have read the *Summa* whole. The *Summa* is extolled as a bulwark of Christian civilization even while almost no one has read it whole. (More surprising still may be how little anyone is embarrassed by this unusual situation. If the Christian Bible is more often cited than read, and if it is most often read cut up into verses or pericopes, there are still many communities that try to read it whole.) Rather than bewail our piecemeal reading or our shamelessness about it, I suggest that we adapt our reading accordingly. Let us begin with the end. We can then turn back to see what difference understanding it makes for the pieces of moral teaching in the middle of the work.[39]

My proposal is not a proud pedagogy. It is a realistic one. It resembles what Socrates in the *Phaedo* calls the *deuteros plous*, the second way of reaching harbor once the winds have died (99d). I do not promise an exhaustive catalogue of the harbor's sights. I am only giving advice about how to row there. This is not another commentary on the *Summa*. It is an exhortation to rereading.

PART I

Sacraments, Gospel, Incarnation

Acting on my own proposal, I begin with the end. The third part of the *Summa of Theology* is Thomas's last work. Hagiographers tell that he broke off writing, in the middle of the consideration of the sacraments, because of a vision during the Eucharist.[1]

Thomas's plan for the whole of the third part includes Jesus as Savior, his sacraments, and the immortal life that comes in rising from the dead with him (3 pro). Thomas had of course treated these topics in earlier works; he had not treated them in this order. The order is significant. To the question of how incarnation, gospel narrative, and sacraments are related, the *Summa* answers by pointing to teaching by bodily manifestation.

Thomas was trained according to an order of theological topics drawn from Peter Lombard's *Sentences*. That creedal pattern pushes the Christian sacraments to a fourth and final book, to the doctrine of "signs" rather than "things." The sacraments are separated structurally from arguments about the incarnation's appropriateness, and the Lombard turns those arguments in any case toward a treatise of human virtues. By contrast, *Summa* 3 draws reflection on the incarnation through a renarrated life of Christ into the sacraments.

Faced with the Lombard's inelegant structure, and needing to incorporate more moral and sacramental topics than ever, Thomas invents a simpler pattern that explicitly expands the creedal order. First, he cuts the creed at a point before the incarnation. God as unity, trinity, and creator goes to a first part of his text. The incarnation and the remainder of the creed are moved to a third part. A new second part is given over entirely to moral topics. Thomas then erases the Lombard's structural division between things and signs, bringing the sacraments and the end of history into the third part, immediately after the teaching of the incarnation. The classical topics of Christology are joined to the sacraments by meditation on the life of Christ.

The incarnation is the decisive event of divine revelation up to the human present. It thus appears in the final part of the *Summa* according to the flow of human history. Christ is announced at the beginning of its last part, in the "fullness of time" (Galatians 4:4, quoted in 3.1.5 sc). God becomes incarnate because embodied human beings need bodily teaching especially when lost in the middle of their historical journey (3.1.5–6). The sacraments then carry on Christ's embodied pedagogy after his bodily departure at the ascension. Indeed, most precisely, they apply to human reformation a particular episode of Christ's life, the passion. Thomas's explanation of the sacraments depends on general conclusions about the appropriateness of God's taking flesh but even more on a sustained reading of the narrative of Christ's life.

The incarnation, the recorded life, and the sacraments are connected by both causality and history. The topics share as well a manner of theological reasoning. In the *Summa*'s questions about incarnation, the most prominent arguments concern whether God proceeded appropriately or in due form—in a manner that was *conveniens*, befitting. Thomas makes such arguments for the fact and the manner of God's assuming a human nature, for Christ's deeds and attributes, and for the institution of sacraments. Read whole, *Summa* 3 is a long praise of the pedagogical appropriateness of God's becoming human.

The arguments for the incarnation's appropriateness conclude that it opens "the way for us to move towards God" (3 pro). A structure of theological teaching that flows from the appropriateness of incarnation, through a narrative of Christ's life, to the sacraments can be found in several of Thomas's sources, most notably in John of Damascus, *On the Orthodox Faith*. John presents the holy mysteries of God as a pendant to a narration of Christ's life. The sacraments extend the time of incarnation and of its narration.[2] They are both remembered manifestations and reiterated ones. It is tempting to see in Thomas's adaptation of this Eastern Christian pattern for structuring theology his affirmation of something like a principle of the icon. Yet, for Thomas the controlling notion of the *Summa*'s third part is not so much a picture as a radiant event. The best introduction to the work is not a laborious paraphrase but an orientation—a turning of the head—that improves a reader's chances of seeing that event on the way to joining it.

CHAPTER I

Incarnation as Instruction

Thomas knows many of the earlier debates about Christ, of course, and he treats them both clearly and generously. In the questions on incarnation, he proposes improvements in technical language. Indeed, the "hypostatic" union of a human nature to a divine person allows him to explore terminologies for individuated acts of being. Still, Thomas is not pursuing philosophical discoveries. Again, in others of these opening questions, Thomas wisely resists entering into the polemics that would preoccupy some of his successors. (With both justification and grace, readers after the Reformation should notice especially what Thomas does *not* ask or argue.) Thomas's main concern in the first movement of *Summa* 3 is neither with adjusting metaphysics nor with quarreling over the tally in justification. He aims rather to show the *convenientia* of the incarnation down to its details as recorded in the scriptures—to display for the reader's admiration the fittingness of how God took flesh for the sake of that same reader's moral reformation.

The whole of the *Summa*'s third part is placed after a question "on the *convenientia* of the incarnation" (3.1). In that question's first article, Thomas explains the key notion: "what is *conveniens* to each thing is what belongs to it according to the account (*ratio*) of its proper nature" (3.1.1 corp). God is the highest good. It belongs to the nature of goodness that it "communicate" itself by enabling others to share in its activity. So the incarnation is the great instance of *convenientia*: the good God's nature is enacted when it brings human beings to share in it (3.1.1 sc).

For Thomas, *convenientia* is obviously not "convenience" in one of the modern English senses. Neither is it the horizontal principle of resemblance that Foucault discovers in early modern science and medicine. In a selection of sixteenth-century authors, Foucault writes, *convenientia* is "a visible effect of proximity," a resemblance by contact or overlapping.[1] Not so for Thomas, who understands *convenientia* principally in its causes rather than its effects. Thomistic *convenientia* is a principle of deliberate expression. The principle operates at every level of being, whether divine or created. It operates as well and perhaps more recognizably in intention or language. For Thomas, then, *convenientia* is not so much an effect of juxtaposition as the reason for juxtaposition. Especially in *Summa* 3, *convenientia* explains divine articulation. It is the logic by which the visible can show the invisible (3.1.1 sc).

In medieval texts, as in modern ones, arguments from *convenientia* are often slighted by contrast with strict demonstrations. Elsewhere, Thomas himself insists that such arguments ought not to be pressed on unbelievers as if they were proofs.[2] Still, if reasoning from *convenientia* is not demonstration, it has its own cogency. It possesses the suppositional or contingent necessity of means in relation to a fixed end. Given a certain goal, something can be strictly necessary as the only means for reaching it. Something can be counted necessary in a wider sense because it is the better or more appropriate way for reaching that end (3.1.2). The most important theological lessons—lessons about how to attain human happiness—depend on seeing the incarnation as the most appropriate staging of divine teaching.

The omnipotent God could have repaired human nature in many ways. A divine incarnation is the better way because it offers the more effective moral pedagogy. It accomplishes both the advance of human beings toward goodness and the removal of evil (*promotio in bonum, remotio mali*, 3.1.2). Divine incarnation moves human beings to the good by speaking to faith, supporting hope, and inciting love. It provides an example (*exemplum*) for right action. It confirms human participation in divinity by showing that Christ became human. An incarnation is also "useful for removing evil." It teaches human beings not to prefer the Devil. It shows the dignity of human nature, which should not be marred by sin. The humility of the incarnation removes human presumption. It heals pride. It frees humankind from demonic bondage. Having offered these arguments, supporting each with authority, Thomas concludes that the incarnation is useful in many other ways "beyond the comprehension of human sense." The cogency of *convenientia* arguments does not require their closure.

This sequence of reasonings about incarnation stands at the beginning of the *Summa*'s third part. I paraphrase it so extensively to show something about how arguments of *convenientia* actually proceed. They are multiplied. They are so many of them partly because of the rhetorical principle of abundance or *copia*—specifically the abundance of "things" rather than of "words."[3] *Copia* is not only ornament. To establish even suppositional necessity for the incarnation, Thomas must show that the incarnation accomplishes the divine purpose more fully than the other means available. So the argument requires an accumulation of considerations and authorities. Thomas gathers ways in which incarnation fulfills the divine purpose of moral reeducation, even if he can never hope to list all. Indeed, a set of arguments from *convenientia* becomes more cogent by admitting that it can never tally all the reasons for divine expression.

The accumulation of arguments from *convenientia* is not haphazard. This opening passage from *Summa* 3 enumerates them carefully in something like a synopsis of morals. Under the heading of the *promotio in bonum*, for example, a reader finds the three theological virtues (faith, hope, charity), the example of a complete pattern for a good life, and the representation of the end of human striving. The passage also highlights central acts of moral teaching: The incarnation gives assurance to faith, builds up hope, excites love, offers example, and displays the human end. Describing the effects of the incarnate God's humility, Thomas quotes Augustine saying that God's grace is "commended to us" in place of presumption, while pride is contradicted and healed. Only in last place does Thomas mention the notion of human liberation from sin by Christ's satisfaction. Even his second authority for that consideration, taken from Pope Leo, reads the incarnate possibility of satisfaction as moral example. If a human being cannot make satisfaction for all of humankind, and if God ought not to do so, Jesus Christ as the union of God and human can and does. As Leo says, Christ applies the remedy as God and "gives example" as human. The implication is clear: satisfaction without example—satisfaction without education—would not be appropriate for a rational creature.[4]

The moral interest of the argument is confirmed indirectly in a nearby article (3.1.3). Its topic is whether there would have been an incarnation if there had not been sin. The article is often cited to contrast Thomas and

Bonaventure—or Dominicans and Franciscans—on the logic of incarnation. Some argue, for example, that Bonaventure's theology is more Christocentric because he insists that there would have been incarnation even without human sin.[5] Perhaps so, though Thomas of course allows for the possibility within divine omnipotence of an incarnation on those terms. Thomas's argument is only that it is more scriptural to regard incarnation as a divine response to an unhappy contingency. He also thinks that it makes better sense of the incarnation's timing (3.1.5–6). Thomas does not mean to reduce the importance of incarnation so much as to emphasize its moral purposes: "The incarnation is principally ordered to repairing human nature by the abolition of sin" (3.1.5 corp).

Incarnation as Union

Convenientia is the great principle animating the third part of the *Summa*. It appears under many forms in Thomas's presentation of both incarnation and sacraments. It also selects and limits the topics that Thomas treats. The pedagogical economy of *convenientia* appears as soon as Thomas turns from arguing the appropriateness of incarnation to explaining its manner (*modus*, 3.2). With this topic, Thomas returns to the bases of Christian faith in the Scriptures and creed. Just because these are the basic professions, he never lets the divine pedagogy slip too far out of sight.

Sometimes the reminder is supplied by the sequence of quoted texts or authorities. At the beginning of *Summa* 3.2, for example, Thomas must establish the basic relation of the two natures in Christ. While remaining distinct, he argues, the divine and human natures belong to one individual being, who is a Person of the triune God. Even the little that human reason can grasp of this suggests much about how rational substances are individuated. For a reader interested in what Thomas has to teach about being (*esse*), his clarifications here of notions like *suppositum* and *hypostasis* are richly suggestive. Still, his point is not to tack on a sidebar for metaphysicians. The authorities remind a reader of what is really at stake in the hypostatic. An effort to understand the creeds is never only doctrinal archeology or analytic exercise. When Thomas comes to explain the union of soul and body in Christ, he recalls an old liturgical verse: "[as] the church sings, 'Taking on an animate body, he deigned to be born of a Virgin'" (3.2.5 sc).[6] The ontological suggestions are absorbed into a confession of faith that is then confirmed by public prayer.

What "the church sings" in its liturgies it also proclaims as doctrine. In *Summa* 3.2, Thomas is not eager to restage the history of technical controversies about Christ. He wants to help the reader understand professed doctrines by seeing them whole. So he constructs a dialectical sequence of likely mistakes and corrective recognitions. For example, a first mistake is to think that divine and human natures were somehow blended in Christ (3.2.1). Such a blending would imply confusion, admixture, or the emergence of a composite superior to its elements. So the union of divine and human must be understood rather as a conjunction or joining in the person of the Son of God (3.2.2). The union brings human nature into divinity without dissolving it. Again, Christ's human nature, including the union of his soul and body, is grounded in the divine Word (3.2.3). No separate entity (*hypostasis*) is produced by the combination of his soul and body apart from the being of the Son (3.2.5). So it would be another mistake to think that the human nature is united to the Word extrinsically, accidentally (3.2.6). Christ's soul is united to Christ's body in God—and only in God.

Correcting this mistake about accidental union requires by far the longest article in *Summa* 3.2. It not only rehearses the Christological heresies of the early church, it connects them to more recent views—indeed, to Thomas's near predecessors. In the old heresies about divine-human union, Thomas identifies two principal errors (3.2.6 corp). One error confuses two natures in one person. Another error separates one person into two so sharply that it can never reconnect them. This second error ends up with weak proposals for union: It is to be accomplished by "inhabitation," affect, shared operation, joint honor, or perhaps mere equivocation in naming. Thomas associates the first error of confusion with Eutyches and Dioscorus. He assigns the second error of weak connection to Nestorius and Theodore of Mopsuestia. He does not stop with the early church. Thomas brings the errors into his present. Following his usual practice, he does not name more recent advocates of related views. He only locates them textually in Peter Lombard.[7] These latter errors are committed by those who, seeking to avoid heresy, fall into it ignorantly. For example, one recent view holds that a certain human being, endowed from conception with body and soul, was then assumed by Christ. It concludes that the one incarnate person contained two entities (*hypostases*). Another recent view goes in the opposite direction: insisting on the unity of the person, it holds that Christ's soul and body, separate from each other, were only accidentally united in the Word. Thomas judges both of these views versions of Nestorian heresy. He considers the second view actually worse than the old heresy so far as it suggests that the soul and body were not really united in Christ.

More can be said, of course, about the history and classification of these views. Thomas does not say it. He moves quickly from this brief taxonomy to what he counts the orthodox position—that is, the truth. The union accomplished in incarnation is neither a joining of two subsisting natures nor a fleeting accident. It happens in an individual act of being, a single subsistence or hypostasis. More important for the progress of the *Summa* than metaphysical implications is a recognition about the consoling place of orthodoxy: "Now the universal faith (*fides catholica*) holds the middle between these positions" (3.2.6 corp). The remark should not be discounted as a platitude. It helps to explain the function of the taxonomy of error that Thomas has just provided. A reader needs to learn the basic arrangement of heresies past or present in order to grasp the truth of the middle position. Heresies serve as markers for Christological insight. They warn the *Summa*'s reader against recurring defects or excesses whenever human imagination tries to conceive divine incarnation.

The middle way of Christological orthodoxy is also the path of dialectical pedagogy. It is the way that Thomas follows, for example, in constructing this question on the mode of union. He tacks back and forth between opposing misconceptions as he builds a coherent reading of authorities that are seemingly or really opposed. The dialectic of selected positions around each particular topic—say, the union of divine and human—is then subordinated to the larger movement of the *Summa*, which wants to imitate as it can the divine teaching that culminates in the incarnation. To fall into one of the ancient or modern heresies about Christ is to miss the path forward.

The motion of the *Summa*'s pedagogy limits error but also useless speculation. At one point, for example, Thomas asks whether a divine person could be united to more than one human being (3.3.7). He reasons from divine omnipotence that the answer must be affirmative. In the next article, he responds to a further question about the incarnation of the Son rather than the Father or Spirit by gathering *convenientia* arguments to remind the reader of the divine purpose (3.3.8). It was most appropriate for the Son to be united to a creature, Thomas begins, because the Son is the exemplar according to which all creation came to be. The creature as partial, moving image of the divine is redirected by the incarnation toward its exemplar and end. Again, the incarnation of the *Son* fulfills the predestination of rational creatures to become adopted children of God. Again, the first humans sinned by desiring knowledge. The word of true wisdom becomes incarnate to lead their children back to God. This style of reiteration draws extravagant speculations back into the forward motion of the text.

The Flesh of Incarnation

According to Thomas's explicit outline, the questions that open the *Summa*'s third part move from the *convenientia* of incarnation through various considerations of its mode or manner. The union is treated first as a relation (3.2), then in the divine and human terms united by the relation (3.3, 3.4–6). This account of the plan is clear enough, but it provides little more than a sorting of traditional topics. Underneath the topics (or above them), Thomas reiterates his chief lessons. I call them "lessons" because they fulfill at least two teaching purposes. The opening questions announce the themes that will carry through the whole of the third part. They also prepare the reader to perform the sort of attention that reading it will require.

When Thomas turns to the human nature that is united to the Son, he first asks whether that nature was "more assumable" than any other (3.4.1). Why didn't God become incarnate as an animal, an angel, or the whole universe? Or why constrain divine omnipotence by creaturely differences at all? Thomas replies that human nature is appropriately assumed because of what it was created to be and what it has unhappily become. He then adds another sort of consideration. Human nature, he says, carries the likeness of an image of the divine so far as it is "*capax Dei*, namely in attaining [God] by its own operation of knowing and loving" (3.4.1 ad2). *Capax Dei* might be translated as "having capacity for God" or "being capable of God." The phrase condenses a passage from Augustine on the human powers of intellect, memory, will.[8] Here Thomas applies *capax Dei* to "human nature" and then uses it as an argument for divine incarnation. Insofar as the human being is an image of God able to share in divine operation, the human is most appropriately assumed by God. God takes up the nature that God created in God's own image so that the nature can be fulfilled in divine life. To say that less carefully: God becomes God's image so that the image might become God.

In these questions, Thomas associates incarnation with representation. He also distinguishes incarnation from mere representation as its fulfillment. He does so by invoking a series of distinctions about kinds of likeness. The first distinction is announced alongside the notion of the human being as capable of returning to God (3.4.1 ad2). It is the distinction between vestige or trace (*vestigium*) and image (*imago*). The likeness of a vestige (*similitudo vestigii*) is found in creatures as a divine impression. It does not imply a share in divine life. Humankind's likeness as image (*similitudo imaginis*) does imply that human knowing and loving are able to join in divine life. Claiming so much, Thomas recalls what he had already written about the human being as the image and likeness of God (1.93.6).

"Image" is a central term for the *Summa*'s structure.[9] Its importance is too obvious to be missed. In the prologue to the second or moral part of the *Summa*, Thomas explains his basic arrangement of topics.

> Since, as [John] Damascene says, the human being is said to be made according to the image of God so far as "image" signifies intellectual [capacity] and free choice and having power over oneself; after what has already been said concerning the exemplar, namely God, and what proceeds from divine power according to God's will; it remains that we consider God's image, that is, the human being. (2-1 pro)

The parts of the *Summa* are built around the relation of image to exemplar.

If a reader proceeds from this salient use of the word "image" to others in the *Summa*, she will find that they occur mostly in its first part, in the discussion of God and creatures.[10] Thomas elaborates technical meanings for the word in dealing with Trinitarian persons or processions (the Son as image of the Father) or with both angels and human beings as *imago Dei*, the image of God.[11] The theologically primary uses of "image" refer not to artistic representations or even mental ones so much as to a Trinitarian person and rational creatures. Of course, Thomas talks about images in other contexts and with other meanings. He does so most extensively when treating the use and abuse of religious artworks, including depictions of Jesus Christ.[12] Still the center of gravity for the teaching about images in the *Summa* is to be found in the first part's discussions of Trinitarian relations and the creation of angels and human beings. This ontology of the image is what Thomas emphasizes in the passage from the third part on the human being as *capax Dei*.

Explaining incarnation, Thomas recalls a related cluster of distinctions between figure and reality or prefiguration and fulfillment. The cluster is first illustrated and then misapplied in an argument *against* the truth of bodily incarnation: "The appearings (*apparitiones*) of the Old Testament, which were signs and figures of the appearing of Christ, did not take place according to the truth of body (*veritas corporis*) but according to imaginative vision (*imaginaria visio*)" (3.5.1 arg3). The objector concludes that Christ, too, must have appeared only as a sort of imaginary figure. Thomas replies that this reasoning mistakes figural fulfillment. "It was thus *conveniens* that the appearings of the Old Testament happen according to appearance (*secundum apparentiam*), as figures; but the appearing of the Son of God should happen according to the truth of body, as the thing figured by those figures" (3.5.1 ad3). Figures point not to other figures but to bodies in history. "One thing is announced prophetically in figures; something else is written historically by the evangelists according to the property of things" (3.5.3 corp).

The bodily truth of incarnation is the fulfillment of figure. It is also the refutation of the notion that Christ's body was merely illusory or fantastical. The body of God incarnate is no *corpus phantasticum* (3.5.1). It is a fully human body, marked by suffering and death. It eats and sleeps and grows tired (3.5.3 corp). Christians believe these things because the evangelists wrote about them. They wrote for faith's benefit what God did to benefit all who would believe. The bodily truth of the incarnation is directly related to its pedagogical usefulness. Though the incarnation is not just a representation, it is indeed a representation. It makes the divine truth visible (3.4.4 corp).

Still the incarnation does not put forth another figure, an imaginary apparition, a fantastical body. It takes place bodily in history. At least some events of that body's life can be narrated as one would with any other human life. They teach partly by their ordinariness. Like so many Christians before him, Thomas emphasizes the full humanity of Jesus Christ by pointing to daily action and passion. He joins Augustine in preferring the sober histories of the gospels to the poetic extravagances of pagan myth. Thomas can assume Augustine's critique of pagan mythology without needing to rehearse it—or being able to do so from his own knowledge.[13] Still the rejection of mythological fantasy is not the only linguistic task to be accomplished in relation to the reality of the incarnation. Theology must also preserve its mystery—especially when narrating it as moral example.

Speaking Mystery

Mysterium incarnationis refers to what remains unsayable in divine incarnation. The phrase appears in the prologue to the *Summa*'s third part. It is then repeated dozens of times across the questions that follow. It even epitomizes them in retrospect (3.59.6 ad3). The mystery of incarnation is both the topic and the compositional challenge for this part of Thomas's book of theology. How does one say what humans can never fully understand in a human language not made for anything remotely like it?

As he corrects heresies to follow orthodoxy, Thomas frequently meets with confusions about the meanings of terms. He responds to them by insisting that human language cannot be other than it is. The ordinary force or meaning of "person," for example, is the one from which theology must proceed (3.2.6 corp, *vis in nomine personae*). Human usage is the source and reference for human language. "Names are to be used according to what they were imposed to signify. [They were imposed] from the consideration of how things are for us" (3.3.7 ad2).

Of course, Thomas inherits something beyond the ordinary uses of Latin or its vernaculars. He must also clarify or defend the technical vocabularies of Christian speech. He has an archive of Latin locutions imposed to signify God's taking flesh. Some of the locutions are to be approved, others condemned; still others should be handled gingerly. As Thomas moves through the questions on the incarnation, he sorts these permissible, impermissible, and imprudent locutions. Indeed, the culminating question of this section of the third part gathers basic lessons about speech for incarnation (3.16.1).

The first lesson is that people can agree on a formula without agreeing on its meaning. All Christians concede that God is human, Thomas says, yet they concede it with different understandings (3.16.1 corp). Manicheans think that the Son of God assumed a fantastical body, and so he is said to be human only as a copper statue might be. Others say that since soul and body were not united in Christ, he can be called a man only figuratively. Still others consider that he was truly human, but God only by a sort of participation. Finally, some affirm the reality of the two terms but cannot make sense of their being joined by the predicate. God, yes; human, yes; God is human—no!

With the majority or "catholic" faith, Thomas wants to affirm both the terms and the predicate. To do so, he recalls a medieval logical doctrine of "supposition," the ways in which terms stand in for things. He applies the doctrine across the following articles, sometimes in tandem with notions about "modes of signification" (3.16.5 ad1). Thomas's analysis of language is interesting in its own right, not least because it disagrees with many later accounts. More important for the reader of the *Summa* is his reiterated caution about the need for care when speaking to avoid falling into heresy.

Thomas recalls a phrase attributed to Jerome: "heresy arises from words spoken in disorder" (3.16.8 corp).[14] Disorders arise in Christological speech both from treating it too simply and from pushing it too far. Speech is simplistic when it makes no allowance for the very unusual ontology required by divine incarnation. Speech goes too far when it entertains frivolous possibilities or tries to settle every detail. So Thomas refuses to enter fully into the adiaphora of possible predications (e.g., 3.16.10–13).

It is easy to take for granted the appearance of old doctrinal controversies at the beginning of the *Summa*'s third part. It seems obvious that the book's intended readers should be tutored in Christological orthodoxy. Why exactly? How do the Chalcedonian formulas, for example, assist their progress to God? Or how might a mistake about incarnation impede it? The standard by which the *Summa* promised to measure its choices in topics was, after all, just what beginners in the study of Christian "religion" most need to hear. A reader should ask: What do the details of hypostatic union have to do with Christian life as a school of formation?

She need not seek long for an answer. On Thomas's reading of the authority from Jerome, Christological heresy is disordered speech. The disorder is more than simple error; it is a moral danger. A heresiarch may innovate recklessly and so cultivate presumption or pride. Those who fall into an old heresy ignorantly or unthinkingly illustrate other risks—not least those that come from misunderstanding what human language can and cannot do. Both oversimplification of Christological language and extravagance in its speculations are mistakes about how to speak a mystery. That mystery is the best divine response to human sinfulness. Mistaking what human language can say about it may lead to mistaking what it teaches.

In the *Summa*, Thomas refuses to offer an exhaustive metaphysics or grammar of divine incarnation. He says enough about ontology to show the possibility of a true union between divine and human natures in a divine person. He recalls enough grammar to defend orthodox locutions and to illustrate the dangers of going beyond them. Both the metaphysical clarification and the grammatical care protect the mystery around incarnation. It is a mystery that can be remembered vividly as narrative even when it cannot be exhaustively explained.

CHAPTER 2

Seeing Gospel Stories

If the structure of the *Summa* is deliberate, it is not always self-evident. A number of the book's transitions call for reflection. One of them comes roughly in the middle of the teaching on the incarnation. Thomas writes (and I translate with exaggerated literalism): "After these [questions], in which has been treated God's union with man and what follows upon union, there remains to be considered what the son of God incarnate in human nature united to him did and suffered" (3.27.pro). What kind of transition does Thomas make here?

The transition has been understood as a shift from Christology to Gospel narrative or even from theory to history.[1] That is not how Thomas describes it. He presents the sequence in what sound like inferential or even temporal terms. There is a union, there are things that follow upon the union, and then there are the actions and passions of the unified being (3.16 pro). In some sense, it is *all* history. In another sense, the account of Christ is all "theory," the contemplation of things shown. A sequence that is at once history and theory might be called a curriculum. So considerations of pedagogical appropriateness govern Thomas's treatment of the union and its consequences as much as they govern the reconsideration of the scriptural telling of Christ's deeds.

Still, the reader can mark a transition at *Summa* 3.27 when Thomas begins to speak of what God incarnate "did and suffered." She might conceive it as moving from the logical time of inference to the narrative time of a biography. Thus, Thomas reasons backward from the fact of the union to its motives and implications before retelling the story of Christ's life, death, and resurrection. The description is apt as far as it goes, but it requires an addition: The events outside of human time are for the sake of the teaching that happens in it. The union of God with the human recorded in the Scriptures is for the sake of what they tell next.

Reading the Bible

Much time—too much—has been spent on criticizing what Thomas says about Scriptural exegesis in two short articles right at the beginning of the *Summa*. The effort is misplaced, as quick reflection on precedent or position will show. Chenu once described these articles as atavistic and extraneous.[2] More gently, De Lubac insisted that Aquinas in the *Summa* is not an innovator on the question of Scriptural interpretation.[3] In the effort to build a whole Thomistic hermeneutics atop two articles, their actual purpose is lost from view. So, too, is the range of Thomas's practice as a commentator on the Christian Bible.

The two articles at the start of the *Summa* recall standard topics. The first asks whether the Scriptures should use metaphors; the second, whether a single text of the Scriptures can have various meanings—indeed, can have the "spiritual" senses enumerated by tradition. Both articles depend on the principle of human learning laid out in the first of them: "It is natural for a human being to come to intelligible things through sensible ones, since all our cognition has its beginning in sensation" (1.1.9 corp). "Representation" is delightful to us, and eminent authorities testify to the pleasures of scriptural figures—as Augustine does poignantly in *On Christian Doctrine*.[4] Still, the Scriptures do not use bodily figures for the sake of pleasure alone. Figures are required by the progress of human learning (1.1.9 ad1). They draw the soul upward (ad2). Again, Thomas puts each of the spiritual senses in relation to a reader's highest end, which is to be sought by coherent action (1.1.10 corp). Christ's reported actions teach human beings both what they ought to do (through the moral sense) and what they should expect in glory (the anagogical sense). The spiritual senses do not encode secrets. They conduct human seeking.

Thomas regularly recalls the moral purposes of the Scriptures when he undertakes to expound them. The prefaces to his detailed commentaries on single books of the Old Testament insist on the point. A helpful example may be the extraordinary prologue to his commentary on the psalms. Following tradition, Thomas regards this book as touching on the whole of theology.[5] It presents the sequence of God's actions from creation through governance and redemption to glorification. The emphasis falls on the last two. The psalms teach about a redemptive incarnation so fully that they appear, Thomas says, to be more gospel than prophecy. Their glorification of God is obvious to anyone who frequents Christian liturgy. Still glorification is not divorced from instruction. If the psalms treat the whole of theology, they also recapitulate the whole of the Scriptures in the manner of petition and praise (*modus deprecativus, laudativus*). Other scriptural books emphasize other manners of speaking. Here Thomas mentions five: narration, admonition, exhortation, precept, and disputation. It is tempting to call these genres so long as the term implies only an underlying compositional motive expressed as a structure or shape.

Thomas emphasizes the connection of textual shape to textual motive, a principle of any rhetoric, when he turns in the psalms-prologue from the modes of scriptural speech to ends. The end or goal of the psalms is to raise the human mind to God. The mind is raised when it admires the grandeur of creation, tends toward the excellence of eternal blessedness, clings to divine goodness, and imitates divine justice by acting. Each ascent is aligned with a virtue. They are, respectively, faith, hope, love, and justice—the three theological virtues and the largest of the cardinal virtues. The moral end of scriptural writing or reading could not be clearer.

I may be accused of stacking the evidence by pointing to Thomas's commentary on the psalms. After all, and by long tradition, Christian readings of the psalms favor moral application. Yet the same moral emphasis can be found in Thomas's other Old Testament prologues, even those for books most remote from spiritual reading or mendicant liturgy. For example, beginning his literal exposition of Job, Thomas stresses the moral consequences of denying divine providence.[6] Those who were moved by the Holy Spirit to teach other human beings strove above all to combat the denial of God's loving rule over cosmos and history. Philosophical errors about providence must be uprooted so that human lives can have some sure purpose. Even as he affirms how masterfully Gregory the Great has expounded the higher mysteries in Job's book, Thomas thinks it worth his time as a teacher of morals to lay out its most obvious sense.

The moral motive can also be found in Thomas's earliest scriptural writing.[7] For his "cursory" exposition of Isaiah, Thomas adapts some of the themes from Jerome's prologue to the work. (He goes on to explicate that prologue line by line.) Thomas organizes his remarks according to the headings of a simple scheme for approaching a work, what medieval teachers called an *accessus*. So he speaks in order of the biblical book's authorship, manner, and material or subject matter.[8] What links the remarks under these headings is an emphasis on the expression of divine teaching as guide to human living. The author of Isaiah—as of any single book in the Scriptures—is the Holy Spirit. The prophet is only that Author's minister: "the prophet's tongue was the organ of the Holy Spirit." Isaiah speaks "plainly" and "openly." What he sees in vision he must explain so that it can become useful.

Following Jerome, Thomas notes especially Isaiah's remarkable style— his "beautiful and masterful likenesses," "the beauty of his words."[9] Such "sensible figures are necessary in the Scriptures," Thomas reminds the reader, because human beings learn from the senses. They learn from Isaiah's beauties how to live. The mysteries that God wrote on the tablets given to Moses must be explained by the prophets for correction and then written into living hearts by instruction. More evangelist than prophet, Isaiah writes so that the reader "may without the obstacle of doubt run by believing in Christ, love by believing, and persevere in love." In case the pedagogical point is not yet clear, Thomas explains that Isaiah's subject matter is the threefold "appearing" (*apparitio*) of the Son of God. He has appeared in human flesh; he does appear in the world's believing; he will appear as figure (*per speciem*) in glory.[10] Isaiah's plain style serves a whole economy of manifestation.

Without adding more examples, I conclude that Thomas's moral preoccupations stand out in his recognized scriptural commentaries. The same is true of his scriptural readings in other forms, especially the questions on the life of Christ in *Summa* 3. These questions recapitulate many years of scriptural study. Even at first glance, they appear to collate or compile a library of earlier readings. Indeed, passages in this section of the *Summa* look on the page like an expanded biblical gloss: They string together carefully selected quotations from patristic authorities just as Thomas had done in his *Catena*.[11] The resemblance to Thomas's New Testament compendium is no coincidence. The *Summa* supports arguments for the meaning of Gospel with the very same patristic sources excerpted for the *Catena aurea*.[12] The meditation of Christ's life condenses centuries of detailed interpretation, much of it newly recovered from the Christian east.

If the *Summa*'s questions on Christ's life can look like a sort of Gospel harmony or synthesis, their main purpose is not to resolve discrepancies. While Thomas does some of that, his main hope is to display the divine pedagogy in a unified narrative. The guiding principle is confidence that everything said about Christ carries a lesson. Arguing in *Against the Gentiles* for the appropriateness of incarnation, Thomas had already stressed the need for moral example: "we are provoked to virtue by both words and examples" (lib.4 cap.54 n.7). In the *Summa*, the principle is expressed more succinctly and more particularly in a traditional motto: *Omnis Christi actio, nostra est instructio*. Christ's every action is our instruction. In Latin even more than in English, the motto has the rhythm and rhyme of a memory-aid. Thomas did not compose it. It saw wide circulation for decades before he wrote.[13] He had already used it before inventing the *Summa*. In Thomas's *Scriptum*, for example, the motto appears regularly, often in liturgical or sacramental contexts.[14] The *Summa* recites the motto only twice, both times in presenting Christ's life (3.37.1 arg2, 3.40.1 ad3).[15] Yet the principle animates the whole of the *Summa*'s concluding part.

Thomas enriches the motto's meanings in several ways. Consider first the word *instructio*. As he proceeds through the life of Christ, Thomas applies it in turn to teaching, to persuasion, and to example. Christ does certain things in order to teach human beings truths about their relation to divinity. So this segment of the *Summa* is filled with verbs of display. Christ's instruction also persuades. So he is said to exhort, to shame, and to move. Finally, Christ's instruction gives humankind an example for imitation. The Latin *exemplum* has technical senses in Dominican preaching and moral writing, as will become clear, and some of these carry over to the *Summa*. Still, a more basic sense of moral example underwrites the range of *instructio*: Christ's life is a perfect pattern for human living.

The motto's other term, *actio*, is both more interesting and more complicated. Elsewhere in the *Summa*, it covers a great range of philosophical and theological cases. There are the expected contrasts between immanent and transient actions or action and passion, as well as the familiar notions of causal action or action at a distance. *Actio* is not confined to matter: Immaterial substances and embodied intellectual souls perform actions that require no material support. By extended analogy, the *Summa* also applies the term *actio* to God. God performs actions outwardly and inwardly, in creation and within divine life. The basis for the Trinitarian processions of the Son and Spirit are so many immanent actions of the Godhead. How then is a reader to understand Christ's "action"?

Christ's *actio* can become *instructio* only once it is known. While his every action need not be witnessed, any action must be narrated before it can teach. No one is reported to have seen Christ's temptations, for example, yet the Gospels record them as lessons (3.41.2 ad1). So Christ's *actio* is not a bare event so much as that event reported and remembered. The Gospel narratives are a way to learn of Christ's action, and Christ's action was performed in no small part for the sake of those narratives. This relation of narratives to actions will reappear in Thomas's account of the sacraments, which require both words and deeds.

It becomes all the more interesting to ask then, as Thomas does, why Jesus wrote nothing (3.42.4). Thomas answers by appeal to the ancient examples of Pythagoras and Socrates: Eminent teachers, they refused to write because they taught their students more directly. This reasoning recalls deeper lessons about incarnation. In the same way that God took flesh to show saving truth, so human pedagogy prizes teaching face-to-face, in the mutual presence of bodies. Since Christ is the most excellent teacher of all, he also refrains from writing so that he can "impress his teaching in the hearts of those who hear him" (3.42.4 corp). Jesus wrote, in the words of Paul, "not with ink, but with the Spirit of the living God, not on stone tablets, but on the tablets of fleshly hearts" (3.42.4 ad2, quoting 2 Cor 3:3). Thomas immediately attributes the same purpose to all of the Scriptures. They are, he says, "ordered to the imprinting of teaching on the hearts of those who hear" (3.42.4 corp). If Christ refrained from writing in order to speak to hearts, the Scriptures are written for the same purpose, though they must accomplish it less directly. The written record of his actions carries on, in some delegated or mediated way, the purpose of the teaching that he chose not to write. In this way, his action becomes written instruction by another kind of bodily instrumentality: The evangelists write as if they were part of Christ's body, his hands.

The justification for Christ's decision not to write has implications for Thomas's writing of the *Summa*. Choosing to write at all, Thomas acknowledges himself a lesser teacher than Christ (or, indeed, Socrates). The fact of the *Summa* is a testimony of obedience. Still Thomas writes in order to help as he can with the ongoing imprinting of human hearts. If the apostles wrote as if they were Christ's hands, Thomas writes only to gesture toward the works of those hands. However well or badly he succeeds in composing the *Summa*, he does so *after* Christ's delegation of writing. Thomas writes by the delegation of a delegation.[16]

As he retells the canonical tellings of Christ's life, Thomas follows something like an ideal chronology of the Gospels. He also retraces the narrative sequence in the great creeds.[17] It can be tempting to explain the pedagogy by analogy to famous Christian allegories. Perhaps it is a series of tableaux like the House of the Interpreter in *Pilgrim's Progress*.[18] These analogies fail, however, to capture the relations of moral telling to living flesh in the *Summa*'s repetition of the Gospels. For Thomas, the stories about Jesus are not an allegorized ideal beyond history. They are memories of an historical life. Again, and however much they mean to teach, the Gospel episodes are not staged fictions. They are the actions of human flesh. That is one reason why Thomas begins his retelling of the Gospels with a mother.

Mary the Mother

Peter Lombard had already included a brief paragraph about the sanctification of Mary among his preliminaries to the incarnation.[19] In the generation before Thomas, this text was appropriated as an occasion to speak more generally about the Virgin.[20] Thomas follows this precedent in his own commentary on the Lombard. When he comes to write the *Summa*, he converts the topical order into a narrative one. The Questions on Mary in the third part of the *Summa* (3.27–30) are a segment of the long consideration of Christ over fifty-nine questions. The four questions devoted to her are themselves arranged chronologically. The first considers Mary's sanctification (3.27), the second her virginity (28), the third her betrothal (29)—three aspects of Mary's preparation for receiving the archangel's announcement. The fourth question (3.30) retells that annunciation. The next four questions of the set describe Christ's conception in its matter, its active principle, its order, and its perfect result (3.31–34).

Treating Mary, Thomas continues to trace a composite scriptural narrative. Of course, he cites many dozen authorities. The theological references draw mainly upon the Latin Fathers (Jerome, Ambrose, Augustine, Bede), though there are frequent mentions of Eastern theologians, especially Basil, John Chrysostom, and John Damascene. Still Thomas is meticulous in sorting scriptural from nonscriptural evidence. Thus, in the article on Mary's sanctification in the womb, Thomas notes that "nothing is handed down in the canonical Scriptures, which make no mention even of her nativity" (3.27.1 corp). So he proceeds to argue "reasonably" (*rationabiliter*) after the manner of Augustine. *Rationabiliter* is used twice in the short body of the article to qualify the sort of assent appropriate to its conclusion. Similar qualifications appear in associated articles where the evidence is largely philosophical or traditional. When Thomas turns to issues that can be settled from the Scriptures, his qualifications disappear. He writes of Mary's virginity in parturition that "it is to be asserted without any doubt" (3.28.2 corp). The evidence is a quotation from Isaiah as interpreted by the Council of Ephesus. Again, in defending Mary's perpetual virginity, Thomas writes with unusual sharpness that "the error of Helvidius is without doubt to be detested" (3.28.3). The evidence here is a pair of quotations from John and the epistle to the Hebrews.

The contrast between scriptural narrative and traditional elaboration is not a dichotomy. Here again Thomas reasons by narrative *convenientia*. Such arguments figure explicitly in three of four articles on Mary's virginity (3.28.1-2,4), in one of the two articles on Mary's betrothal (3.29.1), and in each of the four articles on the annunciation (3.30.1–4). At each of these points, Thomas assumes the abundant meaningfulness of the Scriptures and so is not afraid to press for reasons. He could not ask about the *convenientia* of particular events if God did not guarantee the *convenientia* of the whole of scriptural history.

Thomas begins with Mary's sanctification (3.27). He argues that Mary was sanctified *in utero*, before her birth and yet after her animation. The lures to sin were restricted in her so that she never committed actual sin. The second article in this question has become one of the chief texts in the centuries-long dispute over the Immaculate Conception, settled for the Roman Church by Pius IX with *Ineffabilis Deus* (1854). The discrepancies between Thomas's account in the *Summa* and the (later) dogmatic definition fall under two headings. First, Thomas has a certain view of embryonic development that affects his description of Mary's conception. He cannot understand, within Aristotelian models, how Mary could be redeemed before being "animated," since she could not then have possessed a soul to sanctify. Animation comes after conception, so sanctification must follow conception. Second, more important, Thomas does not see how Mary could be redeemed unless she had, for at least one instant, some share in *original* sin. The *Summa*'s controversial teaching on Mary's conception emphasizes her full participation in humanity's moral history.

For Thomas, Mary was redeemed in Christ: She, too, required redemption. She was accorded an extraordinary privilege of sanctification before birth. Yet she then continued to grow in sanctity. Growth does not imply the failure of any personal sin. Still, in her growth Mary illustrates human moral formation under the action of divine teaching. This is what a modern reader emboldened or embarrassed by the later Mariology is likely to miss. Thomas traces Mary's growth in holiness as a progressive triumph over the passionate readiness to sin (the *fomes*), as an increase in the degree of grace, and as a discovery about her own vocation that led to a vow of virginity.[21]

If Mary has a place in the Gospel stories, she must have something to teach about human living. Before Mary could teach, she had to be taught about the birth of her son. The question on the annunciation is the pivot of Thomas's renarration of the Marian stories. His account moves from the necessity for an announcement to Mary through various aspects of its appropriateness. With each step, Thomas stresses that the annunciation is a moment of holy persuasion.

An annunciation was proper (*congruum*), Thomas argues, for many reasons. Mary should first receive God in mind before receiving God in her body. She should be able to testify to the divine deeds. She should be invited to give herself freely to God before entering into something like a spiritual marriage (3.30.1 corp). Mary learned in the annunciation and then responded to it "in place of all human nature." Gabriel was her teacher—a mediator, repairing the wrong done in Eden by a fallen angel (3.30.2 corp). The annunciation reverses the first act of deceitful "teaching," the sophistry of the serpent. Still Gabriel had to teach Mary in the form of a bodily vision, since even in this privileged moment God would not overpower the limits of human experience by supplying some direct intuition beyond body. The angel came as bodily apparition in service of a triple *convenientia*: He came as a body to announce the embodiment of God; he came to one who would receive God bodily; he came with the certitude of bodily experience (3.30.3 corp).

What was the message? Thomas analyzes Gabriel's speech according to a model from the traditions of the liberal arts (3.30.4 corp). Gabriel's few words correspond to a pattern of Ciceronian speechmaking. Gabriel opens with an *exordium* meant to render Mary attentive to his message. He then instructs her in the mystery of what is about to be achieved—the *expositio*. Finally, Gabriel speaks so as to win Mary's consent—his *peroratio*. Even the details of the angel's speech are construed according to the rhetorician's art: Thomas interprets Gabriel's mention of Elizabeth as an *exemplum*, which means both example and fable or moral story. When an archangel comes to announce the incarnation of God to an astonished virgin, he uses the artful order of human persuasion. Choosing to become the mother of God, Mary also shows herself an apt pupil of divine teaching.

Vision at Nativity, Epiphany, Baptism

The questions on Mary are followed in the *Summa* by many more on the pedagogy of Christ's life. If Thomas will keep his promise to readers, every one of them should contribute to the pedagogy of the whole. Since this is not an article-by-article commentary, I can test that promise only at a few points. I select passages in which Thomas either stresses or amplifies the notion of divine teaching.

As the *Summa* meditates the *convenientia* of Gospel events, it reaches "the manifestation of the newborn Christ" (3.36). Thomas has in mind the episode celebrated liturgically as the Epiphany. The topic leads him to more general principles of divine manifestation. Thomas argues that God's incarnation could not be manifested immediately to all human beings without undoing the *ratio fidei*, the progressive trust of faith (3.36.1 corp). For the incarnation to teach human beings, God incarnate must lead a recognizably human life—beginning as an infant, growing to adulthood. News of the incarnation must also spread in human ways, passing from a few to many. If this is a notion of hierarchical transmission, it is, just as important, a claim that the gospel is entrusted to human means of representation.[22] At their best, human representations fail to figure the divine completely. So too human understanding fails to grasp divinity, and its best descriptions are often negations. Through the *ratio fidei*, God draws human souls beyond their capacities but not beyond their desires.

When God commits news of the incarnation to human telling, God also commits it to human temporality, to history. Thomas justifies many details of the nativity stories as figuring past or future events of salvation history.[23] Some stories prefigure fuller and more complete proclamations of Christ's teaching (3.36.3 ad1). Even before the gospel spreads—before preachers are sent out into the world—there are in distant lands indices (*indicia*) of the incarnation, obscure and miraculous portents (3.36.3 ad3). Nearer at hand, the event itself is framed by "visible apparitions" and "celestial signs" (3.36.5 corp). While the goal is always the "complete manifestation" of God incarnate (3.36.4 ad1), it can be approached historically only within the limits of material representation. So, Thomas says, "the flesh" of the newborn "was manifest, but the divinity hidden." At the birth an angel must appear "with *claritas*" to point out that this infant is actually the "splendor of the Father's glory" (3.36.5 ad1). The divinely assumed body requires more vivid frames or captions—indices at some distance, apparitions nearer at hand. These frames or captions are not Brechtian; they are not meant to alienate the viewer or to draw attention to the frames of representation. They do call for closer inspection of what might appear as only familiar. In that sense, they might be said to alert the viewer to a surprising nearness of divinity in bodies.

There might be other lessons in the play of seeing and unseeing. In his praise of shadows, Junichiro Tanizaki observes that one class of beauties is best appreciated in dim rooms.[24] Some Japanese lacquerware or hanging scrolls show themselves not under fluorescent brightness but light halved by paper screens. The same might be said of certain beauties of Christ's manifestation. The *ratio fidei* offers an aesthetic for dimmed eyes.

The complexity of the aesthetic is confirmed when Thomas treats Jesus's baptism by John. Part of his concern is the relation of John's baptism both to Israelite rituals and to Christian sacraments. The main argument is that Jesus receives baptism from John in order to set an example (3.39. 1 corp [after Augustine], 39.2 ad1). His baptism marks the beginning of his public ministry and so of the fuller manifestation of the truth that he is. This beginning is signified in the gospel narratives by the opening of the heavens (Luke 3, quoted 3.39.5 sc). Following earlier readers, Thomas considers Jesus's vision as he rose from the waters. What kind of vision was it? Certainly it was a spiritual vision, but it might also belong to three other types. It might have been a physical vision, since Jesus was surrounded by splendor. Or an imaginative vision, like those of the prophet Ezekiel. Or an intellectual vision, by which Christ, having sanctified baptism in accepting it, understood that the heavens were now indeed open for humankind (for all, 3.39.5 ad2). Thomas does not choose among these possibilities, since the pedagogy of incarnation can compass them all.

Remember that Thomas is not arguing the *convenientia* of an image of the baptism. He is reading the narration of what he takes to be an historical event. In these remarks on the opening of the heavens, Thomas recapitulates the whole course of visual instruction in the Scriptures in order to apply it to the visible ministry of an incarnate God. Retelling Jesus's birth, epiphany, and baptism, Thomas reminds his readers that the full manifestation of incarnation required deeds in addition to speeches—or, rather, the renarration of events that contained both words and bodily actions. When it comes time for Jesus to leave his followers, he will not hand over a series of painted images or even an anthology of texts (since he has left writing to others). Jesus will institute a series of repetitive events, the performed signs known as sacraments.

Conversatio Christi

The narrative of Jesus's teaching records what Thomas calls the *conversatio Christi*. *Conversatio* is a word that resonates in the *Summa*, easier to paraphrase than to render. It can mean sharing or exchanging, and in that sense it is sometimes treated as synonymous with *communicatio* or even *convictus*.[25] While the souls of the dead before resurrection are separated from the conversation of the living, they join the conversation of spiritual beings (1.89.8 corp). More strikingly, the sharing (*societas*) of human beings with God is *familiaris conversatio*, the exchange of family life (2-1.65.5 corp). So *conversatio* often suggests the word "society" in our sense, if not quite that of Thomas's "*societas*." Human *conversatio* is the field of law and the common good but also of play and pleasure (2-1.107.1 corp, 2-2.168.2–3). More frequently, "*conversatio*" means something like way of life as morally characteristic or distinctive. Under the Old Law, the whole Jewish people and their leaders were set apart by their ways of life (2-1.101.4, 102.4 ad8, 102.5 ad10). So too the "people of the New Law" have a distinctive *conversatio* (2-1.101.4 ad1). Among them, Thomas marks further distinctions, including those of "regular conversation" or life under religious vows (2-2.184.8). Of course, all forms of life properly called Christian take Christ as example.

For Thomas, Christ came into the world principally to make saving truth manifest (3.40.1 corp). Still the *conversatio Christi* instructs us in various registers. It must show, for example, that Christ is both divine and human (3.40.1 ad1). Miracles serve this purpose. They certify Christ's authority while showing who he is and why he has come (3.43.1, 44.1). His *conversatio* must show even more a pattern of restored human life. "Christ came especially to teach and to do miracles for human benefit, principally with regard to the health [*or* salvation] of the soul" (3.44.1 ad4). His life is obviously virtuous. In fact, it shows the range of virtues (3.35.7 ad2, *virtuosa conversatio*).

Jesus teaches both through the form of his whole life and through particular incidents in it. "In his way of life the Lord gave an example (*exemplum*) in all things pertaining to salvation" (3.40.2 ad1). Certain features of the gospel narratives can only be understood as examples. If Jesus appears abstinent at some times and moderately indulgent at others, the explanation is that he wished to illustrate various kinds of human life (3.40.2 ad1). If he allowed himself to suffer temptation, that was "for the sake of example, namely that he would instruct us" (3.41.1 corp). The intended audience for an example can be quite specific. Thinking of his first audience and his own life, Thomas notes that Jesus gave example to preachers both in his periodic solitudes and in his poverty (3.40.1 ad3, 40.2 ad1).

Exemplum is in fact a preacher's word. It refers to a brief and memorable story used to fix a specific point in the mind. If an *exemplum* is something like a parable, Dominican *exempla* from the decades during which Thomas wrote the *Summa* tend to be both more vivid and more particular than Jesus's parables in the canonical gospels. They rely on the sort of detail that makes them sound like the latest news or the tastiest gossip. While mendicant preachers passed around indexed anthologies of these stories, they pitched them to particular audiences by including current references and local allusions.

Thomas does not regard the *exempla* done by Jesus in the gospels as rhetorically tuned fables. He regards them as deeds recorded in divinely authorized texts. The deeds were done for the sake of being recorded: Jesus lived his life so as to give example. His examples are at once deeds and stories, deeds already on the way to becoming stories. The moral narrative is not so much imposed on them as found already in them. If Jesus is the supreme example of a life lived for the sake of moral instruction, he is not the only example. Thomas knows from ancient literature the exemplary lives of heroes. He recalls from philosophy the lives of teachers. He learns from the tradition of his own order that the life of every preacher must be exemplary. A Dominican life not only quotes *exempla*, it performs them.

The notion of pedagogical narrative explains some of Thomas's choices and emphases. It also produces some tensions in the *Summa*'s dialectical unfolding. Thomas regularly argues that the higher mysteries cannot be explained to all at once; they must be disclosed gradually (3.45.3 ad4). Yet he insists more prominently on the openness of Christ's teaching (3.42.3). An episode can be exemplary only if it is reported (compare 3.41.2 ad1). If secrets are kept, they are only kept for a time. The best example is perhaps the episode of the transfiguration. This miraculous transformation of Jesus's body is seen only by a select group of students who are then sworn for a time to secrecy. Jesus is endowed with a splendor that signifies at once his divinity and the brightness of a redeemed world (3.45.2 ad3). Any temporary withholding of that event anticipates a dazzling manifestation, the moment when it will be recognized as the icon it has always been.

The Severe Lesson of the Passion

For the *Summa*, Christ's passion is the culminating episode of his incarnate pedagogy. Thomas does not exalt suffering for its own sake. Neither does he forget the resurrection. Still he judges that human education can only be brought to completion in a terrifying example. Jesus must suffer and die because of the hardness of human learners. In an image that Thomas quotes from Augustine, the cross is a teacher's chair, the *cathedra magistri*.[26]

Approaching the passion, it is particularly important to remember the multiplicity of explanations by *convenientia*. There is not one reason why Christ had to suffer as he did, but five; not one justification for his crucifixion, but seven (3.46.3–4). They are unified by what is required to teach morals to embodied intelligences fallen into sin. The passion of an incarnate God is the most appropriate means for human liberation given history's violence.

Christ's passion and death are needed for human redemption, but Thomas takes pains to prevent a misunderstanding of their necessity. What is required for God to forgive human sin? The strictest answer is, Whatever God decides. Like his incarnation, Jesus's passion and death are not necessary without qualification (3.46.1–2). God could have provided other means of freeing human beings from the consequences of their sin.[27] Indeed, God can forgive injuries done to God without demanding any satisfaction at all (3.46.2 ad3). So, whatever necessity there is for the passion and death of Jesus must be conditional or suppositional.

Three considerations uncover God's choice to redeem in this way (3.46.1 corp). The first has to do with the human condition; the second, with Christ's meriting glory through self-abnegation; the third, with the divine foreknowledge revealed in Israelite prophecies and prefigurations. Clearly, the second and third depend on the first. If the Scriptures foretell the sacrificial death of a savior, that is because God foreknew that death as most beneficial. When Christ merits glory through self-emptying, he reminds fallen human beings of a hard truth they would rather forget. The key condition, then, is the first. The passion and death of Jesus are required by human needs.

Thomas lays out the appropriateness of Christ's passion and death on the cross (3.46.3–4). The arguments multiply here, as a reader should by now expect. Their very multiplicity reinforces Thomas's reasoning. Given the many possible ways of redemption, the most appropriate way is the one that combines lessons (3.46.3 corp). It draws them together by subordinating them to a central motive. Indeed, all of the five arguments for the appropriateness of Christ's passion are moral. The first two obviously so: Christ's willingness to suffer for humankind shows that God loves us even as it enacts a variety of virtues.[28] The virtues include obedience, humility, constancy, and justice, though there are also many others that Thomas does not attempt to enumerate. If the remaining three arguments for appropriateness are less evidently moral, they tend to the same end. Christ's violent death merits a reward that is also the human end; it fixes in human minds the importance of avoiding sin; and it offers humans greater dignity through their rehabilitation. The five arguments for appropriateness taken together confirm what Thomas said at the start of the *tertia*: It was more merciful of God to demand satisfaction and then to supply it—more merciful, because doing so gave human beings more ways to learn their lessons (3.46.1 ad3 with the recollection of 3.1.2).

Moral pedagogy remains Thomas's main concern even when he turns to consider divine foreknowledge of the manner of death. In explaining the details of the Gospel narratives of Good Friday, Thomas frequently invokes a basic principle of Christian typology: Truth must answer to figure.[29] Christ's life gives instruction as it fulfills narrative expectations. Thomas explains, by copious collation of earlier interpretations, how far Christ's manner of dying confirms scriptural predictions. In the main article, he gathers these typological reasons under seven headings (3.46.4). Each of the seven is moral, explicitly or implicitly: The circumstances of the crucifixion give an example of virtues or prepare a way to heaven or show the universality of salvation now offered even as they recall the origin of human sin with the first parents.[30]

The reader may still wonder why teaching morals requires such violence. The question is only sharpened by the typological considerations. Jesus's passion and death fulfill all of the precepts of the Old Law—moral, judicial, and ceremonial (3.47.2 ad1). In particular, Christ's passion completes the ceremonial sacrifices (3.46.10 ad1). Earlier in the *Summa*, Thomas followed Maimonides to find a moral purpose behind Israel's animal sacrifices under the Old Law. The practice was instituted and then centralized in the Temple to inhibit idolatry: It displaced idolatrous rites only in order to claim that God does not want bodily worship for its own sake (2-1.102.3 corp and ad1, 102.4 ad3). Temple sacrifices do not spill blood to appease God. They correct human cruelty by instilling horror.[31] A reader cannot imagine that Thomas would reverse this insight when he reaches Christ's passion. The passion is meant to surpass the Old Ceremonial law, not revert to what preceded it. So any plausible justification for Christ's terrible death cannot rely on expectations of what God demands in sacrifice. Much less can a reader suppose that Thomas is willing to condone human sacrifice. Indeed, Thomas's redefinition of sacrifice does not mention death at all. A sacrifice is anything appropriate done to honor God for the sake of reconciling, placating, or appeasing (*ad eum placandum*, 3.48.3 corp). So why was this killing done?

The verb *placare* is ambivalent. Its several senses call up an earlier passage in which Thomas defends Christ's death. An objector argues that handing over an innocent person to suffering and death is simply unjust. If God surrendered Jesus to his torturers, then God was unjust (3.47.3 arg1). Thomas's reply first emphasizes Jesus's willingness to suffer. God did not hand Jesus over so much as inspire in Jesus-as-human a willingness to suffer for humankind, "in which is shown also God's severity (*severitas*), who did not wish to remit sin without a penalty." This sacrifice—the voluntary death of an innocent—is explained by God's severity. Yet Thomas has already argued that the whole human race could have been redeemed if Christ had willed to suffer only slightly, in *una minima passio* (3.46.5 ad3). If Jesus chose to suffer more, that was not for sufficiency but for appropriateness. What kind of appropriateness? Or appropriateness for whom?

Elsewhere in the *Summa*, severity is frequently contrasted with mercy.[32] Thomas explains in one passage that severity is most technically the part of justice concerned especially with strictness in punishment. The technical meaning would seem to fit in the discussion of Christ's death. God's severity is a refusal to relax the punishment for sin. Of course, God has also set the punishment and, indeed, required that there be punishment. That decision Thomas understands as love. God's severity is an aspect or expression of God's merciful love. This should also be true in human correction of sinners. If the deed of correction shows severity, the proper intention of correction is always mercy (2-2.32.2 ad3). So with the sacrifice of Christ: God's severity in requiring violent satisfaction is mercy for the moral blindness of humankind. Only such an act can capture human attention. Only such an act can persuade cynical observers about love: "in this way, the human being knows how much God loves the human, and so is provoked to love God" (3.46.3 corp).

If Thomas defends the divine severity of the passion, he also suggests another teaching in Christ's saving body. For Thomas, redemption is a kind of incorporation in Christ (3.48.1 corp, 2 ad 1; 3.49.1 corp, 49.3 ad3). The incorporation joins a human being to what Thomas knows as the "mystical" body—a teaching that points forward to the doctrine of the sacraments. Incorporation can also be a sort of configuration or conformation to Christ (3.49.3 ad2, ad3; 3.56.1 ad3). The pedagogy is completed in a sacrifice that breaks through the bulky masks of sin to reshape the embodied soul beneath. If the life of Christ is the great moral example, the end of moral teaching is conformity to Christ so complete that it counts as incorporation. Indeed, Thomas can find no stronger analogy for this conformity than physical contact. Thomas writes: "the resurrection of Christ is the efficient cause of our resurrection by divine power, which alone can bring the dead to life. This power touches all places and times in the way of presence (*praesentialiter attingit*). And such contact by power (*contactus virtualis*) suffices to explain this efficacy" (3.56.1 ad3). What touch is this? "The satisfaction of Christ has effect in us so far as we are incorporated in him as members to the head" (3.49.3 ad3).

It goes without saying that Thomas does not conclude his restaging of the Gospel narratives with the passion and death of Jesus. He continues of course through the descent into hell, resurrection, ascension, enthronement, and eschatological judgment. Thomas follows the narrative out of history to the conclusion of time. Many of the moral themes from the earlier episodes extend into these questions. For example, the appropriateness of the resurrection is defended with five arguments, each of which has moral import (3.53.1). If Christ rises to vindicate justice, he does so even more to instruct in faith, increase hope, give form to human lives, and urge them toward the highest good. Still Thomas concedes that the work of redemption was already completed before Christ rose from the dead. The resurrection is not the cause of redemption so much as its beginning and brightest model, its *inchoatio* and *exemplar* (53.1 ad3). Resurrection is also manifestation (3.55). It completes Christ's work of showing truth—and not only pronouncing it.

The resurrection gestures toward the pedagogy for the future. It inaugurates a third period of history, the stage of the saints (*status sanctorum*), which will be realized only in eternity (3.53.2 corp). Imagining Christ risen, readers can study their own future (3.54.2 corp). Christ's body not only shows triumph over death, it discloses the person with whom the reader might spend eternity.

The retelling of the Gospels as moral instruction ends by gazing forward. Yet, much of the telling has looked backward. Christ's example is for Thomas and all of his readers a remembered example. Gospel stories about the sublime manifestation have been passed down. Something more is needed to carry the work of incarnation forward. So alongside the stories, Christ gave other memorials capable of connecting present to past—of invoking past power in any present. Those memorials are sacraments. They will remind the reader that the example of Christ's action must be completed in ritual enactments that bring him into the present.

CHAPTER 3

Sacramental Bodies

In the *Summa*, sacramental worship is the source and emblem for present Christian living. It is both a "declaration of faith by outward signs" and an indispensable education for coherent action (3.63.4 ad3 and 3.61.1). The larger frame within which to understand the sacraments is liturgy so long as liturgy is neither an aesthetic artifact nor a ritualized social effervescence. For Thomas, liturgy is moral education.

To see how the sacraments together foster moral formation, a contemporary reader may need to approach them along a different path than the one Thomas lays out for the *Summa*'s first readers. (This is a much smaller version of reading the parts of the *Summa* backward.) His questions on the sacraments "in common" ask what they are, why they are necessary, how they have effect, and how many of them there are.[1] It does make good sense to explain what something is before arguing for its importance. Still, a contemporary reader may better understand Thomas's definitions of sacraments (3.60) after reading his justifications for their existence (3.61).

The Human Need for Sacraments

Thomas asks: Are sacraments necessary to human *salus*? *Salus* is standardly translated as "salvation," but here a reader must remember that the Latin word also means "health." Peter Lombard's treatment of the sacraments begins by recalling how the Good Samaritan tended to the wounded man left to die at a roadside. In the same way, the Lombard reasons, "God instituted the remedies of the sacraments against the wounds of original and actual sin."[2] Many commentators on the Lombard's text enrich this medical analogy with their own medical knowledge. Thomas's teacher, Albert the Great, defends the necessity of the sacraments in rather detailed medical terms.[3] While Thomas adopts such medical analogies, he tends to understand *salus* more generally as well-being. God provides sacraments, he thinks, both as remedies and as training.

Taken together, the objections against sacraments that Thomas selects emphasize the sufficiency of direct divine action apart from bodily activity. Thomas answers them from Augustine: Human beings cannot unite in any *religio*, whether true or false, unless they join together in visible signs or sacraments. This argument situates the analysis of sacraments within the analysis of *religio*. That word, prominent in the *Summa*'s prologue, means for Thomas both a specific virtue of worship and the vowed ways-of-life ordered to it (2-2.81 and 186–189). Human beings need sacraments just as they need religion. Christian sacraments may be unique in their origin or efficacy, but they are instituted in response to a general human need.

Deciding this question, Thomas amends a triplet from Peter Lombard. The Lombard says that God gives sacraments to human beings in order to humble them, to teach them, and to exercise them. Thomas reverses the first two elements to begin with teaching. Sacraments are necessary, first, "from the condition of human nature," which is led to "spiritual and intelligible things" by "bodily and sensible things" (3.61.1 corp). Consulting *convenientia* once again, divine wisdom helps human beings toward full flourishing with "certain bodily and sensible signs, which are called 'sacraments.'" The second argument for the necessity of sacraments turns to humility: Since sin subjugated human beings to bodily things, God applies the medicine directly to the disease by supplying bodily remedies. The third argument proceeds from the focus (*studium*) of human action, which is, in the present life, principally concerned with bodies. So God gives human beings something to do with their bodies lest they be tempted either by demonic rites or by sinful actions. Of these three arguments, the second and third respond to the consequences of sin and so seem contingent upon that bleak history. When Thomas changes the Lombard's order to put education first, he suggests that sacraments would be helpful for human moral instruction with or without sin.

Perhaps surprisingly, then, his very next article argues that human beings did not need sacraments before the Fall (3.61.2). The article distinguishes the medicinal model of sacraments from the pedagogical, then agues its conclusion under both. Thomas endorses the argument that the sacraments are remedies for sin and so concludes that they were not needed before it occurred. He adds a stronger argument from the hierarchical perfection of the original human condition: Humans cannot have needed bodily sacraments in Eden even pedagogically because they received both grace and instruction directly from God, without the mediation of bodily organs or powers.

This response and the arguments within it are a close reworking of the parallel section of Thomas's earlier commentary on the *Sentences*.[4] Writing some fifteen years before, Thomas had reported a division of theological opinion, with some theologians holding that human beings required bodily sacraments in Eden for instruction, though not yet as a remedy for sin. Thomas replied there, too, with an argument from the hierarchical order of the human soul, explaining somewhat more fully that human cognition operated differently before the Fall. The sinless human intellect learned its lessons from divine illumination rather than sensation. So it would have been inappropriate for the intellect to approach divinity in subordination to physical things. To assume that the same sort of argument underlies Thomas's judgment here produces puzzles if not inconsistencies. He has argued in the first Part of the *Summa*, for example, that the sinless human intellect understood things by "conversion to phantasms," by reference to the results of sensation (1.94.2 corp). It was even then an intellect in a body. How can Thomas abandon the pedagogy of sensation when considering the necessity of sacraments in Eden?[5]

Several considerations might explain why Thomas seems in this article to set aside principles of embodied learning. For example, he may have failed to revise thoroughly enough. Again, a longer glance at the *Summa*'s other treatments of human minds before sin can ease some of the apparent contradictions. If Thomas affirms that Edenic minds shared limits with fallen ones, he also stresses that their way of understanding was importantly unlike the one they use at present. Knowing in Eden was half way to the beatific vision (1.94.1). Still, it is more helpful to ask what Thomas means to safeguard when he denies that there were sacraments before sin. The answer is plain: He is protecting the superlative orderliness of grace.

The state of innocence was not, after all, the state of nature. Human powers operated then beyond nature by an original infusion of grace. If sacraments are instituted to give grace, already graced human beings could not have required them in any strict sense. To say otherwise would be to doubt the sufficiency of God's provision for Adam and Eve.

If Thomas denies sacraments in Eden to underscore the original gift of grace, he still insists that humans need at present to be taught by and through bodies. Since human nature never appears just by itself, since it is always accepting or denying grace, little enough can be inferred about our natural way of learning from events in Eden. The present "human condition"—as Thomas here uses the phrase—is what can be glimpsed of it after the Fall. A reader cannot discover how humans learn now by speculating on their condition at creation. The need for learning through bodies becomes urgent only after sin.

If human nature must always be studied in some particular epoch, the same is true a fortiori of the sacraments adapted to it. Sacraments are performed in time and for a particular time. There is, Thomas argues, important progress in the transit from Old Testament rites to the sacraments instituted by Christ under the New Law (3.61.3). More important, if more technically, both Israelite rites and Christian sacraments have a temporal reference to Christ as to their source (3.61.4). Since the sacraments are needed because of the contingency of human sin, they draw their power from the contingency of Christ's redemptive acts. Sacramental pedagogy aims to teach by causing particular effects in particular groups of students.

Sacraments as Signs

For Thomas, a sacrament is a sign that causes what it signifies. More precisely, it is a sign of something holy that sanctifies human beings (3.60.2). The basic definition comes from Peter Lombard's paraphrase of an aside in Augustine's *City of God*.[6] Augustine is refuting the claim that Israel's God somehow needed the animal sacrifices or other physical offerings required by the Old Law. It must be, Augustine argues, that the visible sacrifice was a sacrament—"that is, a sacred sign" (*sacrum signum*)—of the invisible, the moral sacrifice of repentance.

Many readers of Thomas, especially since the Reformation, have been preoccupied to establish what exactly the *Summa* says about sacraments as causes. A reader does better to notice that Thomas defines sacraments and justifies their divine provision in the *Summa* before he analyzes their causality. Indeed, he begins by placing sacraments among signs rather than among causes (3.60.1 arg1, ad1). The sacraments are signs first, causes second. A reader also does well to admit that she is unlikely to know beforehand the precise meaning of either term. In these questions, Thomas emphasizes that a sign is a material aid to expression—in this case, the expression of teaching. Among the many meanings of cause, here he singles out instrumental causality. The two emphases are evidently connected: A material instrument is used to bring about a more than material effect. To say that a sacrament is a sign that causes what it signifies is to suggest already that its signification and its causality should be understood together.

Thomas wrote no treatise on signs. If he has a doctrine that differs from those he inherits, it has to be pieced together from what he writes on other topics. His most extended discussion of words as signs stretches over a few sections in his exposition of Aristotle's *On Interpretation*, written perhaps four or five years before these questions in the *Summa*. Unfortunately, the work is a literal exposition of Aristotle's meaning that relies on previous commentators. Something can be learned about signs, of course, by watching just how Thomas intercuts Ammonius (a late ancient commentator only recently rendered into Latin) with Boethius (a long standard interpreter of Aristotelian logic for Latin speakers). Thomas also brings certain characteristic emphases to the Aristotelian text. For example, he stresses the original expressive intention (*impositio* or *inventio*) and the production of the sign as artifact.[7] Again, Thomas elides (Augustinian) notions of the expressive word with the (Aristotelian) correlation between symbols and the mind's invariant impressions (*pathêmata*), just as he elsewhere adds the notion of the "inner word" to Peripatetic accounts of how the mind finds meaning. Still this sifting of the commentaries can only help a little with what Thomas says about signs in dealing with the sacraments.

More helpful are passages in which Thomas tries to understand what happens to the notion of sign in limit cases. Consider the speech of angels. In an earlier disputed question, Thomas treats an objection against the claim that the angels speak. Quoting Augustine (as paraphrased by Peter Lombard), the objector holds that a sign must by definition involve some sensible expression. Since angels do not learn by sensation, they do not use signs and so cannot be said to speak.[8] In reply, Thomas first corrects the definition of sign: The important thing is not so much sensible expression as sequence in learning. "Properly speaking, something cannot be said to be a sign unless it leads to knowledge of something else as if discursively (*quasi discurrendo*)."[9] Human knowledge is sign-based not because it depends on material things, but because it moves through them. Angelic knowledge is not discursive, and so angels cannot be said to use signs in this strict sense. Speaking more loosely, Thomas is willing to count as a sign anything through which something else can be known. Taking "sign" in this wider sense, angels do speak by showing one another intelligible forms (*species*) through which something else can be known. If Thomas is willing to conceive signification without bodies, he cannot conceive it without sequence. Pedagogical sequence defines the sign even in limit cases where there are no bodies.

At present, the human case is simpler—and more evidently familiar. Following Augustine, Thomas stresses the perception of sacramental signs. He contrasts the visibility of sacramental signs with the invisibility of the mysteries they signify.[10] He stresses that "sensible" and "visible" things are used as sacramental signs. When an objector argues that sacraments cannot be necessary for salvation because they are concerned only with bodily things, Thomas rebuts the objection while affirming a qualified version of its premise (3.61.1 arg1 & ad1). The sacraments do require bodily motions, and they do achieve their effects through sensible things—but their effects are not confined to the physical. The more basic point is to realize that it is connatural to human beings to learn through sensation. If a sign leads to understanding something else, then the best signs for human beings will be sensible signs (3.60.4 corp).

Sacramental signs use bodies—dispose bodies, make bodies—to show something not bodily. The showing requires a learnable connection between the sign and what it signifies. This has two consequences. It implies both that God chose specific things as sacramental signs and that God added certain words to them. Sacramental practice directs worship (*cultus divinus*) to human sanctification. Since God alone sanctifies, God gets to determine the signs when instituting a sacrament (3.60.5 corp). While this is a particular divine prerogative, it is also recalls the grammatical notion of original expressive intention: The sign-giver specifies the sign. So, too, in Scriptures, the Holy Spirit determines which particular signs will be used (3.60.5 ad1).

On Thomas's account, and despite divine institution, natural signification is too ambiguous for the sacraments to rely on objects or gestures alone. Their meanings must be specified by words (3.60.6–8). Something like this principle helped Thomas to explain the staging of the nativity. The truth of incarnation requires that Jesus be born as a human baby and that news of the birth travel within human channels, through a human history of reports and representations. Yet, an angelic intervention or miraculous indices and portents are supplied to show that this infant flesh does indeed hide divinity. How to understand this relation so that it does not eclipse bodies by words or render bodies superfluous ornaments to an essentially verbal instruction?

Thomas knows the tremendous range of "word" as a topic for Christian theology. He recalls it to argue that there are several kinds of words in the sacraments. Since every sacrament depends on the "incarnate Word" as the cause of sanctification, the sacrament's objects or gestures are in some sense already words—just because they are already extensions of the incarnation. Still, in human systems of signification, spoken or written words are the preeminent signs. Sacramental signification can only benefit from the addition of ordinary human words. Thomas expresses the relation of spoken words to gestures or objects in a sacrament by a later controversial analogy to form and matter (3.60.6 ad2). The words in a sacramental rite are like its form, he says; the objects and gestures, like the matter. For Thomas, this is only an analogy. (The point cannot be emphasized enough given later controversies.) It is an analogy sustained by the incarnational logic carried in the larger sense of *verbum*. Words ought not to be opposed to other elements in a sacrament. Material forms are typically bound to their matter but in this case especially, since to deprecate or deny the matter of a sacrament would be analogous to denying the bodily reality of incarnation. The sacraments are recollections or reiterations of the principle of their sanctifying cause, who is the incarnate Word.

Sacraments as Causes

Sacraments both signify and cause sanctification through divine institution. Exceeding natural causality, they do not contradict everything that can be known of it. Indeed, their efficacy—which is their pedagogy—is dictated by human nature. Thomas's "*causa*" has a different range of meanings than the modern English "cause." His word names a set of relations and responsibilities that are difficult for contemporary readers to see together, much less to see as causes. In this, Thomas proves himself a thoughtful reader of Aristotle.

Modern summaries usually name four causes in Aristotle: formal, material, final, and moving. The last is often singled out as the one that underwrites most modern notions of physical causality. Still, there is much else in Aristotle, even before Thomas transforms his texts. Aristotle counts many more than four causes, and even his basic lists of them show variations in number and description. Moreover, Aristotle frequently claims that there are multiple causes or causal narrations for any one artifact, thing, or event. Causes of different kinds stand in various relations to one another. They appear or operate in various sequences and ranks. They are disposed in degrees of proximity or propriety. There is also interactive causality—reciprocal causal relations in different axes. An interplay of causes can produce multiple effects, so that a single cause can in some cases be appropriately said to produce contrary effects in combination with other sorts of cause. All of this Thomas finds in Aristotle, especially in a passage like *Metaphysics* 5.2, which tries to sort speech about causes. The sorting shows that a causal relation is predicated of almost anything that can be cited as source, element, circumstance, or end. Causality explains in part by multiplying explanations.

Thomas modifies the Aristotelian causal language in many ways when he describes scriptural rites. In discussing the ceremonial precepts of the Old Law, for example, he has already used "cause" to name the reasoned justification for a particular prescription or prohibition (2-1.102 pro). The cause of an Israelite rite is God's pedagogical intention in it. For the Christian sacraments, there is a similarly specific use. Thomas means by the cause of the new sacraments less their inner mechanisms than their origin in divine power and their celebration by human ministers (3.64). The "cause of the sacraments" is not sacramental causality. It is the sacraments themselves as effects. More important still is the way Thomas reverses the Aristotelian priority of cause over effect. He treats causality only after he discusses the sacramental effect, which is grace. Thomas is most concerned to understand what it means to say that Christian sacraments are causes of *grace*. The uniqueness of the effect requires any number of adjustments in ordinary causal language, beginning with the notion of containment.

Thomas asks explicitly whether the sacraments of the new law "contain" (*contineant*) grace (3.62.3). He affirms that they do in two ways: as signs and as causes. He has just introduced instrumental causes to describe the sacraments (3.62.1). So Thomas adds that Christ's sacraments contain grace only as "a certain instrumental power, which is fluid and incomplete in the being of nature" (3.62.3 corp). In the very next article, he will characterize instrumental power as possessing a kind of "being that moves from one to another" (3.62.4 corp). Some commentators have found this language puzzling or objectionable.[11] Rather than take it literally as evidence of a naive physicalism, I would suggest reading it as a series of reminders about the limits of human imagination or language when it comes to instrumental causes—especially instrumental causes of grace.

Behind these corrections and qualifications, the important thing for Thomas is to recognize grace as the main effect of the sacraments. They cause what they signify, and they signify union with God. The ordinary complexities of causality are here doubled by extraordinary complexities of visible instruments linking an invisible cause to an invisible effect. In this sense, the sacraments are a sort of reverse mime. They show only the instruments, not the figures that move them. To watch a sacrament is like seeing only a moving glass without the hand that lifts it or the quenching drink it carries. What is visible is the least important thing, the intermediary or go-between. But this reversed visibility is precisely the point behind the provision of sacraments. In their present bodies, human beings cannot see God. Neither can they see grace. They see or hear or feel only the sacramental instruments. The sacraments are reminders to look behind them. Thomas picks up those reminders when he rehearses the distinction between "the sacrament alone" (say, the baptismal washing) and the "thing" that it represents (say, baptismal justification; 3.66.1). He does so again when he notices that sacramental signs are sometimes dispensable (say, in the baptism of blood or of repentance, 3.66.11). Still Thomas makes these analytical distinctions in passing, to prevent or correct misunderstanding. His main point is the unity of the sacramental sign and its graced effect: "the sacrament is completed where sanctification is completed" (3.66.1 corp).

Sacramental Character

Thomas comes to the topic of sacramental character, as he comes to most topics in the *Summa*, with a set of conventional issues and attached textual authorities. The compositional challenge in them also varies by topic. In the *Summa*'s question on sacramental character, the authorities are rather few and more confused than contradictory, because the doctrine of character in this sense is rather new. The challenge is to explain it as an integral part of traditional teaching on the sacraments.

Thomas receives this task of explanation from his immediate predecessors. The generations just before his in the schools of Paris handed down two definitions of character.[12] Thomas attributes the definitions only to "some people," *quidam*, his way of naming mentors and colleagues. The first anonymous definition, sometimes attributed to Ps-Dionysius, reads: "character is a holy sign of the communion of faith and of holy ordination, given by a hierarch" (3.63.2 arg3).[13] The second anonymous definition reads: "character is a distinction impressed by the eternal character on the rational soul, through an image by which the creating and re-creating Trinity signs the created Trinity [that is, the soul], distinguishing [the soul] from what is not [so] configured, according to the status of faith" (3.63.3 sc). Each of these definitions goes beyond earlier meanings of the Latin "character" in sacramental contexts.[14]

The new definitions help Thomas to organize and reinterpret other authorities, including two linked scriptural verses. Thomas does not read Greek, but he learns from a biblical reference tool that the Greek *charactêr* stands behind the Latin *figura* in Hebrews 1.3. The Son is the character or figure of the substance of God.[15] Thomas reads this passage alongside Paul's description in Romans 4.11 of circumcision as a *sphragis*, a signet's mark or attesting signature. In Thomas's Latin bibles, *sphragis* has become *signaculum*, little sign, and so character is placed for him within the economy of signification. It distends that economy. The invisible character within the body is a sign in no ordinary sense.

The definitions and the scriptural authorities draw Thomas's attention because they suggest a way of understanding character within moral pedagogy. Let me paraphrase the suggestion as he elaborates it—even at the risk of rearranging, now at small scale, his dialectical sequence. Sacramental character is a principle or source of action rather than an inert product. It is neither a written figure nor an indelible mark. It is instead a role. The role is given to carry out the actions that distinguish Christian life, most especially "worship of God according to Christian ritual" (3.63.1 ad1; compare 3.62.5 corp). Whoever properly receives one of the three unrepeatable sacraments is deputized by God to perform worship and other actions in one capacity or another (3.63.1 corp). Sacramental character enables liturgical participation while supposing it; the sacramental character is received by participating in liturgy. Yet, sacramental character is more than the recounting of voices or plots in idealized liturgical texts. It is also more than an external imitation of episodes in Jesus's life. While it cannot be separated from liturgy, the actions enabled by character reach far beyond what is ordinarily meant by liturgy.

Sacramental character conveys an instrumental power instrumentally: Through the mediation of physical instruments, of bodies, it turns the recipient into a living instrument of God (3.63.2 corp). The specific potency of the character for participating in Christian rites derives from the priesthood of Christ: "believers are configured to his priesthood through sacramental characters" (3.63.3 corp). Indeed, characters are nothing but "participations in the priesthood Christ, derived from Christ himself"

(3.63.3 corp). The proper effect of character is being configured to a greater authority for which the recipient becomes a deputy, vicar, or instrument (3.63.3 ad2). The doctrine of character specifies or illustrates the images of incorporation into Christ that run through Thomas's questions on sacraments. Incorporation into the body of Christ expands the capacities for action.

Priesthood is not principally a social or legal status. The priest's office is to perform "sacrifices." Thomas redefines the word to include any external means for bringing participants closer to God.[16] Priestly performance leads participants toward their created ends. Christ's priesthood is eternal, Thomas has argued earlier, not because Christ needs to be purging sins into eternity but because the consummation of his sacrifice is the entry of human beings into divine life—the entry that he prepared by going ahead into heaven (3.22.5 corp). So far as sacramental character deputizes believers to receive and perform Christian sacraments, it joins them to the fulfillment of human life by giving them means and mediator, sufficient education and promise of consummation. Baptized into Christ's death, the believer no longer lives, but Christ in her. Baptism inaugurates a series of inhabitations or vicarious performances that reach backward, sideways, and forward through a united history.

On Thomas's account, the Christian becomes an instrument of Christ, shares in Christ's priesthood, in order to be moved toward final participation in divine life. Believers see this finality most vividly in Eucharist, which is for Thomas the principal act of divine worship. The Eucharist does not impress a character of its own; the other sacramental characters are given for its sake. Sharing the meal both requires and confirms a kind of membership. Eucharist presupposes the characters of membership given in baptism and (ideally) confirmation, as it presupposes the character of ordained priesthood for its consecration.

The Eucharist is at once the culmination and the limit case for an account of the sacraments. The reader must remember that the sacrament occurs before the host is consumed. On Thomas's account, the central moment of the sacrament is the transubstantiation. This transformation at once completes and denies the principle of signification. The consecrated bread or wine is a sign that actually *becomes* the thing it signifies without in any way resembling that thing. This sacrament seems almost to taunt ordinary perception. The whole substance of the bread and wine are converted into the body and blood of Christ without a ripple in what can be seen, touched, tasted, smelled (3.75.2–8). Even when there is a miraculous vision associated with the Eucharistic consecration, the real body and blood of Jesus are not seen (3.76.8 corp and ad2). Yet, what the senses cannot see, faith claims—and loves.

In an affecting passage, Thomas argues that the Eucharist is gift of bodily friendship (3.75.1 corp). The Christ who came to teach and suffer in his body would not leave the faithful bereft after his ascension. Friends are supposed to live together, and Christ promised his friends his bodily presence as a special gift (*praemium*). So that "his bodily presence would not be lacking in this pilgrimage," Christ left behind the Eucharist "[joining] us to himself in the truth of his body and blood" (3.75.1 corp). Of course, the presence is mute: the friend does not continue to speak. Some of his remembered words are spoken by other bodies at the sacramental memorial of his last meal. Christian communities treasure other words about him—words that he did not write (except vicariously). Even so, the "familial joining" to Christ in the Eucharist is the "sign of greatest love and the uplifting of our hope." The moral teaching of body to body continues even after the Ascension.

Sacramental liturgy makes forms of life available for inhabitation. If inhabiting forms or figures is a kind of incarnation, its sacramental beginning is incarnational in two further senses. The beginning takes place through particular bodies—this water, this oil, this bread and wine, but also these hands, this assembly. More important, it depends upon the priesthood of the incarnate Son who remains miraculously present in his body. The believer is said to put on Christ—by imitation, if you like, but more emphatically by inhabitation, by eating, by loving presence. The believer's body now acts as if she were Christ, acts Christ, but also acts with Christ and as Christ's body.

Sacraments as Scenes of Instruction

Just here a reader reaches what is most striking about Thomas's notion of sacramental efficacy: a bodily event that recalls another event that once befell a friend's body. On Thomas's account, the causal power of Christian sacraments depends not on incarnation abstractly but on a particular episode of Jesus's life, namely the passion. Sacraments are efficacious signs because they are repeated performances of an event that was the culmination of the incarnation as divine teaching. The bloody execution of God is moral teaching for embodied souls that have become savage but that can still learn from what they see. The same pedagogy of divine incarnation continues through the sacraments, which have as their center the (traumatic) memory of the Eucharistic gift that anticipated the spectacle of sacrifice. The gift is a pattern of divine life offered for eating in a repeated and yet singular table scene. You can take that conundrum as a key to Thomas's view of all the sacraments.

The divine teaching of the New Law is not principally a text or picture. It is a sequence of actions that must be repeated in action, as actions, for the divine teaching to attain its goal. Moreover—the second approach—in these discussions Thomas understands words within events. If the sacramental words are not performatives in the strictest Austinian sense, they are performances, and they have their full effect—which is their consequential meaning—in relation to bodies.

The sacraments are teaching events. They are designed to produce an effect of grace while showing as much of it as they can. The effect of the sacraments is grace that arrives as instruction. The lesson is reiterated in the arguments of *convenientia* that Thomas supplies in the *Summa* for each of the seven sacraments. Each of them, down to its details, is an intelligible response to the condition of sinful minds in bodies. This point should not be forgotten in thinking of any sacrament, including the Eucharist. However fascinating the metaphysics of transubstantiation, the Eucharistic liturgy is also an act of mimesis. It is celebrated in obedience to a direct command given by the Lord who is a friend: "Do this in memory of me." Whatever else it is, the Eucharist is learning by repeating what a teacher did first. The believer's body joins the collective recollection of a gift to be consumed.

Such a view of sacramental efficacy as moral (re)formation has many consequences for the rest of the *Summa*. It would suggest that teaching takes place in words but more effectively in (remembered) events of bodily teaching. So the writing of moral theology must display scenes of instruction, recalling speeches alongside exemplary deeds. Thomas believes this. He also sees it in the library left by his authoritative predecessors, who wrote Christian moral teaching in imitation at once of biblical narrative, hagiography, and liturgy.

PART II

Writing Scenes of Moral Instruction

The wager of my reading segments of the *Summa* in reverse order is that understanding the third part will prepare for a better reading of the second. The moment has arrived to look backward—though not yet to the *secunda*. I need first to draw out some lessons for moral reading from the third part. Consider this a reflective interlude, perhaps an *intermezzo*.

The first lesson from *Summa* 3 ought now to be obvious. The incarnation, the events of Christ's life, the legacy of sacraments—Thomas explains all of these as most appropriate responses to the rejection of divine teaching that is human sin. So the moral teaching of the *Summa* hardly stops at the end of the second part. It cannot stop there, because it has not reached the most persuasive forms of ethical teaching, which are the remedial narration and repeated ritual of the third part. Whatever completion of moral teaching the *Summa* can offer comes in its concluding part.

The second lesson ought also to be obvious, though it can be curiously hard for contemporary readers to see. It is a lesson about the compositional forms of ethical teaching. Because human beings learn best how to live from enacted examples, God takes flesh to live an exemplary life, to break open hardened hearts with remembered deeds of love, and to leave behind repetitions of the teaching in sacramental events. One way to respond to Thomas's insistence on this *convenientia* of incarnation is to connect ethics with worship. Recent writers make this connection by reconsidering Christian "norms" as expressions of sacramental community or by comparing those norms to practices of ritual cultivation in other religious traditions. All of that is useful. Still I want to emphasize the often unstated lesson: If the most effective pedagogy for morals is incarnational and sacramental, we ought to write ethics accordingly. Ethics is obliged—as much as any "literature"—to take up the challenge of representing human lives. It is called to speak about embodiment, not despite it.

The lesson about writing applies beyond religious ethics. After all, the divine pedagogy is a diagnosis of human moral learning. So while Thomas draws these consequences from the history of salvation, he recognizes them in the traditions of ethical teaching that he inherits from philosophers beyond Israel and before the birth of Christ. The third part of the *Summa* provides a pattern for evaluating the whole history of moral teaching—including our own.

Christian traditions of moral writing began in competition with scenes of instruction staged by ancient Mediterranean philosophies.[1] The philosophic schools of Greco-Roman antiquity were preoccupied by the relations of teachers to learners and the limits on their effective restaging. To take the obvious example, every Platonic dialogue represents a scene of ethical instruction even as it worries, explicitly or implicitly, about representation itself. Philosophical writers alongside or after Plato offer an exemplary life, a biography, as the privileged pattern for showing morals. Other ancient texts record the daily transactions in a philosophical school: lectures, of course, but also the give-and-take of argument or the scrutiny of ambiguous cases. The ethical works of Aristotle condense his school's ongoing debate, including its gradual revision of terms and arguments. Many ancient works cast instruction as a letter to a distant student. The epistolary form is no mere convention; it reactivates an absent community of relations and so underwrites persuasion. Still other texts are collections of striking sayings meant to be carried through daily life either "in the hand" as a portable reminder (a handbook) or better yet in memory. Then there are what we tend to call "allegorical" readings of canonical texts—like Neoplatonic readings of Homer—or else allegories simply speaking (if allegory is ever simple), including some in which the allegorical covering becomes so satisfying that it raises doubts about whether any further teaching lies behind (as with Apuleius).

I recall this history because Christian moral instruction appropriates all of these philosophical forms as it carries on the teaching of its scriptures and liturgies. Sometimes the appropriation of philosophy is explicit. Ambrose sets out to rewrite Cicero's letter, *On Duties*, for Christian ministers. Augustine redoes the famous Stoic handbook, the *Enchiridion* of Epictetus. Gregory of Nyssa rewrites Plato's *Phaedo* in retelling the death of his sister, the ascetic Macrina, and their final conversation about the soul's immortality. Christian moral readings of the Hebrew Scriptures are now notorious, but they need to be judged alongside other Christian allegories, in all their splendid ambiguity. Boethius's *Consolation of Philosophy*—that remembered, allegorical rehearsal of songs for soul-therapy—can still provoke debates over how far it is a Christian work.

The unbridled polemic of some Christian writers against ancient Mediterranean schools of philosophy should not obscure deeper agreements. Both the ancient philosophers and their Christian successors wrote morals as representations of scenes of instruction. Early and medieval Christian libraries register the importance of the moral scene in dozens of genres—in those I have mentioned and many others: moralized encyclopedias of the liberal arts, saints lives and miracle stories, bestiaries, mystery plays, and, of course, liturgies and sacramental rites. When the "history" of Christian ethics is written in disregard of these forms or genres, much of it is lost. An adequate history must register the importance of the scenes by appreciating or reactivating them, one after the other.

Here I will try for something less than that but more than standard intellectual history. In the three chapters of this interlude, I assemble a set of reminders about Thomas's place in the textual records of scenes of moral instruction, both pagan and Christian. The chapters are arranged in a rough chronology. The first emphasizes Thomas's *past*: his inheritance of what were for him old forms of moral writing. The second turns to Thomas's *present*: his transformation of inherited forms in their repeated citation. The third chapter traces and then projects his book's *future*: a recapitulation of actual reception history that becomes a reverie of how Thomas might yet be received. Seen from another angle, the chapters are parallel efforts to appreciate how Thomas's way of writing differs both from its models and the expectations of many of its readers, past and present. They describe Thomas's writing as a scene of *belated anticipation*.

None of these chapters pretends to be complete. The libraries of ancient and medieval moral writing are large and still poorly known. Many works have been lost. Others are preserved in as yet unedited or uncatalogued manuscripts. If most remain untranslated, some have been translated poorly. I regret these limits, but then I repeat that I am not interested in trying to tell anything like a comprehensive history. My aim is only restore a reader's sense of the compositional possibilities that Thomas transformed in the *Summa*. Whatever there is here of history serves the appreciation of his writing.

A fresh reading of the long arc of Christian moral writing—or a comparative reading—notices quickly enough the gradual eclipse of important genres. The eclipse is caused by the interaction of various movements. One long process is *legalization*, by which I mean recasting Christian scenes of instruction as courtrooms and rewriting Christian ethics into human law. A reader can trace this process in the growing regulation of penance or confession, which takes on both the procedures and the purposes of criminal judgment. She can follow it as well through patterns of moral codification, both in grand schemes for principles and in the meticulous classification of cases. An equally important process is the deployment of moral theology as a tool for *polemic*. It is hard to overstate the effect of continuing controversies on genres in modern Christian ethics. Or of the Enlightened conviction that any religious ethics has to be shrunk, stripped, for the sake of rationalized duty or tolerant peace.

Whatever the causes, the loss of embodied scenes of instruction in Christian ethics is the loss of significant power to represent and shape lives. The reduction—the impoverishment—of the genres for writing Christian ethics not only cramps present teaching, it distorts our relation to the past. We strain to hear what is written in many older works of moral instruction because we have never been taught to recognize the scenes in them.

CHAPTER 4

Scenes of Instruction

A very familiar story about Thomas Aquinas tells that he achieved a "synthesis" of Reason (represented by Aristotle) and Revelation (represented by the Christian Scriptures or Augustine or church authority).[1] To my mind, the story offers little help to reading the *Summa*. "Synthesis" turns attention from the actual features of Thomas's texts to ready conclusions and portable products. It directs readers to look for the *Summa*'s results in abstract sums rather than changed relations to the end of living. It distracts attention from the form of the *Summa*'s teaching and its figuration of the teacher.

On its surface, the form of instruction in the *Summa* corresponds to none of the older forms that it is supposed to be synthesizing or harmonizing. The dialectic of the *Summa*'s questions matches neither the genres of Aristotle nor those of Augustine. It resembles neither the great works of ancient philosophy nor their early Christian transformations. If Thomas "synthesizes" older ethics, then, he seems to do so by disregarding their deliberate practices of ethical teaching. Again, if the *Summa* offers itself as a curriculum for formation in full view of ethical traditions, it does not appear to conduct "spiritual exercises" in the way that pagan philosophers or their early Christian readers did.[2] How, then, can the *Summa* be the continuation of ancient or early Christian genres of moral writing?

I take this as a useful question rather than a decisive objection. I concede at once that some features of the *Summa* make it difficult to recognize any resemblances to older traditions of moral writing. For example, the size of the *Summa* renders its largest structures invisible to most readers, who can manage to read only a few bits. The few readers who do attempt the whole text easily lose themselves in thousands of distinctions. By another optical illusion, the standardizing format of Thomas's disputations can suggest that he has no interest in persuasion. These *are* illusions. A disputed question is indeed a scene of instruction, and the *Summa*'s scale measures the time required for staging them across the minimum selection of inherited topics and languages.

To dispel the illusions, I need to present something of the range of compositional forms for ethics that Thomas receives. I start from the ancient notion that writing ethics is not so much confecting arguments as presenting scenes.[3]

Setting a Scene

In ancient moral writing, a scene of instruction is typically a *place*, real or imagined. Some scenes of instruction spread out in luxurious detail: the exact plan of a room or walled garden, with its furnishings and decoration; its sounds—laughter, quarreling, sighs, music—or deliberately none; a fragrance or a stench; drowsy heat or alerting breezes; the display of implements readied for a feast or an execution. Other scenes take place on a bare stage where the wavering background only hints at shapes, while the props are few and unstable. Either way, the space of the scene already begins to teach readers about ethical instruction. Is the scene to be public or private? How may one enter it? How is it connected to other places—to the kitchen or bedroom, the marketplace, the temple? Is it a place in which some normal expectations are suspended or severely enforced?

A scene of instruction is also a *time*. The moral teaching may begin at a specified hour or fall on an anniversary. Summer brings cicadas to the overhanging tree, or the night promises a torchlit procession to honor a Thracian goddess. (These are the times of Plato's *Phaedrus* and *Republic*.) Other scenes refuse to settle on any fixed calendar. They unroll outside of time or roll time back over itself. Still, every scene of instruction, even one that happens in a visionary moment, becomes a sequence, the steps or stages of learning. So the scene's time leads quickly to other questions about ethical teaching: How much time does the scene's pedagogy require—fifty minutes, a year of late adolescence, more than a lifetime? What must happen before the scene can begin? What hopes or fears forecast its future?

Together, the place and time of a scene set the stage for its *characters*. Characters are more stylized and diverse than human beings. For example, they do not always possess bodies, though disembodied characters—souls, virtues, demons, deities—are often lent bodies for the scene's duration. During a scene, the body may express or enact a lesson. It can also change, resist, suffer, fall away. Characters are patterns for thoughts, passions, and words as much as deeds. Some characters present a fixed pattern, yet there can be no scene of instruction unless at least one character can change. A scene of instruction is an occasion for bringing new meanings into action, for binding new words into bodies. At least one character is liable to be remade by it. The change in that character is the scene's chief action.

Scenes display, perform, and address characters. Some ethical characters, the most obvious, are held up for praise and blame. They are simple examples. Be like this! Do not be like this! *Example-characters* tend to matter more in the writing of premodern ethics than principles, rules, or cases. More consequential still are the characters that constitute the scene as instruction: the learner, the teacher, the witnesses or bystanders. I sometimes distinguish these as *protagonist-characters*. The relations enacted by the protagonist-characters are usually both the means and the substance of ethical teaching. Their relations make ethical teaching significant, effective, and memorable. More important, they make it possible.

The various characters in a scene of instruction are not bright drapery for moral lessons taught more accurately in the form of rules or theories. If they exemplify certain actions concretely, they *teach* action only through certain affective relations they enable for a learner. The function of the scene is to establish and cultivate moral relations through which teaching can take place. A learner may feel such relations with any of the figures in a scene, but the decisive relations typically run to the figure of the teacher— or constitute one figure especially as teacher. Ancient scenes of instruction represent relations of teacher to learner in order to strengthen such relations. The scene of instruction that exemplifies a learner's proper disposition to teaching becomes an occasion for practicing or exercising that very disposition. This practice often leads through a sort of conversion. A student who has come to learn something trivial stays on to learn something important. A fan drawn to a display of rhetoric catches fire with another love. These changes occur in the relations to the figure of the teacher.

I have been talking so far as if the scenes happened right before our eyes. Some of them do—or once did. Much ethical instruction in antiquity was carried out in "real time," on living bodies. A teacher would address a group of students or give private counsel to someone seeking care. Still, and early on, these embodied scenes of instruction were doubled by written scenes. A teacher might become famous enough to merit the circulation of transcripts. Or a passionate and gifted student might forgo writing dramas to record the acts of a master who died too soon (a story told of Plato). Or a teacher might choose to present scenes that could only be written: episodes of divine instruction in a mythic or visionary past. Once scenes are retold or represented in texts or pictures, another set of characters arrives. To the characters *within* the textual frame are added the characters *of* the frame: the author and reader, the dramaturge and viewer. I call them *frame-characters*. Written scenes can sometimes incite or begin moral conversions: A mere author can become a persuasive teacher.

The effect is neither automatic nor free of risk. There is an old worry in Mediterranean traditions about transcribing moral scenes. Some powerful authors express sharp doubts about them—as Plato does in both *Phaedrus* and the so-called seventh letter. Those doubts do not keep the authors from writing. Few ancient schools are reported to have refused writing altogether (though some held back choice secrets). Even teachers who vigorously resisted erudite forms and emphasized bodily action encouraged the passing down of illustrative stories. At the same time, few writers presumed that the representation of a scene of ethical instruction could be literal or complete. It was more likely to be related to events of teaching ironically or emblematically. It could represent them by its failures and silences. It was a script or set of directions that would only make sense when performed. Representation did not capture ethical instruction so much as incite or reactivate it. Of course, written instruction need not be a mere transcription of oral teaching. If it raised new problems, it also provided new possibilities. Perhaps a text could even accomplish some things that a living teacher could not—if only by a sort of action at a distance.

Heirs in so many ways of ancient philosophy, early Christian teachers regularly write with the confidence that representing scenes can produce important effects. This belief is a corollary of the Christian trust in Scriptures. It is also the principle of incarnation. To receive Scriptures—especially Gospels—is to accept the power of moral formation through writing. Once written down, scenes teach through the features peculiar to writing. Take Matthew's telling of the Sermon on the Mount. Christians encounter this scene not by direct experience but as textual construct. The scene is enriched with textual devices of allusion and symmetry. It displays a variety of characters, both exemplary and enacted. As inherited text, it elicits new relations in communities that transmit or interpret it. Thomas believes that the Sermon on the Mount was an event, but he expounds it by referring to the material memory of an authorized narration.

The Gospels' patterns of teaching and learning pass down into the many institutions of Christian teaching. Thomas lives them as a baptized Christian, a communicant, and a Dominican. He comments on them in reading the Scriptures. He imitates them in other teaching relations. He expects the scenes to have strong effects, especially in relation to the Teacher and his students or delegates. For Thomas, it is obvious that a student should practice reverence for a teacher (2-2.103.4 corp). It is so obvious that Judas's kissing Christ at the moment of betrayal might be explained not as cynical display but as the last trace of a communally shared habit of reverence.[4] Thomas also believes that teachers can be said without scandal to love their students with the affect of *dilectio*. The teacher's affect is associated with John, the disciple whom Jesus is said especially to have loved.[5]

The more fully a reader appreciates the affecting and effective writing of ancient philosophy or early Christian formation, the more sharply the original question presses. The *Summa* is not written in the form of a Gospel narrative. If its third part reassembles Christ's narrated life as moral exemplar, it does so in a string of disputed questions. When Thomas analyzes the elements of human action or sorts the relations of virtues and vices, he does not present a succession of detailed cases or a parade of moral characters. He does not even seem to solicit or elicit a reader's attachment. How then can the *Summa* be regarded as the continuation of ancient or early Christian scenes of instruction? How is it anything other than their formal rejection, page after page? Let me begin addressing these questions with Thomas's relation to traditions of philosophical writing, then turn to theology.

Thomas and Philosophic Writing

Why does Thomas reject the teaching forms of ancient philosophy? One answer to the question would be a plea of ignorance: Thomas could not read many of the ancient works. They were unavailable in Latin or preserved in rare copies. Thomas had no direct acquaintance with the Platonic dialogues, the transcripts of Epicurus's teaching, or Diogenes

Laertius's collection of the lives and sayings of teachers in many ancient schools. Much less could Thomas have known the vivid satires of ancient philosophic life in Aristophanes or Lucian. These hazards of transmission prevented him from knowing as much about ancient philosophic writing as his "Renaissance" successors soon would.

Unacquainted with many of the finest texts from antiquity, Thomas did know criticisms of them. He receives in the Aristotelian corpus both complaints against the early cosmological poets and more precise objections to Plato's composition of dialogues. Thomas repeats both complaints and objections. He further inherits Augustine's critiques of ancient mythography and the philosophical excesses to which it led.[6] So, Thomas retraces a double judgment on the use and abuse of image in ancient religion and philosophy. He repeats that the ancient poets and philosophers sometimes veiled truth under delightful fables accommodated to the understanding of their readers.[7]

Thomas agrees: Fables are indeed delightful. If a performed representation delights, so too does a representation in words. Indeed, "fable" refers properly not to falsehood but to this artifact of representation that moves the viewers to understand something hidden.[8] Just here Thomas's doubts begin. He has learned that the earliest philosophers were "theologizing poets" who composed in meter.[9] His harsh view of the limits of poetry prevents him from regarding their products as anything more than a prelude to philosophy.[10] Sometimes the problem with a fable is that only its author knows what exactly it means. A fable taken one way can be reprehensible, taken another way, laudable.[11] After all, heretics are also fond of fables.[12] So to say that a philosopher writes "fabulously" is not to speak praise.[13]

Thomas's worry over the abuse of concealment does not mean that he always holds every philosopher to full disclosure. His judgments are more particular. In expounding Aristotle's *On the Heavens*, for example, Thomas explains the difference between exoteric and esoteric genres, between teachings meant to be read by the many and those to be heard only by a few.[14] He gestures toward the same distinction in the traditional subtitle of Aristotle's *Physics*.[15] If Thomas sometimes allows Aristotle to distinguish the many and the few, he does not approve the consistently poetic style of Plato. According to some ancient commentators, he reports, Plato wrote to conceal his true teaching behind stories and enigmas.[16] These commentators fault Aristotle for attacking only the surface meaning. Thomas shrugs off the controversy as beside the point of his exposition: he means to get through dialectically opposed opinions to the truth about things. So he reproves the obscure style of the Platonists and justifies Aristotle in attacking the misunderstandings to which such a style inevitably gives rise.[17]

In these scattered remarks, Thomas expresses a worry that embellishment in a philosophic text may undo teaching. The taste for exotic concealment can give rise to errors or hide those already committed. Would Thomas have amended his judgment if he had known more of the library of ancient philosophy? The question cannot be answered confidently, but I suggest that the evidence counts against amendment. Other medieval writers who knew even less of ancient philosophic writing adopted its narrative or figural genres. (Call to mind Alan of Lille in the *Anticlaudianus* or *The Plaint of Nature*.) In contrast, Thomas seems to have been persuaded of the greater usefulness of both the language and the genres of the Aristotelian corpus. I do not attribute this to an innate or acquired Aristotelianism. It is at once Thomas's judgment about genre in philosophy and his reminder that he needs philosophy at the service of theology.

Thomas complains against poetic cosmologists and Platonists that they are needlessly obscure. He objects to the loss of directness in teaching even as he recognizes ancient teachers' motives for it. Thomas is not ruling out certain genres (the dialogue, the narrative) so much as he is criticizing writing that undoes itself in clever conceits. In the Aristotelian texts, he seems to admire the tireless effort to rectify philosophic speech by making it at once truer and clearer.[18]

Thomas admires the composition of the Aristotelian corpus. He is not trying to repeat it because does not mean to write philosophy.[19] He uses philosophical words in another sort of text. The reader has been told that the *Summa* is the holy teaching (*sacra doctrina*) needed for Christian religion (*religio*). The plainer the form of the philosophical text, the more easily it can be appropriated for that sort of theological composition. The discursively organized excurses of the Aristotelian corpus are easier to incorporate into the forms of academic theology that Thomas adopts. Records of ongoing debate, the Aristotelian texts that Thomas receives resemble the forms of his classroom. Accepting Aristotle's judgment on more poetic forms of writing, Thomas both confirms and enables his own choice of philosophical genres useful to theology.

Thomas and the Narration of Christian Theology

Nothing in Thomas's critique of ancient mythography or philosophical fable excludes figure and narration as forms of Christian truth-telling.

Indeed, and from the beginning of the *Summa*, Thomas has explicitly defended the use of poetic devices in Scripture. Philosophy should proceed with a minimum of fable or figure; theology cannot do without them.[20]

Thomas returns to the defense of theology's reliance on image and narrative at many points in the *Summa*. Let me mention two. The first—the more obvious—comes in the justification of Jesus's parables (3.42.3).[21] Parables seem to suffer all the defects of poetic obscurity. Thomas describes them as a veil or fabric (*tegumentum*) over spiritual teaching (3.42.3 corp). He admits that they provoke incomprehension in many hearers.[22] Still, he finds it appropriate that Jesus speak to the public in parables. The Lord explains them to his chosen disciples, who then go on to spread his message over time and as appropriate. Moreover, Jesus does not always teach in parables. Often he speaks plainly to the crowds that follow him (3.42.3 ad3). (Thomas elsewhere suggests that some in the crowd may have learned how to listen through his parables.)[23] When Jesus chooses to speak parables, though, he does so to cover for a time or for some hearers the highest spiritual truths.

Thomas links parables to the narrative form of the Gospels. The four canonical books narrate material signs because human beings learn best through them, especially about difficult things. There is no way to remove narrative from theology without undoing the fundamental pedagogy of Scripture. So Thomas applies the term *narratio* to the Gospels without hesitation or qualification. He repeats the phrase "Gospel narration" as a sort of pleonasm (3.5.3 corp, 4 corp). The Gospels are wholly narration because they seek to register the scene of instruction that is the whole life of the incarnate God.

The point should be underlined. The Gospels are constructed as stories because the action of God incarnate was the best form of moral instruction for embodied intelligences fallen into sin. Thomas explains the divine choice of narrative. He also imitates it when he retells the Gospel events. So Thomas's objections to ancient philosophic styles cannot disqualify narrative or embodied representation altogether. They are either complaints about excessive artifice or recognition of philosophy's limited role in the hierarchy of learning. For Thomas, theology is not bound by the limits of philosophy. Its range of styles is much greater. It can—it must—use narrative and other forms of poetic representation. But that only brings back the impelling question: Where is narrative in the *Summa* beyond the retelling of the Gospels? And how is disputation an effective form of narration?

Thomas's repetition of Gospel stories raises a still sharper doubt. His emphasis on the uniqueness of the Gospels' narration might imply the impossibility of any further narration, of any later scene. There could be only one pedagogical scene: the historical unfolding of the one incarnation. What then does it mean to write morals after the Gospels, alongside their sacramental extensions? What scene of instruction is possible to a *Summa of Theology*?

The Scene of the Summa

Thomas hands on theological traditions that emphasize the role of the embodied teacher. He insists in the *Summa* that the privileged form of Christian moral instruction is a narrative of the manifestations in divine incarnation. Yet Thomas does not write the *Summa* in explicitly narrative forms. Instead, he seems to presuppose narratives in order to explicate and reorder them.[24] What, then, is the scene of instruction represented by the *Summa* itself?

Textual inheritance is the obvious feature of the *Summa*'s construction. It might offer the best clue to its scene. Thomas writes at a certain time in the communication of divine teaching. He inherits theologies that emphasize the uniqueness of the incarnation, its record in the canonical Scriptures, and its pedagogical legacy in sacraments. Jesus Christ has accomplished the manifestation of the full truth for all, commissioning his own preachers to spread the good news. He instituted sacraments to continue miraculously the healing ministry of his presence. No preacher can do again what Christ did. Certainly, no preacher can do more. At most, a latter-day preacher can proclaim what has already happened elsewhere and then invite hearers to share in its mysterious, ritual repetition.

The Christian theologian is constrained by a stronger *belatedness*. If preachers are sent out into the world before Scriptures were written, if they aim to assist a faith that comes from God through hearing, the theologian is a reader of sacred texts who wants to continue writing after them. Whenever Thomas writes theology, the revealed texts precede him. They give ground to his writing; they also encircle it. Thomas presumes that the typical readers of the *Summa* will have heard about how to live from more authoritative texts than his own. Readers will reach the *Summa* already tutored in Gospel narratives and in commentaries on them or disputes occasioned by them. The *Summa* comes afterward. Indeed, for Thomas theological writing is belated by definition, since theology is defined by its dependence on a historically transmitted revelation. So the *Summa*'s scene of instruction must look at once backward and forward to the lessons of a more powerful teacher. It occupies that place in time.

Thomas also inherits fragments of ancient philosophical traditions that value the intimate scene of instruction as the site of moral formation. Many of them describe a correction—sometimes a lifelong correction—of faulty lessons learned earlier from family or city. Much of ancient philosophy is a project of reeducation. Thomas stands in very different relation to his pedagogical inheritance. The theological traditions he affirms place any human teacher outside and after the most important scene of moral instruction. The original scene is not to be corrected. It can only be cited reverently. If Thomas knows a little of the pedagogy of ancient philosophy, a reader must still suppose that the shape of his writing would not have changed much had he known it all. Thomas's writing would always have displayed his dependence on the teaching of an incarnate God recorded by revealed texts and reiterated in sacraments that transform a community of students into a church of pilgrims to beatitude.[25]

The *Summa* constructs a series of scenes that are belated and *anticipatory*. The setting for its teaching is not the desert of Moses's revelations or the shores of Galilee. Nor does the *Summa* sample the speech of heaven, even if it claims that theology depends on what the blessed know. Instead, every article in the *Summa* is a simplifying imitation of classroom teaching in the present. Each article rehearses a disputation. In the full performance of public disputation, the presiding master first supervises the presentation of arguments and authorities on several sides of a controversy. After reflection, the master determines the issue by arguing a position that does justice to all the authorities. The master's determination answers a question while reconciling or at least sorting competing languages. The master obviously sets an example of how to speak better. What other sorts of example does the master give? Or what are the virtues of a classroom disputation considered as a scene of belated instruction?

Describing the scene of the *Summa* is never easy. Thomas prefers to perform examples of disputation rather than set out rules. Still, some passages help explain how he proceeds. In the *Summa* itself, for example, there is an article on disputing publicly with unbelievers. In it, Thomas usefully distinguishes several kinds of disputation. Those who hear a dispute about theology may be "instructed and firm in faith" or else "simple and hesitant."[26] The simple and hesitant are further divided between those who inhabit regions without conflict over orthodoxy and those who live where they are "solicited and buffeted by the unfaithful." Faced with heretical solicitations, the master in dispute must be ready to "confute errors" (*errores confutare*). The phrase recurs later in the article when Thomas writes that "one ought not to dispute about the things that are of faith as if doubting them, but in order to make truth manifest and to confute errors."[27] Simple, hesitant believers need to hear error corrected so that their faith is strengthened and the ability of heretics to deceive is checked for the future. Dominican preachers in training need to be prepared to perform that ministry for others. But even those "instructed and firm in faith" need to be shown a fuller truth. That purpose of disputation holds as much in university halls or Dominican houses of study as in regions of heresy and unbelief.

Thomas makes the connection himself in one of his brief "quolibetal" questions. He is asked whether a master when determining theological questions should use reason or authority. He answers by distinguishing two purposes for disputation. The first is to remove doubt "whether it is that way" (*an ita sit*).[28] To accomplish this first purpose, Thomas says, a master should use whatever authorities are admitted by those with whom he (not, in context, she) might be disputing.[29] Of course, disputation may have another purpose. A master disputes "in schools" not to remove error but to "instruct those listening so that they may be led to an understanding of the truth that he intends" (*ad intellectum veritatis quam intendit*). In this case, the master must proceed by reasonings or definitions to investigate "the root of the truth" (*radix veritatis*). Those listening must be brought to understand how what the master says is true. Otherwise they will learn nothing and go away empty.

The passage from the occasional question and the parallels to it are usually read for what they say about the relation of reason to authority. They may say more about the purposes in a scene of theological disputation—and so the virtues required in a master who presides over it. Elsewhere Thomas adds a bit more. In his inaugural lecture as regent master, he distinguishes three "offices" or duties of the "teachers of Sacred Scripture": preaching, reading (or expounding), and disputing.[30] Teachers must lead exemplary lives in order to preach effectively. They must be illuminated in order to teach correctly when expounding. Finally, the *doctores* must be well "armed" or prepared in order to "confute errors by disputing." What strikes me in this passage is not only the presumed unity of the three offices but also the moral expectations for each.

Thomas emphasizes both the moral purposes of teaching and the moral example of the teacher when describing controversial settings—the master not in school but in public disputation with those who doubt or deny Christianity. In the opening of *Against the Gentiles*, Thomas considers at length the prospects for argument in relation to two kinds of truth. In "what we confess of God," some truths exceed every power of human reason" while "natural reason can also reach" other truths.[31] The distinction justifies the plan of the whole work, so Thomas picks it up again in the last prefatory chapter. Truths that human minds can discover should be set forth by demonstrative reasons "through which the adversary can be convinced."[32] The teacher should not try to "convince the adversary" about higher truths by the same arguments. The only way of "convincing the adversary" about the higher truths is by the authority of the Scriptures confirmed in miracles. Still, if a teacher's arguments should not try "to convince adversaries," they can serve for the "exercise and consolation of the faithful."

What does Thomas mean by "convincing" an adversary—the phrase he repeats five times in a few lines from *Against the Gentiles*? Is the master's work only to refute the adversary's views in some abstract logical space?[33] No, a fuller persuasion is required. After all, this passage completes the prologue to *Against the Gentiles*. The prologue began with a praise of wisdom. The highest wisdom looks to the universal end. The universal end is the good of intellect, namely, truth. "And so divine wisdom clothed itself in flesh and came into the world to testify for the manifestation of truth."[34] The teacher of Christ's wisdom is called both to speak truth and to fight against error. The master does so in virtue of a double temporal reference. Errors that hamper human living *can* be convicted because God took flesh to lead a teacher's life. Errors *must* be convicted on the way to a fuller showing of a truth. A master's moral example cannot stop with logical refutation. Any theological refutation succeeds in view of a promise. The principal virtue shown by a master in disputation is belated *anticipation*— or inherited hope.

The task of theological disputation is to investigate the root of a truth that those listening profess but cannot yet understand or possess.[35] The investigation may be helped by establishing creedal teaching and refuting attacks on it. Still, it requires more than notional assent or verbal consistency. The theological teacher seeks to show the truth by showing what Thomas has called its root. The root is a reason but also an embodied testimony—the testimony of Wisdom itself taking on flesh. Thomas says earlier in the *Summa* that any teacher is like a physician helping the body to heal itself, not least by "strengthening" it (1.117.1 corp). The teacher of Christian wisdom is more precisely like someone who leads the student home. Presiding over a public disputation, the master exercises gifts and virtues by making a determination within a tradition—standing late in it while urging toward its culmination. This anticipating belatedness is not a species melancholy so much as matured desire.

Thomas does not write the *Summa* as a narrative because the teacher's virtues he means to show are those of inheriting a narrative more persuasive than any he could write. His task is to clear the way for its persuasion. More: He cannot perform this teaching in isolation. The *Summa* is not meant to persuade on its own. Thomas teaches after and in relation to ongoing scenes of scriptural preaching and sacrament. The *Summa* supposes them from article to article without needing always to recall them. Christ remains the teacher throughout the *Summa* whether he is named or not. A reader might picture the *Summa* as a marginal comment alongside Gospels and sacraments. Thomas's writing everywhere supposes their scenes without having to mime them.

Thomas does not write narrative because the plot that most interests him is the one traced in readers' souls by the graced effects of the authoritative narratives he recalls—narratives spoken and acted, written and repeated. Thomas does not want his stories, his fables, to compete with those being written by the Trinity onto hearts. In the *Summa*'s prologue, Thomas undertook to help beginners by strict selection of inherited texts and topics. That minimalism can now be appreciated as a moral example, an expression of the theologian's belated anticipation, which is the *Summa*'s scene of instruction. The anticipation begins in the present as hope that the reader will be changed inwardly by God.

The scene is a *via*, a way, that has been cleared by the teacher. Thomas's promise to provide only the useful is a promise not to distract from the divine pedagogy that continues to unfold in recounted revelation, sacrament, and vowed community. Thomas means to draw attention to that grand pedagogy. He hardly wants to put another story in its pace. To say that his scene of instruction foregoes its own narrative in yielding to the prior narrative of divine pedagogy is hardly faint praise. For Thomas, at least, it would be no praise at all to say of the *Summa* that it scribbled over divine grace. The book has its own beauties, but they are the beauties of belated anticipation. Written between incarnation and eschaton, it contents itself to help another teaching—more powerful, more urgently necessary.

CHAPTER 5

From Scenes to Authorities

If there is such a thing as "Scholasticism," it is something like a style of composing arguments around ranked quotations.[1] The style is distinguished by its way of quoting—by the balance of obligation and ownership, of subservience and invention. The quotations are called *auctoritates*. The term resists translation into current English. It might be rendered as "precedent" except that an *auctoritas* is usually not treated so roughly as a precedent in American law. Neither is an *auctoritas* a "source," even if modern editions track *auctoritates* in what they call a "source-apparatus." Nor is an *auctoritas* just a sort of footnote moved up into the body of the argument. Its function is neither documentary nor probative. Let me try to say what it is while suspending the question of translation: I will transliterate *auctoritas* as "authority."

An authority consists of *words*. The words are usually attributed to someone who deserves a hearing—though sometimes they are misattributed or else correctly attributed to a person who can safely be ignored. The words of an authority are recalled so that they can be applied to a particular topic—though they are sometimes not truly pertinent to it. At all times, and whoever originally spoke or wrote its words, the effective meaning or import of an authority is open to dispute.

The authority's words are typically transmitted as *separate* sayings, as a discrete unit. Indeed, it may mislead to conceive an authority as an excerpt from a larger text. Often an authority is deployed with scant awareness of any larger context except the context of the immediate argument. An authority resembles instead a separately remembered Gospel saying or other *dictum*. Thomas does sometimes refer to the whole texts from which authoritative quotations have been taken. He seeks to restore their authors' original "letter" or intent. In some cases, obviously, an authority will recall a larger argument or a striking example that Thomas may endorse or embellish. Still, for Thomas as for so many of his contemporaries, a theological dispute is not constructed by scouring whole texts anew in search of something pertinent. Disputation relies instead on practiced memories (or handy memory aids) that collect texts already parsed under topics. The "Scholastic" theologian's library is filled with anthologies of sayings, and a theologian may well assemble personal indexes as supplements to them.[2]

An authority is a *textual genealogy*. It might be compared to the Talmud's recording both rabbinic sayings and how those sayings were woven into a tradition. When Thomas recalls an authority in relation to a topic, he often tacitly calls up its various functions in earlier disputes. He further constrains its meanings by a criterion of pertinence to the matter at hand. Thomas's procedure discourages sentimentality about original meaning. It recognizes that authorities have often been twisted to make unlikely or outrageous points. By habit or by temperament, Thomas prefers to read authorities charitably, even when he disagrees with them. If an opponent alleges an authority in support of an error, Thomas often replies by denying the error while noting that the authority can mean something else.[3] Offering better readings, he may rebuke an obvious misinterpretation or decipher an enigma. Sometimes Thomas will trump one authority with another, much plainer, from the same author, or he will overcome a lesser author with a greater one. Mostly Thomas is content to remain within the confines of an authority rather than reaching behind it to a larger view of its author. He seems not to worry that the very procedure of arguing from authorities erases something essential to them.

Thomas applies authorities to all the topics across the *Summa*. His contemporaries disputed with authorities in every field of knowledge from grammar and logic through physics and metaphysics to medicine and law. There may still be something surprising when Thomas marshals topically excerpted authorities for *moral* teaching. The shift from narrating scenes of instruction to disputing disaggregated authorities looks to be a profound change in moral pedagogy. Indeed, it seems to repudiate the bases of the older teaching. The change does not coincide with the move from pagan philosophy to Christian theology. Earlier theologians, and precisely the ones Thomas counts as authoritative, had exerted themselves to imitate and then transform ancient moral genres. The change happens with Scholasticism—or we use the word "Scholasticism" to name the change without quite explaining it. Let me abandon the word's abstraction to study the change of form concretely in the *Summa*. I ask again: How can Thomas be faithful to the very traditions of *Christian* moral writing that he means to claim when he cuts up those texts and affixes them to disputed topics?

I can clarify the force of the question and begin some responses to it by using the relations among three texts. The first is Cicero's *On Duties*. The second is Ambrose's rewriting of Cicero as *On the Duties of Ministers*. The third linked text is the moral part of the *Summa*, in which Thomas conducts disputations—writes articles—using authorities from these works by Cicero and Ambrose.[4] In the textual relations among the three, a reader can study not only Thomas's transformation of ancient moral genres but also the transit from scenes to authorities—or the fashioning of new scenes from authorities.

From Cicero to Ambrose

Cicero's *On Duties* is a letter from a father to his son who is away at school. The writer is a Roman orator, the reader a student in Athens of philosophy. The father writes to commend his own example as a sometime student who cooled Athenian extravagance into Latin wisdom.[5] Cicero addresses his son again and again at prominent places in the text, such as the beginning and end of books.[6] He intends, of course, that his letter serve other readers, but he fuses that intention into a letter. When he claims at the very end to have taught as a fatherly gift, he has in mind two kinds of children—by blood, by reading. His text stages a scene of instruction for both kinds.

The familial address of Cicero's *On Duties* is reiterated in apostrophes or tacitly reinforced by allusions to the elder Cicero's accomplishments.[7] It is also required by the moral arguments. Cicero's typical argument appeals to example. Most of the examples have force only on the presupposition of prior relations. So *On Duties* contains some blunt appeals to family pride.[8] Then, more grandly, it summons Roman examples, the deeds of "our" elders or predecessors, the history of "our" polity.[9] *On Duties* draws dozens of figures from Roman history, especially in its second and third books.[10] Their examples are reinforced by reminders of the accumulated authority of Roman culture, of Latin poets, playwrights, and orators.[11]

If familial or civic address that calls to moral imitation empowers Cicero's teaching, it is also the pivot for a Christian rewriting of him. Ambrose declares in his title, *On the Duties of Ministers*, that he will appropriate and correct Cicero. He begins by altering the rhetorical address: "As Cicero wrote to educate his son, so I too write in order to form you, my children; nor do I love you less for having begotten you in the Gospel than if I had gotten you by marriage."[12] Ambrose speaks from love, a love as strong as a philosopher's teaching and a parent's anxiety intertwined. Yet, the motive of Ambrose's address is not the love of biological family or earthly city. Both must yield to the new community of church. So Ambrose replaces Cicero's unblushing use of himself as exemplar with a humble refusal of that role. Ambrose's children are not to imitate him—except perhaps in his self-denial before holier figures and other Fathers. With so many later teachers, including Thomas, Ambrose pictures himself as a mere pedagogue: He is a servant who leads even more ignorant students to school.

In Ambrose, examples are drawn from "our Scriptures," which provide Christians at once with the story of their family, their nation, and even their new species.[13] When he speaks of "our elders" or "our fathers," Ambrose means a parade of Old Testament figures.[14] Our "father" is Abraham, and Moses is "our Moses."[15] So far as a Christian becomes the spiritual child of God, she exchanges a biological genealogy for the lineage traced in the Scriptures. She can now hear the Hebrew Scriptures as direct address. "For whom was it written, if not for each of us," Ambrose asks of a verse in Sirach.[16] More emphatically, he rejects an abstract enumeration of virtues in order to introduce them by "the examples of the elders."[17] The figures stand before the reader, demanding response: "Look! Judith offers herself to you as admirable."[18] The only fit readers of Ambrose's text are those who become its children.

Through much of *On the Duties of Ministers*, Ambrose presents Israelite examples, making only brief allusions to Christ.[19] Then, at a crucial moment in Book 3, Ambrose discloses that the figure of Christ has been standing behind the Israelite stories.[20] Christ is revealed again, more strikingly, at the end of the whole treatise. Here Holy David is quoted, but the Lord Jesus speaks after him, more fully and more decisively, to offer the promise of eternal friendship. When Ambrose reveals Jesus speaking through David, a reader can perhaps recognize another sort of rhetorical correction in regard to Cicero. If the love that impels Ambrose is more urgent, the moral response he wants is quicker and more complete. Ambrose's reader does not receive an erudite reminder from a distant father who hopes that writing may protect his son from Athenian folly and so better prepare him for the mantle of Roman service. Ambrose demands from all who read an immediate acceptance and unreserved confirmation. There is, he urges, no other moral education than the education of Christ.

Ambrose announced in his title an appropriation and correction of Cicero's rhetorical address. Ambrose has carried out that work on multiple levels: in revising the motives of address, in appealing to a different history, and in intensifying the urgency of the imitation proposed. Through all these changes, Ambrose preserves the importance of Cicero's whole text as a scene of instruction. He has shown why and how a Christian theologian should imitate the genres chosen by ancient moralists even while transforming them. Thomas knows Ambrose's compositional choice. He chooses otherwise.

From Ambrose to Thomas

In the *Summa*, a reader encounters both Cicero and Ambrose. They appear without the rhetorical shapes or topical arrangements they devised and polished. They are both reduced to *auctoritates*. Using them in this way, Thomas not only chooses against Ambrose's rhetorical imitation of Cicero, he also appears to cancel the old genres of instruction altogether in favor of piecemeal contention. Is that appearance right?

The number of authorities in the *Summa* requires that any comprehensive study of them be statistical. So it is with Cicero and Ambrose: any thorough representation of their use by Thomas requires tables. Yet tables of citations cannot settle questions about reasons for the striking change in form. Without compiling them all, I want to note a few features of Thomas's citations to *On Duties* and *On the Duties of Ministers* in *Summa* 2-2.

Thomas invokes the two earlier works dozens of times from beginning to end of the *Summa*'s second part. As always, he repeats particularly useful citations. Certain text-units are affixed to particular topics; others are paired in patterns of affirmation and denial. The authorities also perform various functions in Thomas's arguments. Some quotations from Cicero and Ambrose become maxims. Ambrose is used, for example, to assert that the generous should not neglect their relatives or give ruinously to anyone (2-2.9. ad 2, 32.10, 117.1). Other quoted sayings define or classify. So

Thomas returns to Ambrose when he describes temperance (most extensively 2-2.141 and 144).

Thomas often cites Ambrose and Cicero together, as if interchangeably. Indeed, almost half of the citations to *On Duties* in *Summa* 2-2 fall within articles where *On the Duties of Ministers* is also cited.[21] In some articles, the two books are pitted against each other—for example, when Cicero figures as an "objection" and Ambrose in "on the contrary" (2-2.58.11, 77.3). In other passages, the two books are combined. In one "objection," for example, we read: "[Cicero] proves in *On Duties* that nothing can be expedient that is not honorable. The very same point is had from Ambrose in *On the Duties of Ministers*" (2-2.145.3 arg3). Just before this passage, in the two preceding articles, Cicero has figured twice as a prominent authority on the honorable.[22] So Ambrose here confirms a Ciceronian teaching that develops across several articles.

More interesting still is the second article of *Summa* 2-2.168, which asks whether there can be any virtue in play and relaxation. The query is not as silly as it might sound given the ferocity of Christian asceticism. Ambrose himself is quoted as urging his readers to forgo laughter and jokes altogether (2-2.168.2 arg1). Yet when Thomas sets about distinguishing permissible from impermissible play, he freely intermingles advice from Cicero and Ambrose. Indeed, if a reader is not careful, she will lose track of whose "book on duties" is cited in a given sentence.

Thomas uses the linked books by Cicero and Ambrose side by side or interchangeably. His procedures of combined citation appear to abolish the carefully crafted differences of voice that separate Ambrose from Cicero. The reduction to authorities seems further to ignore each author's preoccupation with the staging of moral persuasion. It is not just that Thomas mingles excerpts from their larger scenes. He neglects other textual features altogether. The examples that figure so importantly in both Cicero and Ambrose disappear from the *Summa*; so, too, do the resolutions of difficult cases. In their place, Thomas's reader finds the rapid dialectic of terminological and argumentative clarifications.

The question (or charge) is easy to generalize. Cicero and Ambrose are evidently not Thomas's only authorities in morals. They are not even his most regular authorities. Statistically, they fall somewhere in the middle range of frequency. Yet, even the most frequent authorities seem to lose their specific pedagogy when cut up into authorities.

For example, *Summa* 2-2 is filled with references to Aristotle's *Nicomachean Ethics*. Not all of them are equally interesting or—indeed—

characteristically Aristotelian. A tabulation of the citations to Aristotle will show that some are ornamental allusions, some superficial misreadings, some general maxims; some are peripheral while others are terminological; and only some are both topically specific and decisive for constructing the argument at hand.[23] Still, no number of disconnected authorities from Aristotle can carry the pedagogy of the *Nicomachean Ethics*.

A related if sharper question occurs with the *Summa*'s use of authorities from Gregory the Great. Gregory's *Moral Readings of Job* provides Thomas with many of his central terms and topics for moral matters. It also illustrates a way of reading the Christian Scriptures for moral instruction. I have suggested that the memory of an authority might bring with it some of the examples, cases, or arguments around it. The same holds for modes of scriptural reading. An accumulation of authorities from the *Moral Readings* might remind a reader of a whole art of interpretation. But no collection of discrete authorities from the *Moral Readings* can repeat Gregory's textual pedagogy in that book.

So the puzzle returns. What has happened to moral pedagogy in the transit from Christian imitations of pagan moral writing to the fragmentation of authorities in the middle part of the *Summa*? But perhaps this reiterated questions conceals a confusion. Fragmentation may subordinate the memory of authorities to deeper Christian memories. The greatest moral examples for Christian living are *not* recalled for the *Summa*'s readers by its quotations. They are brought into the living present by preached Scriptures and performed sacraments. The remembered teaching of any moral authority like Cicero or Ambrose must fit within the stronger memory of grace incarnate. The wholeness of graced memory is what Thomas tries to picture in the *Summa*'s procedure.

Textual Memories

The structure of each article in the *Summa* recalls the performance of disputation. That performance takes place within a rather specific community, one that believes in the Christian revelation and practices Christ's sacraments. This is not a historical remark about Thomas's circumstances or those of his readers. It points, rather, to pedagogical assumptions that give structure to his text. The presupposed continuity of Christ's more powerful scenes of instruction underwrites a teacher's confidence in the pedagogical coherence of theological traditions. The teacher trusts not only that a determination is possible, but also that it can be achieved without rending the inherited hierarchy of authorities. More: On Thomas's account, confidence in the coherence of theological languages is compatible with reminders that none of them can fully express God's essence or saving actions. The coherence is not accomplished by measuring all other languages against the one of them judged complete. They are measured rather against the living rule of faith or the expectation of divine presence. They are measured against the future goal shared by all inquirers. (That is the hope in belated anticipation.) These habits of theological interpretation rest on a confidence in the unity of the universal faith across times and places. The unity of faith derives from the specific unity of a divine gift, a theological virtue. It also gains from the unity of the act of human judgment of truth through multiple articulations, none of which can claim to exclude the others.

The multiplicity of languages introduced into a dispute is like the multiplicity of languages Thomas encounters when comparing Latin and Greek theologians. In his *Against the Errors of the Greeks*, Thomas tries to explain why certain passages in older authorities strike later readers as doubtful or dangerous. One reason is the difference of theological speech in Latin and Greek. "[M]any things that sound right (*bene sonant*) in the Greek language often do not sound right in Latin, since Latins and Greeks confess the same truth of faith with different words."[24] An exhortation follows: "it belongs to the task of the good translator, in translating what belongs to the catholic faith, to preserve the judgment (*sententia*), while changing the manner of speaking (*modus loquendi*) according to the particularity of the language into which he [or she] translates."

The same exhortation applies to the theologian when determining a question posed by contending authorities. Nominal differences must be distinguished from real ones—or, better, a single truth of faith must be recognized under different formulations. Again, unusual or even imprudent formulations in older authors have to be judged in relation to their intention, not the reader's later scruples.

In *Against the Gentiles*, you remember, Thomas writes that theological arguments are given for the "exercise and consolation of the faithful."[25] The exercise in handling authorities is easy to see. Resolving doubts by disputation not only strengthens conviction, it stretches memory and builds the capacity for recognizing truth across topics and languages. It may encourage some students to turn back to a continuous reading of particular authors while giving others material for more effective preaching or refutation. The enumeration of benefits could go on. But I want to emphasize the other part of the quoted phrase: Disputation through authorities must also count as consoling meditation of divine truth—and so an act of wisdom as Thomas describes it in *Against the Gentiles*.

Thomas's practice of disputation depends, I said, on a hopeful confidence in the coherence of theological traditions. It might be better to say that it trusts in continuing divine instruction. The gathering of contrary authorities in an article of the *Summa* is a risk, at least in some formal sense. It exposes a seeming contradiction in the inheritance of revealed narratives and so risks failure in resolving it. It raises the possibility of contention among revered authors but also of a collapse of language into nonsense. The teacher's task is to offer the gathering of contrary authorities as an oblation of human languages in the confidence of continued speech.

Contemporary readers struggle quite understandably with the *Summa*'s authorities. Thomas cites so many unfamiliar authors and texts. Worse, he seems to cite familiar authors badly. He jumbles technical vocabularies without explanation. He conflates texts from different periods and traditions. Indeed, he commits what many now regard as large mistakes of historical interpretation. Still, I suggest that the cause of the reader's struggle with authorities lies elsewhere. Thomas's main compositional forms are especially vulnerable to disruptions in the means of moral education that they assume. Far from being a timeless system true across all cultures, the *Summa* is a deliberately belated teaching that depends on community practices of Scripture and sacrament for its sense and (more important) its persuasion. Its authorities are like points in the tracing of a silhouette. They have effect only when the fuller figure is supplied by the teacher's public anticipation of the coherence and continuity of a divine teaching.

CHAPTER 6

The *Summa* in (Our) Libraries

Once written—or once circulated as a work never to be completed by Thomas—the *Summa* takes up its place in libraries.[1] The libraries eventually offer it to communities of learning that it did and did not anticipate; they juxtapose it with texts that it could and could not know. Even in medieval Dominican libraries, the *Summa* appears from the first as an alternative or rival to other texts, including its immediate predecessors and contemporaries. It is then read and put to use by successive generations of its scattered readers. With surprising speed, it assumes starring roles in the histories of ecclesiastical and educational institutions. The book plays these roles down to the time of its latest readers today.

So far as the *Summa* aims to be a moral curriculum, these moments of reception cannot be disregarded as if they were entirely outside it. Some of them, at least, are part of its later operation and so perhaps of its meaning. Of course, all readings of the *Summa* are not equal. Some are intimate and attentive engagements with the work. Others are so hasty or obtuse or doctrinaire as not to be about the *Summa* at all. The readings must be sorted as better and worse, pertinent and impertinent (in several senses). Still, the history of readings cannot be dismissed when thinking about how the *Summa* teaches. A reader might even wonder whether the overall balance of better and worse readings shows something about the work's composition. How are we to judge the "success" of ambitious moral writing if not in terms of its effects over time on readers? What conclusions should we draw if many readers—perhaps most—seem not to experience the text's pedagogy?

While the question should not be evaded, it must not be taken at face value—not, at least, if a reader wants to think about Thomas with Thomas. Within the *Summa*, Thomas analyzes direct and indirect effects of moral teaching, recognized and unrecognized consequences of it. Most important, he conceives his own pedagogy always in service to a divine pedagogy handed down in the Scriptures, the sacraments, and community of life. Thinking with Thomas about the *Summa*'s effect on readers will require many distinctions of agency and much humility. For later readers, it also requires reflection on the *Summa*'s relation to dozens of Thomisms, not least those officially enforced.

In this chapter, I pursue the question about the moral implications of long misreading by looking at three groups of readers. I sort the relations chronologically, but I emphasize that what follows is not a history of Thomism or even of the reading of the *Summa*. Those histories are too complicated for quick telling and too poorly known for confident synopsis.[2] They are also no more than a starting point for the question about misreading. While I will proceed in some sense chronologically, I am not trying to outline a history. I review some modes of reception as examples of how habits of reading might matter to a work like the *Summa*.

Thomas and His Dominican Rivals

If the *Summa* was written in part to fill a gap in Dominican education, it did not begin to circulate in empty space. It entered libraries alongside many other books of theology, including recent ones by Dominican authors. How did it differ from them? What did it add to them? The *Summa* itself encourages these comparisons both explicitly and implicitly. Explicitly, it criticizes recent Dominican projects for organizing moral matters; implicitly, it borrows from them. So the *Summa* complains about current ways of ordering the moral part of theology (2-2 pro; compare 1 pro). Thomas appears to have in mind particularly the *Summas of Vices and Virtues* by his Dominican predecessor, William Peraldus. Right alongside such complaints, a network of borrowings links passages from the moral part of the *Summa* to another Dominican work, Raymond of Peñafort's *Summa of Cases*. Let me take these two as examples of the books sitting beside the *Summa* in a medieval moral library.

William Peraldus's paired *Summas of the Vices and Virtues*, when combined, are about ten percent longer than the moral part of Thomas's *Summa*. On Thomas's judgment, the double work is much longer than it needs to be. It digresses into various patterns for organization and it amasses various sorts of material, including cases. The *Summa of Vices* is organized around the seven capital sins, with pride allotted almost as many sections as the rest combined. A host of lesser sins is attached to the seven, and a loquacious appendix treats sins of the tongue. In the *Summa of Virtues*, Peraldus strings out other familiar schemes: the virtues in common, the theological virtues, the cardinal virtues, the gifts of the Holy Spirit, and finally the beatitudes. For each list, he favors a recurring sequence of subtopics. A cardinal virtue, for example, is given its several senses, then described, next commended, and finally divided into parts. Regular mention is made of helps and hindrances to a virtue's exercise. And so, indefinitely, on.

We have already heard Thomas's complaints against disordered moral writing. His *Summa* proposes both to simplify by eliminating needless detail and to rectify by concentrating on what is properly fundamental. Organizing the moral part of his *Summa*, for example, he rejects the basic plan of Peraldus's *Summa of Vices*. Thomas treats the seven capital sins separately and not as an organizing principle.[3] There are less obvious corrections. For example, Thomas replaces his predecessor's direct exhortations with a display of the life of the incarnate Word. Instead of upbraiding and exhorting, the *Summa of Theology* extends Gospel narrative into sacramental event. The rejoinders to Peraldus would have been obvious to a contemporary Dominican moralist on reaching the middle part of the *Summa*.

Something else would appear in Thomas's borrowings from another Dominican standard, Raymond of Peñafort's *Summa of Cases*. In it, Raymond attempts for a smaller segment of the medieval moral library something like what Thomas's *Summa* does for theology as a whole. Raymond codifies the reasonings of confessors' casebooks according to a simple schema of crimes. Crimes are committed against either God or one's neighbor, and they are fully direct, less direct, or indirect.[4] Raymond also adopts a list of typical questions, reinforcing the schema in repeated application.

Comparing Raymond's *Summa of Cases* with the moral part of Thomas's *Summa* shows at least three things. First, Thomas covers almost all the topics in Raymond's first two books while omitting particular cases. Second, there are closely parallel passages where Thomas uses Raymond rather regularly for both authorities and arguments.[5] Thomas also borrows definitions of some key terms, arguments, and schemes for judging cases or justifying punishments.[6] Third, most important, Thomas completely reorders and reworks the material taken from Raymond. Thomas covers much of the same ground, but he does so within a unifying theological context.

Thomas reworks his predecessors in the name of pedagogical improvement. Did he succeed? From the evidence of early Dominican reception, the simplest answer would be, No. Or at least, Not immediately. The *Summa* is no sooner read than unread. Its principal structural accomplishments—the features that distinguished it from its rivals—are almost immediately undone.[7]

Within a few years of Thomas's death, John of Vercelli, master general of the Dominicans, commissioned an abridgment of the *secunda secundae*. The moral matter was not only extracted but also condensed.[8] A few years further on, the Dominican John of Fribourg rewrote Thomas's moral teaching into a confessor's handbook.[9] The handbook was in turn abridged, simplified, and alphabetized. The new texts proved more popular than Thomas's original; there are between two and three times as many copies of one alphabetized summary, the *Summa Pisana*, as there are of the *secunda secundae* of the *Summa*.[10]

Thomas was altered not least by his disciples. Masterworks of fifteenth-century Dominican morality cite Thomas's *Summa* respectfully while actively resisting its structural innovation. For example, the *Theological Summa* of Antoninus of Florence refers to Thomas ostentatiously for many of its definitions and a few of its arguments, but it revises Thomas in two ways. First, Antoninus's entire *Summa* is concerned only with moral matters. Antoninus makes moral teaching a separate species of theology rather than an integral portion of it. Second, more important, Antoninus organizes his *Summa* not according to the structure of Thomas's *secunda pars* or either of its subparts, but according to a series of older schemata, including both the Ten Commandments and the seven capital sins. Like so many others, this decision to retain the traditional moral schemata is the decision to cut Thomas's plan into pieces.

Given all of this, it is not surprising that Thomas also failed to persuade the Dominicans to replace Peter Lombard's unsatisfactory order with his own.[11] That replacement would come later—and as a result of other forces. Before turning to them, it is worth summarizing what the early Dominican reception might suggest about the *Summa*'s proposal to reform moral pedagogy. The obvious possibility is that Thomas was simply wrong about what his Dominican confreres needed. Alternately, and just as obviously, he may have been right about what his first readers needed though wrong about what they wanted. There are more interesting possibilities. For example, Thomas may have been right but at the wrong scale. The *Summa* may be too large to be taught or, indeed, to be appropriated easily even by another teacher. Again, it may be that the *Summa*'s correction of moral teaching was right but too early. Perhaps intermediate steps were required for its pattern to become pedagogically persuasive.

Whatever the causes, many of the early Dominicans who excerpted or revised the *Summa* as a moral curriculum understood at least this much about Thomas's project: They took him as centrally concerned with moral teaching. They applied the *Summa* to the care of souls. When the *Summa* finally replaced Peter Lombard as the standard curriculum, it did so on a different understanding. Its institutional success would be another and deeper misreading.

From Thomas to Thomism

Reception has its own reversals. By the sixteenth century, Dominican reform movements advocated reading the *Summa* whole. Detailed attention to its structure is proposed and practiced by Conrad Koellin, Thomas de Vio "Cajetan," and Peter Crockaert (the last of whom is traditionally credited with having replaced the Lombard's *Sentences* with the *Summa* as classroom text). Yet, these early modern advocates rehabilitated Thomas not as a contested reformer of moral curricula but as an exemplar of right doctrine. Thomas does not appear in sixteenth-century Paris or Lombardy or Salamanca as someone who wanted to change teaching habits in morals. He rises up instead as the Angelic Doctor allied to the doctrinal purity of the Roman see.

The transformation has many consequences. Attention slowly shifts from the "pastoral" middle of the *Summa* to the more "doctrinal" segments of the first and third parts. The tone changes from dialectic to apodictic. This transformation eventually requires that the *Summa* become whatever orthodoxy understands itself to be, in form as much as in content. Just here the *Summa*'s pedagogical purposes are particularly liable to distortion by stronger programs of human power.[12] I speak of "power" in an effort to disentangle two sources of change in the *longue durée* of the reading of the *Summa*.

Any exegetical tradition will change along with "intellectual context" (for lack of a critical term). Such changes are often imperceptible to those inside them. They are concealed behind textual continuities. A reader of the *Summa* can discover such changes by tracking the succession of Thomistic readings for a single passage or term. Consider the case of natural law as read from the sixteenth century through the nineteenth—say, by Cajetan, Vitoria, Suarez, the Salmanticenses, and Liberatore. Each of these authors wants to be faithful to Thomas. I do not deny that wish in them any more than I do in myself. I mean only to notice that the conception of natural law mutates as they read. Cajetan brings to the *Summa*'s questions on natural law not only the objections of Albertists, Scotists, and Ockhamists but also the epistemological expectations of early modern notions of "science." When Vitoria applies natural law to Spanish claims of dominion over the "New World," the emphasis falls on the communal discernment of natural law. He also voices the hope that any human being who does her best to live according to natural law may count on divine revelation about Christ.[13] For Suarez, to say the obvious, the notion of law has shifted fundamentally. It is now defined in terms of a *regula* that imposes intrinsic obligation apart from divine command.[14] Two and a half centuries later, Liberatore refutes Kantian ethics by performing detailed demonstrations from Thomas's natural law—precisely on terms that a post-Kantian would recognize.[15] The same passages from the *Summa* are cited across these authors. The meanings assigned change like colors in a kaleidoscope. The same passages are not the same.

As I said, such mutations are to be expected in any long tradition. They accelerate when traditions are enforced by different regimes of power. Once the *Summa* is designated an official textbook in modern Catholicism's enormous system of intellectual regulation, mutations of reading are at once constrained and amplified. Readings of the *Summa* can no longer mutate on their own, as it were. They are too important. They are also increasingly scattered. Thomas is cited on all sides in modern Catholic thinking and so against himself. For these reasons, among others, I no longer wish for a history of Thomism. I suspect that most of the historical Thomisms misunderstand Thomas's purposes. In particular, I fear that the ascendancy of the *Summa* during certain periods is directly correlated with its distortion. The work's genre is deformed into an encyclopedia of orthodoxy. The balance of its moral emphasis is ignored. Its function within communities of learning is roughly redirected to institutional ends. Even so, I remain grateful to official Thomisms for assuring not only the material persistence of the text but also institutional provision for its study. Most of all, I want to learn from the most monstrous offspring of official Thomism something about the limits on what a reader can safely expect from any human text.

The Situation of the Latest Reader

Already in the early hagiographies, the memory of Thomas elicits fantasies. William of Tocco, for example, presents a parade of Old Testament
heroes and heroines as the saint's prefigurations. Thomas is at once Isaac,
Jacob, the Israelite Joseph, and many times another Moses.[16] In the encyclical *Aeterni Patris*, Pope Leo XIII is less scriptural but no less exuberant.
He describes Thomas as gathering the *membra disjecta* of patristic learning
into a single body and so becoming "the unique bulwark of the Catholic
faith." The pope (or perhaps his ghostwriters) then quotes Cajetan to seal
the point: Thomas unites in his one mind all the most important insights of
his Christian predecessors.[17] It would be easy to multiply examples of hy-
perbole since Leo wrote. If Vatican II or its implementation marked a step
back from enforced Thomism, it also freed Thomas for use as a fantastical
figure of the reaffirmation of threatened orthodoxy.

The lure of Thomas reaches far beyond Catholic cultural politics. The
Summa is a featured stop on many itineraries for pilgrims seeking different
ends. Sometimes they colonize the text with fantasies of invincible argument or timeless terminology. At other times they want a rigorous antidote
to the clammy sentiments of some pastoral counseling—or a philosophical
complement to the relentless literalization of the Scriptures. Indeed, many
readers demand of the *Summa* what no human text can provide. That is a
legacy of official Thomism, which sometimes makes Thomas an idol.

To ask whether Thomas's *Summa* has "succeeded" is to enter this space
of impossible wishes. Succeeded at what, for whom, for how long? It would
be better to set aside the criterion of success to realize how modest are
Thomas's expectations. He does not offer a method for resolving all doubts
in moral theology. He does not even provide a field guide for quick iden-
tification of moral types. Thomas is skeptical of human powers of moral
recognition, and he does not pretend to the easy verification of moral schemata in embodied lives.

The same modesty applies inwardly. What is Thomas watching as he
writes the moral part of the *Summa*? The answer *cannot* plausibly be: He is
watching his own experience. Many of the experiences he discusses are
damaging. Others are simply not accessible to attention. The infused virtues, for example, are ordered to future beatitude. Even in a state of grace,
the wayfarer's hope gives no cognitive certainty about that (2-2.18.4). Any
felt certainty comes by participation in the motion of infused faith—which
is precisely not knowledge.[18] Again, absent the special privilege of a direct
revelation, a believer cannot have certainty in this life that she possesses

grace (2-1.112.5). At most, Thomas suggests, she can reason about such things by conjecture, which yields only "incomplete cognition" (*cognitio imperfecta*, 2-1.112.5). The same applies more strongly to judgments about grace in another person, since some of the best evidence for conjectures about grace consists of private signs that cannot be communicated to another human being.[19]

The moral part of the *Summa* is then not a phenomenology. It is, instead, a dialectical examination of inherited languages for analyzing human action—some of the languages authorized by revelation, others not. Once examined, the languages of virtue cannot be applied to particular situations automatically. The plurality of languages is a constant reminder of the limits of each. No single language can pretend to replace all others, much less to capture divine action entire. Even if one is convinced of having the best language available for describing a particular situation, many fallible discernments have to be made before it can be applied to that situation, much less to a whole life. However he sorts conflicts among inherited languages in aid of souls' progress, Thomas cannot make the language of *viatores* do the impossible. On the contrary, he takes himself to be showing the limits even of the best-ordered language for talking about human souls or to them.

Thomas does not offer the certainties that ardent readers have often presumed to discover on his behalf in the *Summa*. Nor is he interested in policing the boundaries between a knowable nature and a supposedly more knowable grace. Thomas wants rather to open possibilities for unexpected divine action—say, by providing some form of revelation beyond the boundaries of Israel and church (2-2.2.7 ad3). He is also always eager to recognize the operations of grace outside the ordered plans of his new curriculum. A moral curriculum for a Christian is, after all, a proposal for trusting cooperation with divine action. It is a gesture of hope both in divine generosity and in the choices of divine pedagogy. The hope may well be fulfilled in unexpected ways.

On these terms, how can a reader expect to address the question of the success of the *Summa*? Does she imagine that she can measure an increase of divine action after someone has understood so many pages of the *Summa*? Does she think that she can tell when a person is getting better? Even if she persuades herself that she can discern when souls are improved, is she so sure that she could trace the causes of their improvement? Could it be that the divine grace works as well in distortions of the *Summa*'s curriculum as in its proper applications—or that divine action regularly overleaps all curricula?

I postpone indefinitely any question of how to reckon the *Summa*'s success in the face of centuries of misreading. I move it—as Thomas would—into the future of a divine judgment that can only be discerned through hope. Our own situation as the *Summa*'s latest readers is conditioned by the belated anticipation that constitutes its scene of instruction. We read the book after seven centuries of mixed reception, much of it distorted by official enforcement. We may suspect that much of the *Summa*'s historical influence is based on misunderstanding. (If Thomas had been read more attentively, he might have been read less often.) We must always be skeptical of our own readings after so many disheartening examples. That is a feature of our belatedness. Our anticipation holds that the book might yet work on us if only we come to it embodying attention.

PART III

Moral Theology on the Way to Its End

For Thomas, the period of moral formation is the span of mortal life. At every point this side of death, human beings are still wayfarers, *viatores*. They are more like the adolescents of ancient ethics than its adults. Moral maturity, on Thomas's account, happens beyond death. Thomas thus conceives every divine disposition for present human time as pedagogical. Dependent as it is on both grace and revelation, his teaching in the *Summa* is even more time-bound. Thomas inherits moral languages that point forward to an end not yet reached. He writes in the middle of the history of salvation: after the divine incarnation and before the Lord's return in glory. He addresses a reader who has already heard the good news and shares in Christian sacraments but who still requires correction, exercise, and consolation. The *Summa*'s structure traces circles of memory and desire, of recollection and foreshadowing, prototype and fulfillment. A reader can study the circling especially in the relations of the second part to the third. The middle part of the *Summa* prepares for and depends on the last. The analysis of human action is both an anticipation and a sequel of the retelling in incarnation and sacrament.

The elaborate analysis of virtues at the center of the *Summa*'s second part is only an analytic moment on the way to fuller representations of human fulfillment in incarnation, Gospel, and sacrament. The *Summa*'s moral middle culminates in the depiction of ways of life for confirming and integrating the virtues. This culmination is only more articulate yearning for what is yet to come—at the end of history but also within the *Summa* itself. Those ways of life still require the grace and the sacraments of a divine-human priest for their enactment. The middle part of the *Summa* does not pretend to be a freestanding ethics. Certainly it cannot offer a self-contained virtue ethics—not least because its most important virtues are not contained by human agency. It presents instead a pedagogy of graced characters called to share in divine life—which is to say, an intrinsically sacramental ethics. Sacraments are the reiterated evocation and conferral of a troupe of moral characters that make virtues livable.

In the present tense of human history, the reader's motion between the third part and the second of the *Summa* never stops. The third part completes the whole work only as a sketch of the historical motion of human lives. The *Summa* does not finish the reader's formation even when it looks forward to beatitude and the end of history. It sends the reader back instead to the practice of virtues and vices with a fuller appreciation of their means and end. The teaching on the sacraments in the third part returns the reader to the present life depicted in the second.

The second part of the *Summa* is by far the longest in the extant work. It contains almost three times as many questions as the first part. Even if it had been finished, the third part is hardly likely to have reached the 189 questions of *Summa* 2-2, much less the 303 questions of the whole second part. The detail of the moral inquiry puts off many readers, even specialists. Yet, truncating the second part of the *Summa* takes from a reader both some of Thomas's boldest innovations and the persistence of his efforts to write the circumstances of human life. The moral part of the *Summa* shows again and again how human beings are to be taught through bodies while reminding them of what bodies cannot comprehend.

Summa 1 concludes by placing humanity at the boundary between intellects and bodies. The emphasis on embodiment carries forward into *Summa* 2-1. One obvious example is the space given over to the passions: the group of twenty-seven questions is one of the largest. Such sustained attention might seem to contradict Thomas's promised selectivity by digressing from theology into natural philosophy. In fact, Thomas spends attention on the passions partly because he wants to show in their treatment the limits on theology. He begins by explaining that the passions are not only automatic bodily reactions; they are morally good or morally bad insofar as they "lie under the command of reason and the will" (2-1.24.1). In the questions that follow, images of command, obedience, and rule or measure (*imperium, obedientia, regula*) appear on every side. Political and regal governance is exercised in a city by means of education, habituation, and rational persuasion; so, too, within the soul, in its relations to the bodily affects and impulses that power the passions. The space given to the passions reminds the reader that the project of moral education begins in intimate relation to the body. The reader also learns how the soul's appetites draw it to what it cannot yet see or ever comprehend.

The importance of embodiment appears in another way in the delayed entry of grace and its pairing with law. In Peter Lombard, grace appears immediately after the discussion of free choice.[1] The analogous position in the *Summa* would be in the first part, around question 84. Thomas in fact delays the treatment of law and grace for more than a hundred questions, putting it at the end of *Summa* 2-1. The reader is brought to law and grace from inside the human soul, as it were, from the prior study of the internal aptitudes for rational action. Thomas's slow approach to grace does not deny God's assistance. It helps readers by starting with what is nearer to hand. *Summa* 2-1 begins with the highest human end because it is implicated in any human willing. The sequence of questions then follows the human approach to the end, beginning with the primary possibility of choice and ending with the uniquely efficacious gift of grace (2-1.6 pro, 2-1.113.pro).

Thomas makes his boldest rearrangement of traditional topics in the book's next section. *Summa* 2-2 is at once his most lucid and most detailed representation of the complexities of embodied life. He begins by acknowledging that the great temptation for any more detailed moral teaching is to run on endlessly, through every variety of virtue, gift, vice, precept, and counsel, illustrating each with abundant cases. Thomas proposes instead two simplifying principles. First, he unites in a single cluster of questions a virtue, the corresponding gifts, the opposed vices, and the attached affirmative or negative precepts. Second, he sets intellectual virtues aside and traces all of the moral virtues back to the three theological and four cardinal. He insists that the vices—favored by theatrical preachers—not distend this list of seven. Vices are treated compendiously in relation to virtues, and they are distinguished by real differences rather than accidental ones (2-2 pro).[2] The bold reorganization in *Summa* 2-2 depends on rejecting all secondary classifications, however vivid, in favor of the essential.

Thomas's emphasis on essential classifications of virtues and vices reinforces his main theological lessons. He reminds the reader that sin can
be understood only as defect or derailment. More fundamentally, if not
more obviously, the entire effort to teach the virtues and vices presupposes
that sin is something of which human beings can repent. This possibility
of moral instruction after sin follows from the conditions of embodiment.
For angelic minds and wills, Thomas has taught, there is no possibility of
repentance (1.64.2). Fundamental choice fixes them immutably. For human souls, the cognitive and volitional circumstances of embodied learning open the possibility of repentance up until death—that is, until (temporary) disembodiment. The possibility of repentance is the precondition
of moral reeducation. In this way, the project of *Summa* 2-2 presumes and
displays human embodiment, not least by calling for a teaching that can
address fallen souls convincingly.

The *Summa*'s moral reorganization has its compositional costs. Inserting morals into the middle of the creed interrupts the narrative pattern
with what may seem an overly tidy taxonomy of virtues and their correlates. I hope to show that if the moral part interrupts the narration of the
creeds, it also enacts a rhetorical narrative of exhortation.

The scale of the second part means that I cannot describe it whole in
what remains of this book. I cannot even sample it adequately. My style of
reading must then change. I will look only at a few portions of the text that
best reveal its pedagogy. Each teaches the reader something about how to
move toward God while drawing attention to her motion through the curriculum in the *Summa*. For the sake of balance if not quite breadth, two of
my topics come from the *prima secundae*, two from the *secunda secundae*.

I begin, as the moral part itself does, with questions on the last end of
human willing (Chapter 7). In them, Thomas rewrites ancient patterns
of philosophical exhortation to direct the will beyond its bondage to lesser
goods. He qualifies and completes these patterns when he argues that the
untellable circlings of will and intellect depend from the start on the lure
of God.

I jump then to the long sequence of questions on law and grace at the
end of *Summa* 2-1 (Chapter 8). I try to correct positivist misreadings of
natural law as moral system by recalling that Thomas treats it within histories of human legislation and divine correction. In structurally prominent questions on the Old Law, Thomas performs symbolic or typological
readings of Israelite ritual. He not only prepares the lessons of incarnation
and sacrament, he unfolds a sort of moral tapestry that points towards the
minimalist aesthetic of grace.

My third selection comprises the questions on the gifts of the Holy Spirit that are distributed across *Summa* 2-2 (Chapter 9). By insisting on the need for these gifts, Thomas not only circumscribes the cardinal and intellectual virtues, he also approaches the intimate motions of human response to divine incitement. In certain moments of these questions, Thomas's description of the gifts becomes at once lyric and prayer.

I turn finally to the end of *Summa* 2-2 (Chapter 10). In questions on states of life, Thomas revises ancient genres of exhortation to take up a way of life that pursues the good. He urges the reader to see that moral formation requires a choice to join a community that can serve as a sacramental school.

Those accustomed to standard renderings of Thomas's ethics in the *Summa* may well find my selection perverse. My plea is that these four topics are among the most significant structural features of the *Summa* 2. They are moments at which the reader is moved simultaneously toward God as end and toward God's incarnate teaching as it will appear in *Summa* 3. Perhaps I can justify my selection more convincingly in the next chapters. At the same time, I hope to test the usefulness of reading the *Summa* "backward." If my counterproposal has worked, the structure of the book's moral part should look different coming to it from the last part. It does indeed.

CHAPTER 7

The Good That Draws the Will

The *Summa* inaugurates its teaching about human action by describing the highest human end. The description is both an appeal and a correction. Thomas appeals to the will as a rational appetite already drawn toward its end, however inarticulately. He attempts to correct any misdirection. His persuasion neither denies nor obstructs the human need for grace in order to reach its end. What is more, he represents the circling interaction of will and intellect within the human being to show God's role at the beginning of human willing. The dependence on grace for reaching happiness is adumbrated in the different dependence of the will's first motion. Thomas's persuasion is a reminder in words of God's persuasion by first presence.

Where to Find the Good

Thomas's questions on the human good occupy a crucial position in the *Summa*. Inaugurating the moral part, they show in high relief his assumptions about the possible effects of teaching. They show them most clearly as structural innovation. Before the *Summa*, the discussion of the highest good for human life was a moveable element in Thomas's theological compositions. Its placement in the *Summa* resolves both a conflict in the inherited authorities and a puzzle in his own writing.

Peter Lombard investigates the end of human life according to its position in salvation history; he reaches it at the very end of his last book.[1] There, too, it appears in Thomas's first commentary on the *Sentences*.[2] Putting human happiness at the end of theological instruction delays any discussion of the cause of human action. The fundamental motive in human life has been left for last and so deprived of pedagogical force. Already in this commentary, Thomas tries to remedy this difficulty by inserting a discussion of the highest good and its relation to the will in the very first distinction of Book 1. There the Lombard applies Augustine's dichotomy of use and enjoyment to a variety of topics, including the elements of human moral life. Thomas knew from his predecessors—indeed, from his mentor, Albert—that the Augustinian dichotomy could do more.[3] So Thomas inserts questions about the human enjoyment of God at the very beginning of his *Sentences*-commentary.[4] Of course, that insertion still splits the discussion of the human good between the beginning and end of a sprawling text. It also dissociates happiness and the highest good from the virtues, which Peter Lombard disperses across his *Sentences*.

An obvious alternative to the Lombard's arrangement is offered by Aristotle's *Nicomachean Ethics*. By the time he first commented on the *Sentences*, Thomas had read through the *Ethics* carefully with Albert. He copied out Albert's readings in his own hand.[5] Albert makes prefatory arguments about happiness as the subject (*subjectum*) of moral science, and he establishes the highest end as what unifies deliberate human actions.[6] If Thomas feels the difficulties of the Lombard's failure to place happiness properly, he learns from Aristotle interpreted by Albert that moral teaching proceeds more surely when it glimpses the last good from the start.

Thomas uses the lesson to create an alternate order for moral pedagogy in *Against the Gentiles*. There his plan combines elements from philosophical and theological models. On the one hand, it makes room for the technical description of the beatific vision inspired by the Lombard's *Sentences*. On the other, it allows both for a general argument about the universal hierarchy of goods and the specifically moral appeal of Aristotle's comparison of ways of life. It does all of this in a single, continuous treatment. Still *Against the Gentiles* is not *Summa* 2. The remaining chapters of *Against the Gentiles* 3, placed under the broad heading of providence, fail to offer anything like an exposition of the constituents of human action or a synopsis of virtues and vices. Thomas accomplishes the unified treatment of morals only with the invention of the *Summa*.

There are risks in placing beatitude at the beginning of the *Summa*'s moral account. One risk comes in the need to talk about the highest moment of grace before the topic of grace has even been introduced. Thomas says relatively little in these opening questions about the enabling "light of glory" or the limits on the human's beatific vision of God. He also avoids questions about beatitude that might be raised by the Last Judgment.[7] A second risk of the *Summa*'s order is more general. If the end of human life is depicted so clearly at the beginning of moral teaching, how can the teaching make any narrative progress? Isn't the rest of moral teaching reduced to anticlimax? Thomas has both doctrinal and rhetorical responses to this second risk. The doctrinal response, as will be clearer in a moment, recalls that there can be no deliberate motion whatever without some view on the end. The rhetorical response comes in the very structure of the first five questions. They exhort the reader toward more explicit desire without pretending to satisfy it. They offer a glimpse of a distant goal. Thomas's depiction of the good here is not denouement. It is overture.

I can show this in miniature from *Summa* 2-1.2, which argues that none of the things commonly considered good can provide happiness. Its individual arguments are not sophisticated. More interesting is the sequence of candidate objects considered and rejected. Happiness cannot be found, Thomas argues, in wealth, honors, fame, power, or any bodily possession or pleasure; it does not arrive in the present with any good of the soul; it is not supplied by any creature whatever (2-1.2.1–8). The possible objects appear in ascending order of plausibility, with the last being the most plausible candidate for the locus of happiness but also the most general.[8]

This form of argument was famous in Mediterranean antiquity. Most of the ancient exhortations to philosophy contain a *synkrisis* or comparison in which the claims of a divine wisdom are argued against the lures of beauty, riches, power, and pleasure. The classical examples were largely unknown to Thomas.[9] He did have before him one of their late variations: Boethius's *Consolation of Philosophy*. The whole of the *Consolation* is a protreptic to return to philosophy and, through it (or her), to the wisdom of Christ. The book also contains particular passages that hope to reveal how unsatisfying the goods of this world are in comparison with those beyond. Boethius's personified Philosophy performs a comparison of possible goods twice.[10] The second time around, she argues that the image or shape (*forma*) of the good that mortals commonly seek can be reduced to five things: wealth, honors, power, glory, and pleasures.[11] Philosophy's list of apparent goods is exactly the one Thomas considers in the *Summa*. This is no coincidence. Thomas cites Boethius's *Consolation* six times in the eight brief articles of

Summa 2-1.2. Four of the citations occur prominently and decisively in the *sed contra*.[12] Thomas not only solves a structural problem in teaching morals, he also recapitulates through Boethius an ancient genre of rational persuasion to the good.

In Thomas, as in many of his predecessors, the persuasion is importantly apophatic. It is an ordered negation of misleading possibilities: "Not here . . . Not here. . . ." Thomas begins the apophasis with the relatively external temptations, easily seen through. The wealth even of the natural world, and much more the artificial wealth of human currency, is clearly sought for the sake of something else. Honor and glory ought properly to follow upon blessedness; they do not grant it. Power is notoriously fleeting, the cause of more unhappiness than happiness. The temptations of pleasure may be sharper—and not just because of bodily cravings. The frequent temptation is to reverse the relationship between pleasure and happiness by taking any pleasure as the sign of happiness. A similar but subtler inversion occurs in cultivating goods of the soul, since it is quite true that the last human end is the soul's possession of the highest good. Still, beatitude is a good *for* the soul, not within it.

Having rehearsed the sophistries by which humans deprive themselves of what they most desire, Thomas insists that their desire is too large to be contented with anything less than the unbounded intensity of the uncreated good. This end cannot now be spoken except as a promise. The excess of human desire over the presently available goods is the way to God but also the confirmation of limits on God's present appearance. The rhetorical structure of the persuasion must support desire so that it does not stop short. How does it do this—and for which kind of reader?

Rhetorical Movements Toward the Good

Human beings act for ends—as all things do. These ends give character to human actions. Indeed, there must be ends in order for human actions to be undertaken at all. Arguing this point, Thomas reads universal natural teleology as the background for human actions and so specifies arguments from Aristotle's *Physics* with those from specifically Christian sources.[13] Once the teleological principle is applied, Thomas begins a triple ascent to the final cause by winnowing arguments. The first winnowing establishes the unity and universality of the highest good (2-1.1.5–8). The second is the *synkrisis* of candidate goods I have already recalled (2-1.2.2). The final step locates this good at last: it is an operation of intellect, and not primarily of sense or will; it is speculative, though contained neither in human science nor in a vision of created immaterial substances; it is the vision of God (2-1.3.2–4, 4–7, 8).

The next step in Thomas's rhetorical structure aims to show that while the human good is attainable, something must be done to reach it (2-1.4–5). Question 4 asks what is required for beatitude, then sweetens its answer with some consideration of beatitude's delights. The passage has an almost relaxed rhythm in comparison with the three preceding questions. It makes its point about the need for willing, then expands on the satisfactions, the *bene esse*, of beatitude. Question 5, by contrast, drives toward the single conclusion of the whole account of the highest good: Beatitude cannot be reached by one's natural powers or with the aid of some other creature (2-1.5.5–6). Only God can give what all creatures desire (2-1.5.7–8). Having argued the existence and character of a unique good, Thomas now proposes that it should be gotten in the only way possible—namely, by seeking rightness of the will as disposition to further seeking. The question's rhetorical effect is like that of a peroration after a deliberation. Thomas has argued that all act for the sake of a good. He has shown what that good is. He concludes by proposing what must be done in order to reach it. There could be no clearer call for action—or, more exactly, for the action that consists in letting God act.

How can Thomas pursue that sort of persuasion? A reader might concede at once that a Greek philosopher needs to convince pagan youths that they should abandon the pursuit of money, pleasure, or civic power to pursue wisdom. She might see, though perhaps not so immediately, how a Christian writer could appropriate such arguments to help Christians fallen into despair—as Boethius's narrator fell. Still a reader might object to Thomas's appropriating these rhetorical forms for teaching students of *theology* about human action. Presumably, those students are not pagan, or without philosophy, or in despair. Isn't protreptic rhetoric inappropriate or useless as theological rhetoric?

A number of partial answers suggest themselves. It could be, for example, that Thomas wants to provide exemplary persuasions for theologians who might need them in their missionary or pastoral work. Or he could wish to make explicit for young theologians some tacit suppositions of faith that they have never yet articulated. Or it could be that Thomas seeks to include specimens of philosophic reasoning within a properly capacious theology. Still, a satisfying answer would surely have to refer more directly to the *Summa*'s main motives. The protreptic argument at the beginning of the *prima secundae* must belong to the essentials of Christian religion that Thomas offers to his beginners.

The kind of protreptic that Thomas here recapitulates is more than an ancient philosophic genre preserved in Boethius. It is a staple of Christian preaching generally and mendicant preaching quite particularly. The sorts of arguments Thomas makes against wealth or power or glory are found in many medieval sermons contemporary with his writing.[14] More strikingly, Thomas himself puts the protreptic pattern to homiletic use. His two surviving sermons for All Saints present the halves of the *Summa*'s protreptic to the highest good. The sermon *Beati qui habitant* moves up through the possible goods toward the vision of God. The later sermon *Beata gens* confirms the persuasion by arguing that the blessed enjoy all good things.

Beati qui habitant is probably the earlier sermon and may come from Thomas's years in Italy—before or as he conceived his final masterwork.[15] Interestingly, it shares arguments and authorities with this part of the *Summa*.[16] Thomas begins the sermon by claiming that many have been deceived about the location, the duration, and the operation of happiness. Where then is happiness to be found? Happiness is threefold, replies Thomas the preacher. One is worldly: It comes in enjoyment of the earth's goods. But these things can be secured only with much toil and care, with lawsuits and wars, or by means of narcotic pleasures. So too with the second happiness, the political: There are a few good kings, yet more often devouring tyrants. Finally, third, there is the happiness of contemplation, the greatest and most divine. Philosophers sought it by studying truth and disputing for authority. God teaches a shorter way, through cleanness of heart. In fact, God offers to the holy whatever is really good in all the forms of earthly happiness. Thomas concludes his preaching with a ringing description of eternal life and a doxological petition to the Son, who alone can lead those listening to the happy life.

In *Beati qui habitant*, Thomas may be addressing a mixed audience mired in worldly enticements or lured by them. Yet, the form of persuasion is not limited to those still "in the world," just as preaching is not only for the laity.[17] In the later sermon, *Beata gens*, Thomas address his university audience in Paris with assurances of pleasure. The saints in glory have everything they desire and more—in pleasures and delights, riches, knowledge.[18] Should any hearer remain unconvinced, Thomas adds immediately a refutation of old errors about the location of happiness. If he blends such arguments in university preaching, he must think them useful for educating Christians. He can also see no contradiction between rational exhortation and liturgical edification.

If the only exhortation useful to Christian life occurred before baptism or when rescuing those in despair, there would be little for Thomas to say in the moral part of the *Summa*. In fact, he has a great deal to say, precisely because Christian souls benefit from a lifelong education, a continuous protreptic, as they progress toward the human goal. Thomas writes out his understanding of the care of souls in the *Summa*.[19] He defends his own teaching activity as both contemplative and hortatory, as intending both to present truths for contemplation and to bring lives to sanctity. It would be ridiculous to suppose otherwise. Because his teaching belongs to the divine pedagogy he describes, it cannot be inappropriate for him to use homiletic forms—including protreptic forms—when he addresses his Dominican students or a wider audience of readers at many different stages of the *via*.

Protreptic is not demonstration. Its persuasion does not presuppose that the final end can be perfectly shown in the present. Just the opposite: An apophatic persuasion to the highest good is needed precisely because it does not appear evidently at hand. Given human sinfulness, it is all too easy for anyone, including the reader, to misidentify the location of the highest good or to misdescribe it. The space of human sin is the realm of means, which offers the misguided choice of a partial, immediate good over the complete, future good. Protreptic fastens on means. Unable to represent the final good completely in the present, persuasion can still remind that nothing now available will satisfy human desire. Preventing mistaken attachment, it urges the reader to wait for the end—indeed, to wait on God for providing the means to the end.

Exhortation and Divine Gift

Thomas explicitly exhorts his hearers or his readers to an end that is not in their power. He has insisted that the vision of the divine essence lies beyond the means of any creature. It can only be attained by the grace of God. What sense does it make to exhort to such an end? More emphatically, what sense does it make for creatures to have such an end—to have a good beyond their natural capabilities?

This is a famous crux of Thomistic exegesis over which many pages and not a few reputations have been squandered. Across the centuries of Thomism, the debate recurs. Recent or current episodes have looked particularly to Henri de Lubac's controversial book *Surnaturel: Études historiques* (1946).[20] With the larger debate, so with the fate of this book: Every time Thomas's teaching is vindicated, it is assailed again as heterodox. At the risk of heterodoxy, let me pass over the persistent debate to read Thomas.

From the questions already discussed in *Summa* 2-1, the following points stand out. The last and complete happiness of the human intellect lies in the vision of God's essence (2-1.3.8 corp). This teleological fact is expressed as a motion in the will toward the universal good and in the intellect toward the universal truth, both of which are found only in God (2-1.5.8 corp). Neither the will nor the intellect can be fulfilled short of union with God. Many humans mistake the site of this complete good, and so they seek it where it will never be found (2-1.5.8, 1.7). Deliberation about the true site should proceed not from the opinions of the wicked or the stupid, but from the reflective judgment of the well disposed and wise (2-1.1.7, 2.1 ad1). Finally, the complete good cannot be obtained by human natural powers or, indeed, by the natural powers of any creature (2-1.5.5).

Taken together, these points imply that human beings have by nature a desire for an end that can only be attained by means beyond nature. The points do not imply, of course, that humans are endowed either with intuitive recognition of that end or the means for attaining it. An inarticulate inclination toward a complete good is experienced perhaps most sharply as disappointment with any actual or possible good of creation. The *via* to God is indicated by the excess of deep desire over the ends at hand.

A few questions further into this part of the *Summa*, in considering the passion of love (*amor*), Thomas will locate desire (*desiderium*) rather precisely as the middle step in a sequence of three: desire comes between love and joy (2-1.26.2 corp). Love in this sense is the *complacentia*, the special attraction or agreement, of an "appetite" with its object.[21] It is a power's affective recognition of what it has been created to seek, its resonance or fittingness for it. When an appetite begins to move toward its object, love becomes desire. When the appetite comes to rest in the object, there is joy (*gaudium*). Desire is love in motion toward its end. To say that human beings have a natural desire for God is to say that their unimpeded motion would be toward God.[22]

To deny that the natural end of human life is the vision of the divine essence is to deny the explicit construction of the opening of the *Summa*'s moral part. Thomas begins with beatitude, he says, because arguments about human actions can only be made in view of their end. Unless beatitude is the end toward which human life is ordered, then its consideration at the start is an impertinence. If there is some other "natural" end of human life, if human beings as such are "naturally" ordered to something other than the vision of God's essence, then Thomas must describe that other end and postpone any discussion of the beatific vision until he introduces grace. He would then have to explain how something that is not a creature's natural end can be the source of its highest happiness, since happiness is supposed to come from complete actualization of the form. That conclusion from ontology is supported by Thomas's adaptation of Boethius. Just because human beings desire a complete good with certain features, just because they will not come to rest in anything less than the complete truth, a protreptic argument can pull them away from partial goods or truths and toward what they really seek. If there were no natural desire for the vision of God, the structure of Boethius' *Consolation* would be inexplicable and Thomas's adaptation of it would be vain.

The difficulties in holding onto this rather obvious reading of the *Summa* are partly illusory and partly real. The illusory difficulties are those that come from the introduction of an alien terminology (such as *potentia obedientialis*) or an alien problematic (such as the exaggerated notions of divine freedom spun off from the much later controversy *de auxiliis*). The real difficulties are of two kinds, some textual and some conceptual.

In the hail of citations that falls upon the debates over "natural desire," only one cluster of texts seems really to say anything different from what is said here in the *Summa*, in the corresponding arguments of *Against the Gentiles*, and in many other places. That cluster of dissenting texts comes from the questions on evil and has to do with the penalties for original sin.[23] Referring to this text, de Lubac said that Thomas did not contradict himself in it so much as concede the "very paradox of human nature (or rather of the created spirit)."[24] I take this to mean that the text from the questions on evil reports an apparent contradiction because it responds to an apparently contradictory subject matter. The contradiction can be explained, as many have shown, but a reader is not obliged to explain it in order to hold to the evident meaning of the *Summa*. The burden of proof actually falls on the other side. Why abandon the plain sense of the *Summa* because of a contested reading of another text?

If there are no textual difficulties that careful reading cannot unravel, there are still conceptual difficulties with the notion of a natural end requiring more-than-natural means for its achievement. Thomas gives voice to these difficulties in one of the objections (2-1.5.5 arg1). A human being must be able to acquire beatitude by the powers of her own nature (*per sua naturalia*), the objector reasons, because a nature cannot lack in something essential. Thomas replies that just as nature did not supply the human being with natural weapons and protective hide, giving her instead the ability to acquire these, so the human being has the ability to acquire beatitude by turning to God, who will make her blessed (2-1.5.5 ad1). The seeming paradox of a natural end requiring means beyond-its-nature is addressed (if not quite dissolved) in the claim that God will provide freely what God had intended to provide from the first. Gilson captures this nicely by saying that Thomas sees nature as "nature-willed-by-God-in-view-of-grace."[25]

The invocation of God's generosity not only resolves the long-running debate, it acknowledges a question that has been lurking from the beginning: Where is the body in blessedness? The protreptic ascent through all possible goods in this life puts highest happiness beyond death. It thus seems to put it beyond the body. Thomas recognizes as much in the second All Saints sermon, when he writes that the church's "whole concern (*totum studium*)" is to move human beings through contempt of earthly things to desire of the heavenly.[26] Perhaps so, but faith claims that the heavenly things will include by grace a resurrected body. Are the body's desires—or the desires of an embodied intelligence—sacrificed in progress toward the vision of God? Is it only equivocally that one can say that beatitude satisfies the desire for pleasures and delights? Thomas's final answer would have been given in the part of the *Summa* he did not live to write. Still the answer begins here, in the promise of a gift of grace that will satisfy nature's desires beyond nature's abilities—not least by raising bodies from the dead.

The *Summa*'s argument about human happiness ends with a reiteration of two points: All human beings desire the vision of God and each must do something in order to hasten its attainment.[27] Human actions neither produce grace nor compel its provision. They do cooperate with God in preparing the soul to receive it. More will be said later in the *Summa* about the role of grace even in this preparation. The important thing at this point in the structure is to notice that another set of questions has lurked all along in the very performance of a protreptic. Thomas's brief ascent to the highest good appeals both to reasoning and to desiring. It assumes that intellect and will cooperate in moving the human being toward God. How does that cooperation happen? How must the human being be constituted in order for protreptic to produce movement?

The Will as Appetite

Thomas turns from the discussion of human happiness to questions on the will. He explains the turn as a search for means to reach the highest end just described. Since beatitude comes by human acts, the reader must learn about them in order to find beatitude (2-1.6 pro). But the will is a means to happiness in a very unusual sense. It is the means by which all other means are chosen. Or it is the movement within the human from which all other voluntary motions follow. Thomas's questions on the will discover important limits on the theologian's ability either to describe or to explain human motion. If a theologian rightly resorts to protreptic when writing or preaching, the protreptic can neither fully disclose nor originally actuate the will that is its target. There are riddles in rational persuasion that arise from the circular interactions of intellect and will. In these questions, Thomas tries both to present the riddle and then to resolve it by appeal to the God who is both the end of human life and the constant companion along the way.

With so much resting on them, the questions can seem curiously superficial. They are certainly brief enough, and rely almost mechanically on a set pattern of subtopics (visible in 2-1.11–17). Moreover, given that human responsibility seems the indispensable foundation for any moral account, Thomas's quick treatment of it here would hardly seem sufficient. After all, Thomas himself wrote earlier in the *Summa* that without free choice, "all counsels, exhortations, precepts, prohibitions, rewards and punishments would be in vain" (1.83.1 corp).

The brevity of these questions can be explained partly by pointing to the division of topics between the parts of the *Summa*. At least four questions from the first part have to be remembered here in the second for the discussion of will to make much sense. A reader must recall the general account of appetite, together with its divisions into sensuality and will, as well as the association of will and free choice (1.80–83). More important, a contemporary reader must abandon expectations about what sort of doctrine is on offer. Thomas's account is not produced out of experience, whether by introspection or phenomenological inference. He speaks from critical reflection on a host of inherited terms and models. He does not attempt even to illustrate his distinctions by appeal to experience. The account cannot be illustrated from introspection, since it distinguishes acts too swift for separation or separates aspects of a single act only notionally distinct. For these reasons, among others, Thomas nowhere stops to construct an example in which all the steps of willing are presented in sequence.

A contemporary reader may also be surprised that Thomas is not motivated by a desire to rebut skepticism about human freedom. Thomas recognizes the worries, of course. No fewer than five objections were raised in the first part on the question of free choice (1.83.1). Still, in the *Summa*, Thomas is not especially concerned to address the doubts about freedom recorded in texts he inherits. Thomas rests his discussion instead on the broad basis of moral education. Human beings make choices for which they can be held responsible. They can be taught to make better choices.

Their choices largely determine what becomes of them. This account may seem naïve, but it explains both the apparent ease with which Thomas approaches some questions and the conciliatory answers he offers to them.

Without rehearsing all of Thomas's steps in presenting free choice in the first part, let me reiterate his basic lessons as a series of consequences. First, a created will faced with the highest good cannot will otherwise than to rest in it. Second, absent a direct vision of the good, the will desires whatever it apprehends as leading to it and so chooses it. But, third, the relations of means to end are not now known with certainty. Moreover, because everything except the highest good has an admixture of evil, the will has considerable latitude in its choices, including its determinations of where the good itself is most likely to be found. Fourth, Thomas's account in no way excludes divine influence on choice, either so far as God is the first cause of everything that happens or so far as God might strengthen or dampen certain particular motions of the will. What is excluded is God's exercising a violent or coercive causality on the will. To do so would contradict the nature of the will and so God's own intention in creating it. Fifth, finally, the analogy between the relation of intellect to reason and the relation of will to free choice suggests that free choice tends to resolve itself back into simple willing, from which it arises. The discursive calculation of alternative means is done for the sake of possessing the end reached through those means.

When he takes up will and choice again in *Summa* 2-1, Thomas seems more concerned to catalogue the types of act traditionally ascribed to the will than to repeat basic arguments already given in the first part. The catalogue sorts a bewildering variety of terminologies. More important, it multiplies the interconnections of understanding and willing. The interlocking of willing and knowing is the deep note running underneath the confusingly disposed and rather technical questions in the *Summa*'s moral part.

Structurally, the questions on the will in *Summa* 2-1 resemble a dictionary or, more exactly, a philosophical lexicon in the manner of Aristotle's *Metaphysics* Book 5. A number of terms are introduced, characterized, and then related to adjacent terms. Thomas's order is not immediately clear. There is a broad division between elicited acts and commanded acts (2-1.8–16 against 17), and the elicited acts are sorted by their relations to the end (2-1.8–11 against 12–16). But the relation of means to end is then immediately confused by saying that acts having to do with ends have also to do with means if taken loosely. Moreover, and without justification, Thomas treats the acts otherwise than in their order of occurrence (as noted, e.g., 2-1.13 pro, 17.3).

There are other puzzles. The allocation of questions in this cluster gives special importance to will (*voluntas*, 2-1.8–10), yet it treats other acts or partial acts structurally as of equal importance. Each of them is given a single question. Even sympathetic readers may balk at this artificial tidiness. Indeed, almost everyone thinks that Thomas is here guilty of an unnecessary eclecticism. While trying to accommodate divergent traditions, they complain, he ends by making oversubtle discriminations that he could have avoided if he had been less interested in harmonization. This sort of judgment leads some to amend Thomas's terms—or else to concede that the structure of the *Summa* is here defective.[28]

In fact, Thomas's textual order reflects the order of finality, which is the reverse of demonstration or efficiency. For actions, the place of principle is taken by the end. Though obtained last, it has to be considered as underlying the entire chain of considerations and actions. That is why beatitude comes first in the *Summa*'s moral part. That is also why *voluntas*, the radical power of appetite for an end, appears first in the questions on the interlocking motions of will and intellect. Other acts are reached by reasoning backward from the end. So the sequence *voluntas, fruitio, intentio* moves from the radical power of appropriating an end, to its application in enjoyment, to its appreciation in teleological view of the end as last term. Since all three acts consider the end, they precede the acts that have to do with means. Those acts are ordered according to the same principle—that is, by relation to the end. Here a second inversion of textual order appears: the chronology of the acts. *Voluntas* comes first causally and teleologically and even chronologically, so far as some willing must be presupposed underneath the process of motion. Yet, the acts of appetite by which means are taken up are teleologically prior and chronologically posterior. Thus, the sequence of questions begins properly from the point of view of the end, causing a reversal of the chronology of means.

There is a further complication in Thomas's textual sequence. Each of the questions is careful to discuss various reflexive and reciprocal causalities linking the acts named. So, for example, the will is moved by the intellect but also by the sensitive appetite, by itself, and by external objects (especially God) in several ways still to be clarified (2-1.9.1–4). The will also embraces the particular acts of the intellect and moves the intellect to those acts. The reciprocal causality is illustrated more particularly in the second part's question on the act called *imperium*. It is an act of reason based on a prior act of will. Thomas explains this combination by noting a general fact: "the act of the will and of the reason can apply to each other so far namely as reason reasons about willing, and will wills to reason. It happens that an act of will precedes an act of reason and conversely" (2-1.17.1 corp). So, too, for the other acts catalogued here. An act of *imperium*, which presupposes a prior act of will, embraces within its control a whole range of faculties. Thus, *imperium* can control the will, reason, the sensitive appetite, and the actions of exterior members (2-1.17.5–7, 9).

It is impossible, then, to regard Thomas's linear presentation of acts or partial acts of will as more than a heuristic device. It does not represent any actual sequence. It may be possible, for very important moral decisions, to construct a kind of pattern by which deliberation proceeds from apprehended good, through its being willed, into counsel, and finally onto choice of means (compare 1-2.15.3 corp). Still this much reduced (Aristotelian) schema is a static and clumsy rendering of actual processes. In fact, and especially with regard to the most important things, the will seems always already to be in motion toward some final end, however obscurely, and the dialectic between choice and deliberation seems to go forward by rapid mutual adjustment beyond description.

Thomas has several purposes in pushing the description to this limit. One is to safeguard the difference between the will and the intellect. The will is an indispensable source of motion because it is an appetite for the good. Another purpose may be to show the limits of our languages even for describing what we think we know best. But the main purpose must be to slow that motion does not begin in a closed loop within the human being. A closed loop could not set the soul in motion. If it will move, the soul must be drawn to something outside of itself.

This dependence is taken up explicitly in the article that asks whether the will is moved by some external principle (2-1.9.4). A first answer is that it obviously is, insofar as it is an appetite for something external to it. A second and subtler answer is required, since the will also depends on an external principle for its being moved to exercise. Whatever is intermittently active must be actualized by something already in act. It is obvious that the will is intermittently active with regard to particular desires. The will begins to want something in particular by wanting it as end under which the particular falls as means. This requires an act of counsel, which in turn requires a prior act of will to set the end about which the counsel deliberates. If there is endless regress, there is no action. The will's first motion, which begins the alternation of willing and deliberating, must come from outside. Thomas seals this conclusion with a reference to Aristotle's *Eudemian Eth-*

ics.[29] Curiously, in view of his use of that passage elsewhere, he does not here specify what the external principle is. It is God. Something like a divine presence is required to set the will in motion.

A protreptic presentation of the highest good must presuppose that readers have within themselves some desire for the good, however mute or confused. That assumption is abundantly confirmed in Thomas's account of the will. Nothing can be willed except within the inclination of the will toward its highest good. That inclination is natural and inescapable. Moreover, the central analogy between willing and knowing has insisted that the end serves not as conclusion, but rather as premise for the process of willing. Still, there is a significant difference between how willing and knowing attach to their objects. As Thomas repeats in a variety of contexts, will attaches to the thing itself, not its "intention" or abstractive representation. Indeed, the soul is drawn to something more by appetite than by apprehension (2-1.22.2 corp). If complete cognition requires knowing a thing singly and in its constitutive components, love requires only being drawn to it as it is. Something can be fully or completely loved without being fully known (2-1.27.2 ad2).

The function of Thomist protreptic cannot then be to provide a perfect representation of the end, even if one were possible. The will does not need to be told about God as if it were unexpected news. The protreptic must aim rather to help the will's natural love for God find its way through distracting means and false ends. If the protreptic can correct or clarify the notion of end, then the will can begin to follow out the "consequences" of that premise in the choice of actions. The first motion of human wills was elicited in view of an end that must be sought through the means at hand. The possibilities for choice are limited by the implanted end, by the actualized appetite. That limitation in no way diminishes the importance of choice for attaining the end. More important for any theory of moral teaching, freedom requires education about means. If Thomas argues from rationality's freedom in concluding to freedom of choice, he asserts freedom of choice more strongly because of the evidence of moral education. Since human beings can be educated by "counsel, exhortations, precepts, prohibitions, rewards and punishments," they must be free (1.83.1 corp). The reader's own education through deliberative disputation is proof of her freedom. Her freedom requires ongoing education.

The presumption of educability goes together with the notion of freedom as deliberation under a natural inclination. If there were no possibility for deliberation, moral education would be useless. It would also be useless if there were no natural inclination, since then there would be no coherence in actions and so no possibility of instruction. A naturally implanted inclination aimed at a shared good enables not only the protreptic but also the whole project of moral formation to proceed. Of course, moral education that wants to help the reader to keep on searching for the not-yet-present end may require stronger consolations, stronger inducements, than an apophatic protreptic. What is needed is an embodied pattern of living that can be loved without committing idolatry and so derailing. The soul needs to look beyond bodily ends; being a soul in a body, it needs a body that can be loved as part of the pedagogy. "A human being can tend more toward God by love, passively attracted as it were by God Godself, than being led by its own reason" (2-1.26.3 ad 3). The Thomist persuasion to seek the highest good shows the need for more direct moral pedagogy. God has provided.

CHAPTER 8

Stages on Law's Way

The *Summa*'s questions on the sequence of laws are the most famous of Thomas's moral texts. They may also be the most misunderstood. One reason is that readers often encounter them as contextless excerpts from which they are told to extract timeless maxims or "exceptionless" norms. In context, within the *Summa*, law teaches the embodied reader in other ways.

Thomas treats law toward the end of the first section of the *Summa*'s middle part. The whole section concerns the elements and motives of human action. It opens with the exhortation to the final end of all human acting. It closes by depicting the most powerful means for attaining that end, namely grace. The questions on law, which are not now and have never been a separable "treatise," come immediately before grace. Law and grace are paired by the *Summa* as incomplete and complete, anticipation and fulfillment. If grace animates the new law of Christ, earlier kinds of law prepare to be fulfilled in it.

Thomas emphasizes the pairing as he introduces this segment of the *Summa*. Law and grace are, he explains, external principles of human actions (2-1.90 pro). There are others. The devil is an external principle inclining human beings to evil by temptation. More important, and more consolingly, the external principles of human action culminate in God, who moves human beings toward the good. God does this in two ways: instructing by law and helping by grace.

God instructs us by law: *nos instruit per legem*. Thomas chooses the verb carefully. From his earlier writings forward, and often enough in the *Summa*, Thomas repeats that the law is for instruction.[1] In Thomas's lexicon, law is, of course, not the only thing said to instruct. Instruction is given by God, Jesus Christ, the Holy Spirit, angels, bodily creatures, revelation, apparitions, sciences, infused virtues, and even inner instincts—to recall some frequent phrases. Still, law also instructs, and instruction is the most important thing that it does. Its pedagogical function is particularly resonant in the *Summa*, because the claim that God "instructs us by law" recalls the work's opening words: "Since the teacher of catholic truth should instruct not only the advanced . . . " (1 pro). Law belongs to a divine pedagogy that includes the teacher of Catholic truth. Before the reader reaches the four-part definition of law, she hears that law is an instruction given by God as an external help in the human pursuit of the good. She hears as well that it is linked to the more direct help of grace. Whatever else a reader learns about the law must be read back into that fundamental characterization, which determines its position in the *Summa*.

The notion of instruction conditions the meaning of another word that Thomas repeats when explaining law: *praeceptum*, the ancestor of the English "precept." In the questions on law, *praeceptum* functions as a genus comprising a number of species. Within the Christian Scriptures, it will name what English-speakers call the ten "commandments" but also the liturgical ordinances and political arrangements of ancient Israel. It will also refer to various exhortations or instructions from Jesus. For Thomas, following Jesus, the greatest precept is to love God (2-1.100.10). Outside the Scriptures, *praeceptum* refers to various kinds of civil legislation, ethnic custom, and moral instruction. It comprises more specific terms like *mandatum, justificatio*, and *testimonium*. Still, the analogical extension of the word's meaning is weighted toward scriptural examples of divine instruction.

Earlier in the *Summa*, precept was one of the signs or aspects of divine will (1.19.11 corp). *Praeceptum*, strictly speaking, concerns a good to be sought. There are negative precepts, of course, but they are given as part of a gradual pedagogy that ends in positive precepts about the good (e.g., 2-1.72.6 ad2). Later in the *Summa*, after the questions on law, groups of precepts will be discussed in relation to each of the main virtues, with most attention paid to the precepts of charity.[2] In each of these discussions,

Thomas will insist on both the pedagogy of precepts and their connection to virtues.[3] Indeed, the meaning of "precept" might be said to inform the meaning of "law" rather than the other way around.

For Thomas, law falls within the larger meaning of precept. This may be why he does not adopt the patterns of the Decalogue or the Beatitudes for the *Summa*. Both patterns had been used by his predecessors, sometimes at large scale. Certainly Thomas defends the patterns as appropriate summaries of moral teaching. Once rightly distinguished, the precepts of the Decalogue show a proper number, order, and articulation or formulation (2-1.100.4–7). The Sermon on the Mount contains "the whole forming (*informatio*) of Christian life" (2-1.108.3 corp). But these patterns are still, in Thomas's evident judgment, less clear or comprehensive than the pattern of the virtues. If law falls under precept, precept falls within the more comprehensive ordering of moral instruction that puts the great virtues at the center.

From Eternal Law to Natural Law

The *Summa*'s questions on law begin by compiling a definition from four elements: "law is an ordering of reason for the common good, by the one who has care of the community, [that has been] promulgated" (2-1.90.4 corp). Some readers want to exclaim: This is what Scholastic method is supposed to look like! Their enthusiasm may lead them to forget that the definition hardly captures an essence of law. It is, in the terms of Aristotelian logic, a dialectical definition, an agreed starting point from which further inquiry can proceed. Like every other key term in Thomas's theological speech, "law" moves over a range of meanings held together by analogy. The further one gets from the word's origin in human practice, the greater the analogical distension. For the most important cases of law—the eternal law and the divine law—each of the four elements of the original definition will be profoundly qualified, if not reversed.

The fame of the fourfold definition should not distract from the other principles Thomas invokes in this opening question. For example, he recalls another basic analogy, between demonstration and practical reason. As speculative demonstration descends by syllogism from principles to conclusions, so practical reasoning moves down from law to inferences about what is to be done. The analogy is only an analogy. Laws are not principles of demonstration; they rather take the place of principles in the sort of syllogism that practical reasoning uses (2-1.90.1 ad2). More pertinent for contemporary readers may be the reminder that speculative syllogisms are themselves related to ideals of teaching. Demonstrable knowledge is eminently teachable knowledge.

The question on the nature of law allows Thomas to fix other starting points as well. Two of them are connected. If law can be likened to a rule or measure, the main reason for giving a law is neither to judge nor to classify. Law aims instead to "induce" the one receiving it to some action (2-1.90.1 corp). The inducement addresses both reason and will. The cooperation of two faculties is required for human action, as we have seen, and it already illustrates the rule for law in producing it. "Reason commands (*imperat*) what belongs to the end. But the will for what is commanded must be regulated by some reason (*ratio*) if it is to have the sense of law (*ratio legis*)" (2-1.90.1 ad3). The last end of the action undertaken by reason and will is "beatitude"—which seems to mean here both the happiness of human community and the blessedness promised for the afterlife (2-1.90.2 corp). Law induces human beings to move toward their end. If law must be spoken using meanings most familiar in human cities, its dialectical first definition already reaches upward to include a heavenly "kingdom."

Law descends from the Ruler of that kingdom. Thomas recalls from his sources four kinds of law: eternal, natural, human, and divine. This is a taxonomy but also a hierarchy and a history. The other laws depend on eternal law. Since a hierarchy is a pedagogical sequence, they come after it in the order of presentation, each with a particular role in history. Natural law is a rational participation in God's goal for embodied souls. It is both incomplete and vulnerable (2-1.91.2 corp). Its general and variously discernible precepts are meant to be specified by human law and custom. When sin more and more obscures natural law, divine pedagogy responds with other stages of law that can lead to the fulfillment of the Gospel.

I say stages. Thomas speaks of *status*. The word is usually translated into contemporary English as state, condition, or circumstance. Each of those renders a part of the Latin word without exhausting it. We could get more of the meaning if we still had the older English sense of "station," as in "one's station in life." For Thomas, *status* refers technically to social role and rank. A sermon *ad status*, a staple of Dominican preaching, is a sermon directed at a particular group of people—merchants, the married, the nobility, and so on. There is yet another range of moral meanings for *status* that is best rendered by our word "stage." These are the meanings that matter most in the discussion of the law.

In the *prima secundae* of the *Summa*, before the questions on law, *status* refers most often to the stages of human progress toward beatitude. In a quotation from Boethius that Thomas both recalls and uses, beatitude is itself a *status*.[4] It is the same as the stage of "glory" or "the homeland" (*status gloriae, status patriae*). Before beatitude comes the stage of the present life; before the marred present, there was innocence, the first *status*. This life is a stage in which humans can still improve morally (*status merendi*), as opposed to the condition of those already blessed or damned (2-1.93.6 arg3). The sense of *status* as moral epoch is applied directly and repeatedly to the kinds of law, perhaps especially divine law. Thomas relies on Paul in Galatians 3:24–25 to compare these stages with human aging. The *status* of the Old Law was like a youth still being led to school by a pedagogue; the *status* of the new is adulthood (2-1.91.5 ad1).[5] But Thomas is more concerned to understand the stages of all kinds of law as corresponding to the changing stages of human understanding (*status cognitionis humanae*, 2-1.101.2 corp). So there are "three stages" of the Old Law corresponding to steps in Israel's perception of the divine will (2-1.102.6 ad5). More significantly, Thomas distinguishes three stages of "interior worship" that correspond to three kinds of faith and so to three times of worship: under the Old Law, under the New, and among the blessed in heaven (2-1.103.3 corp).

If Thomas reiterates the word *status* most often in speaking of divine law, he assigns to each of the kinds of law a temporal reference. To ask for the time of a law is to ask for its exact purpose. Eternal law is the "reason of the governance of things existing in God as in the ruler (*princeps*) of the universe" (2-1.91.1). Here the reference is to eternity. It is not only the first law in every sense, it is the law that subtends all others as their ground. Eternal law is divine providence. Much earlier in the *Summa*, the reader learned that providence in God is only notionally distinct from creation (1.22.1). Describing eternal law, Thomas stresses again the pairing of the creator's art and the provider's ordering. Both creation and providence are teleological: Their end is God. God's law is none other than God's self (2-1.91.1 ad3). The common good contemplated by eternal law is the teleological return of all to God. That may seem already to stretch the notion of common good beyond any political sense. Thomas stretches the notion of promulgation even further. The eternal law is promulgated verbally in the Trinitarian procession of the Son as Word (2-1.91.1 ad2). It is promulgated in writing by "the book of life"—that is, by God's knowledge of predestination conceived "metaphorically" as a book (1.24.1 corp). Thus, the promulgation of eternal law occurs entirely within God. There can be no promulgation to creatures (2-1.91.1 ad2).

The analogical application of the four elements of law might seem easier in the case of natural law, especially because Thomas can rely in discussing it on numerous and familiar authorities drawn from civil and canonical law. Each of the compilations of Roman law commissioned by Justinian begins with remarks on a law of nature and a law of peoples. Written into all living creatures, the law of nature impels them to survive and procreate. The law of peoples is the rational ground under local laws.[6] The two laws are mixed by Isidore of Seville. In his *Etymologies*, natural law includes imperatives of mortal life but also of life in community. Common property, equal liberty, and simple justice all belong to natural law.[7] Gratian takes up these texts from Isidore in his definitive compilation of church law. For the *Decretum*, natural law, first and invariant, comprises common principles binding on all human beings; it overrules human laws that would contradict it.[8] Still Gratian's most striking remark on natural law may be his first: for him it is "contained in the Gospel" and epitomized in what English-speakers call the Golden Rule.[9] The list of Thomas's legal sources for natural law continues into his immediate, Dominican predecessors. Raymond of Peñafort begins his *Summa of Law* by listing five elements of natural law, including every precept of divine law.[10]

This crowd of authorities does not agree about natural law. Some of their disagreements or confusions had been negotiated in comprehensive theological works before Thomas began to write. For example, the *Summa* "of Alexander" contains a lengthy treatment of four kinds of law that correspond roughly to Thomas's own: eternal, natural, Mosaic, and evangelical.[11] There are about four times as many articles in the Franciscan *Summa* as in the corresponding questions of Thomas's work. Moreover, the Franciscan authors marshal a wider variety and greater quantity of authorities. By contrast, Thomas is laconic. He wants the reader to see through his selection of topics and pruning of authorities to the history that leads from law to grace.

Thomas is less concerned to canvass all the authorities than he is to place natural law properly within the sequence of laws. For him, natural law is "a participation by the rational creature in eternal law" that produces "a natural inclination to the due act and end" (2-1.91.2 corp). Where lower animals have mute instincts, rational souls affirm their appetites as participations in God's teleological creation. If all laws are derived from eternal law, natural law is derived first in the very act of creating rational animals. The promulgation of natural law is the reception by the human mind of an impression of divine light. It is not a set of propositions handed over by God after the fact. It operates rather as a fundamental inclination (2-1.94.2). Since it is articulated by reason, natural law remains subject to the conditions of cognition, in individuals and their groups. The question of what kind of participation underlies natural law is less urgent than another question: How much can we still know of it?

Thomas's treatment of natural law is a long exploration of its cognitive limitations. Although Thomas introduces law by drawing an analogy between speculative and practical reasoning, he emphasizes for natural law a decisive disanalogy.[12] In speculative matters, the premises can be known by all equally; the same conclusions are drawn, though not with equal facility. The more difficult the demonstration, the fewer will be able to reach its conclusions with certainty. In practical reasoning, the first principles are also known to all. The conclusions, by contrast, are not, either in content or in clarity of apprehension (2-1.94.4). Natural law is precisely not like Euclidean geometry, which yields the same conclusions everywhere.

Something more stubborn still produces disagreement in practical reasoning. The reasoning is distorted by moral condition. Many disagreements about practical conclusions can be blamed on the interference of passion, bad custom, or defective disposition (2-1.94.4 corp, 94.6 corp). The same forces afflict culture. On the authority of Julius Caesar, Thomas reports that ancient Germans considered theft not to be a crime even though it is "expressly against the law of nature" (2-1.94.4 corp). If that law's first principles can never be entirely erased from the human heart, the law can be "deleted" (*deleri*) both individually and communally by desires and passions, by wicked arguments and corrupt customs (2-1.94.6 corp).

The effective application of natural law is further limited by the scope of practical reasoning. The difficulty of descending to particular cases from very general principles requires help for specification. Thomas distinguishes three levels of precept in the natural law according to three basic human inclinations: toward the good of being (self-preservation), toward the animal good of reproduction, and toward the rational good of knowing God and living in political society. Thomas gives only a few examples of precepts for each level. So, for example, reproduction includes the "education of children," while political life requires "that a human being avoid ignorance and not offend others, with whom he [or she] must share community" (2-1.94.2 corp). Thomas does not attempt to deduce all of the conditions for fulfilling each inclination. A complete deduction of the implied virtues cannot be performed. Natural law includes the inclination to act rationally, which is the same as acting virtuously. It does not include a complete list of virtuous acts. Virtuous acts are discerned in political life (2-1.94.3 corp).

Thomas considers no particular set of human laws in any detail. The fullest description he provides of exemplary specifications of natural law precepts comes in his discussion of the moral precepts of the Old Law. His best example is the Decalogue. God revealed its precepts as something more than remedies for logical slips. The revelation responded rather to a dramatic history of universal deviation. A reader understands the actual limits of natural law only when she grasps something of God's purpose in giving Moses written tablets of *natural* law.

The Old Law and Its Ceremonies

The law of Moses is an essential moment in God's teaching of the human race.[13] For Thomas, the Old Law is good simply speaking because it is fully in accord with reason. It restrains unruly desire and prohibits sins. It leads human beings toward eternal happiness. Its deficiency is an incompleteness of means. If Mosaic law teaches truly about the highest human end, it cannot yet invoke the full grace required to reach it. Thomas holds that there was grace in the time of the Old Law. He affirms that some in Israel were saved. Still they were saved, just as Christians are, not by law but by faith in a mediator (2-1.98.2 ad4).

Following tradition, Thomas divides the principal precepts of the Old Law into three groups: moral, ceremonial, and judicial. There are other elements of instruction in the Hebrew Scriptures, but they are subordinated to the precepts in these three classes (2-1.99.4). These classes are distinguished both by content and by historical span. The *moral* precepts of the Old Law, which reiterate or make explicit the conclusions of the natural law, hold always just in the way that natural law does (2-1.100.1, 11). The *ceremonial* or ritual precepts bind the Jews alone and only until their fulfillment in Christ, after which it is in fact immoral to fulfill them (2-1.101.3–4). The *judicial* or political precepts bind Israel until the coming of Christ, after which they become merely another in the repertoire of political regimes (2-1.104.3).

The temporal distinction points toward the notorious difficulty of separating the Torah's precepts for Christian appropriation. The scheme does not fit neatly onto the scriptural text. Even Christian Bibles could not label the Mosaic precepts by kind. For example, Thomas will say that the ceremonial precepts are the ones that concern the worship of God (*cultus Dei*), but he will then go on to show that worship is a form of moral education (2-1.101.1 arg1 and corp). His defense of the rationality of particular ceremonial precepts will often argue that there are moral reasons behind apparently "ridiculous" regulations (2-1.102.6 arg10). This underlines the textual challenge: in what Christians call the Old Testament, precepts later distinguished as moral and ceremonial appear side by side, pronounced with the same gravity and backed with equally severe penalties for their infringement. More important, the moral pedagogy of the Old Law is not restricted to the moral precepts. Moral, ceremonial, and judicial laws teach together. The bare list of ten commandments is not meant by itself to perform the re-education of fallen humanity. The Israelites need civic and ritual schools alongside the moral reminders. So it is understandable that Thomas nowhere proposes a complete textual division between moral and ceremonial. He relies instead, as many Christians have, on the continuing customs of Christian community. If a precept has not been observed by communities recognized as Christian, and especially if it has been prohibited by them, it must be ceremonial and not moral. Current versions of Christian practice are projected backward. The temporal distinctions among precepts in the Old Law are in fact retrojections of Christian history.

Having conceded these doubts about the division of precepts, let me begin with them where Thomas does. On his account, the moral precepts of the Old Law reveal the principles or conclusions of the law of nature (2-1.98.5). God revealed what could be inferred from nature both because of the limits on human practical reasoning and because of particular gaps in the conclusions reached. To explain, Thomas divides cases for moral judgment into three groups (2-1.100.1). Some human actions are so clear that they can be approved or reproved by quick reference to first principles. Others require longer consideration by someone wise. Still other actions can be judged only with the help of divine instruction. These three groups correspond to three levels of precepts in the natural law. The first level contains practical principles knowable by everyone: "Honor your father and mother," "Do not kill," "Do not steal." The second level consists of precepts knowable only to the wise: "Rise up before the white head, and honor the person of the elderly" (Leviticus 19:32). The third level comprises precepts that all human begins must learn directly from God: "Do not make a statue or any image [of God]," "Do not take the name of God in vain."

All of the examples are scriptural because Thomas correlates the three grades of moral precepts with the commandments of the Decalogue (2-1.100.3). The ten commandments, as we call them in English, offer precepts of both the first and third levels. The precepts of the second grade, those known only to the wise, are conclusions from the Decalogue rather than principles of it. What Thomas earlier called "first [or primary] precepts" of natural law—the inclination to continue in being or to live in community—are the ontological grounds behind the Decalogue's explicit commands. The commands do not create the inclinations. They are revealed because the inclinations have lost their way.

God announces basic moral truths because they are too important to be left to the contingencies of discovery or deliberation. For the same reason, God also reveals some speculative truths that could be known by demonstration because they would have been known only to a few, after a long time, and with an admixture of error (1.1.1 corp, 2-1.99.2 ad2). The *disanalogy* of speculative and practical reasoning makes the revelation of moral precepts more urgent. Human capacity for moral inference has been "darkened" by the "the custom of sinning," by "the abundance of sins" (2-1.99.2 ad2, 98.6 corp). God reveals natural law precepts after human beings have experienced the humiliating failure to achieve human happiness by their own power (2-1.98.6). The natural law slips further and further into darkness until God calls Moses up to the mountain.

The grim history should remind the reader that natural law was never some state of pure nature. For Thomas, the state of nature is a hypothetical construct. It is posited as backdrop for explanation, not as historical episode.[14] Human beings were created in grace, with the gift of what Thomas knows as the "rightness of the first *status*" (1.95.1 corp). God gave this grace freely to the human species at its creation. If human beings had not fallen through sin, each generation would have been born, by God's intention, into the renewed gift of a supernatural justice (1.100.1). They would thus have been born with a knowledge of the universal requirements of law, and they would have possessed this knowledge "much more fully" than they now can naturally (1.101.1 ad3). Human creatures chose sin. They fell, not into pure nature but nature deformed. They came to need the revelation of important parts of natural law—and more besides. From the beginning of his discussion of Mosaic law, Thomas urges that its revelation, while complete as doctrine, is not complete as formation. If the Old Law could reach so far as to teach acts of love, it could not supply the grace for doing them (2-1.11.10 corp and ad3). At most, Thomas thinks, it could look forward to a future in which some redeemer would supply that grace.

The law given to Moses is the first stage of divine law. It is a first step in law toward the incarnation. It also contains implicitly God's diagnosis of how humans learn when they have fallen far away. The giving of the Mosaic law is one of the most familiar scenes of instruction for Christian imaginations. Childhood memories of stone tablets should not trick us into thinking that the divine law began only as a short list of prohibitions. It was accompanied, on Thomas's reading, with an indispensable schooling for bodies. Having learned already the importance of sacraments for continuing the moral instruction of Christ's life, a reader might be especially alert to a corrective law that prescribes rituals.

The Old Law teaches anticipation of the redeemer most effectively in its ceremonies. Thomas's questions on Levitical worship are an indispensable (if neglected) part of this teaching on law. They are a prominent feature of the architecture in this segment of the *Summa*. The book's longest single article explains the rational pedagogy of the sacred objects and structures of Israelite religion (2-1.102.5). Indeed, the last three articles on the rational "reasons" (*causae*) behind the Old Testament's ceremonial ordinances take up as much space as 21 or 22 average articles in the earlier questions on law. The treatment of the Old Law's ceremonies might even seem to distend the structure and so to violate the principle of pedagogical economy announced for the whole work. It might also be tempting to think that Thomas were hastily copying himself, except that these extensive articles have no parallel in Thomas's other works.

What accounts for this extended treatment? One clue is given in Thomas's reliance on Maimonides. "Rabbi Moses" is mentioned repeatedly in the articles on Israelite ceremonies, and he is relied upon more often than he is mentioned.[15] With Maimonides, Thomas strives to explain how even the details of ceremonial prescription drew worshippers away from idolatry and toward the single God, from whom they were taught to expect a further and final stage of instruction. God did not give meaningless rituals to the Israelites, and the Israelites did not invent them on their own.

The effort to justify ceremonies is also, of course, an effort to justify the Scriptures that record them. The distension of articles on the ceremonies of the Old Law responds to the extraordinary detail of Leviticus or the architectural descriptions of 1 Kings. To dismiss the ceremonies as irrational or unpedagogical would cast doubt on large portions of the Scriptures. More: Thomas's emphasis on the rational pedagogy of the ceremonial laws applies the larger principle that God does not waste teaching. It reinforces the *Summa*'s lessons about how to teach embodied, rational souls. Like the Christian sacraments, the Israelite ceremonies are not arbitrary or nonsensical. Like the narrative of Christ's life, they frame examples for rational living.

The detail of Thomas's explications of ceremonial law makes them impossible to summarize. I hope only to gather some principles reiterated in them. Thomas starts from the defense of the need for ceremonies under the conditions of the present life. Human beings cannot now see the divine truth directly; they must approach it under "certain sensible figures" that prefigure what will appear in beatitude (2-1.101.2 corp). During the period of the Old Law, when the surest way to reach God had not been revealed, the rites stood one step further back. They could only prefigure the incarnation of Christ, who is the full figure of the glory to come. The reasons for certain rites lie in the future, in relation to an end that has not yet appeared and is so far anticipated only by a few (2-1.102.1 ad3). If it is not true that ceremonial precepts are defined by the hiddenness of their reasons, it is true to say that their being figures of a future truth means that their reasons cannot be immediately evident (2-1.101.1 arg4 and ad4, 103.2 corp).

At the same time, Thomas insists, it is possible to discover *literal* reasons or causes in the old ceremonies (2-1.102.2). The chief literal motive behind all is to educate the Israelites out of idolatry and toward the worship of the true God (2-1.101.3 corp, 102.5 corp, and so on). Thomas invokes this principle regularly. When no other explanation appears, it suffices to say that something was prohibited because the idolaters did it or used it. There are more satisfying applications of the principles, of course. The institution of animal sacrifices and their eventual centralization in the Temple are both meant to inhibit idolatry, displacing idolatrous rites while reminding the Israelites that God does not want bodily worship for itself (2-1.102.3 corp and ad1, 102.4 ad3). God must wean Israel from idolatry slowly enough, indulgently enough, that it does not relapse into the attractions of demonic rites (2-1.101.3 ad3). Thus, education against idolatry also implies a broader education of appetite or sensibility. The ceremonial precepts repress disordered desire. They correct cruelty by instilling a horror of bloodshed.[16]

The doubling of literal and figurative meanings recalls the layers of meaning in Old Testament exegesis. A crucial argument *sed contra* moves from the multiple senses of scriptural history to the double justification of the ceremonial precepts (2-1.102.2 sc). Paul writes that many things happened to the Israelites in figure. Thomas adds, "But in the history of the Old Testament, beyond the mystical or figural understanding, there is also a literal understanding. So also the ceremonial precepts, beyond figural justifications, have as well literal reasons."[17] As later with the Gospels, the history (*historia*) of the Old Testament is understood to mean both historical events and their narration in the Scriptures. The literal and figurative meanings of old rites can be discovered in the canonical texts. Thomas applies to the figurative meanings of the rites a threefold division of spiritual senses in the Scriptures. The rites can refer figuratively to Christ and the church (allegory); to the *mores* of the Christian people (morality); or to the glory toward which Christ leads (anagogy). These meanings are found both in the scriptural ordinances for ritual performances and in the rites themselves. Rites and descriptions of them give practice in figurative reading. Indeed, this is the only section of the *Summa* that gives extended practice in reading the whole of Christian liturgy or iconography. Lessons in reading the rites of Israel are also lessons in reading the rites of the Church. Those lessons will prove important in the *Summa*'s third part.

The rites of Israel are figures. They prefigure Christ, and so they can seem pure indexes of an obscure future. Still, prefiguration is a species of figuration rather than its root. The category of figure has to be understood beyond prefiguration and in some sense before it. Here as in many other places, Thomas wants to distinguish figuration from the deceit or obscurity of poetic ornamentation (2-1.101.2 arg2; compare 1.1.9 arg1-2). He is particularly careful here, because the rites are not only texts. They are performances. The lurking threat is not poetry so much as theater—a term that almost always has negative connotations in Thomas.[18] If a performed representation is not theater, what is it? One possibility is that it might be like an example. Thomas uses the logic of example in many positive ways and especially to explain certain gospel narratives about Jesus's life. But the logic does not fit here. The old ceremonies do not in fact offer discrete moral examples. Their representations are meant to teach the mind and shape the body more indirectly than by direct imitation.

As against example, a figure suggests concealment. To understand indirect teaching, Thomas turns as so often to Ps-Dionysius: "in the stage of the present life, we cannot intuit the divine truth in itself, but the ray of divine truth must illuminate us through (*sub*) certain sensible figures, as Dionysius says" (2-1.101.2 corp). The implied reasoning is filled in a few lines later. If human beings were shown divine truths before they were ready for them, their incomprehension would lead to contempt (2-1.101.2 ad1). God's grandeur must be veiled just as the Holy of Holies was in the tabernacle or temple. "The matter of the four elements is the obstacle (*impedimentum*) by which incorporeal substances are [now] veiled from us" (2-1.102.4 ad4). The logic of figuration itself is figured in sacred architecture, not least because the structure represents the whole created order. Its figures teach observers how any figure can teach.

The indirectness of figuration favors certain styles. A sort of exaggeration is required since spiritual things must be represented "more manifestly" for human beings to understand them (2-1.102.4 ad6). The invisibility of God is, of course, explicitly affirmed, yet the divine absence must be marked vividly. The incompleteness or imperfection of the old rites leads to another sort of emphasis: figures of Christ are multiplied. Their number shows their limitation. The principle of multiplication leads Thomas into kinds of reading most readers do not associate with him or at least with his *Summa*. He provides many detailed interpretations of specific figures. Some are evidently edifying, like the comparisons between Christ and the grain offering or the altar (102.3 ad12, 102.4 ad7). Other interpretations are more surprising. Commenting on dietary restrictions, Thomas offers a moralized bestiary of two dozen birds (2-1.102.6 ad1). These articles of the *Summa* strew figures and their explanations.[19]

Some of the figurative readings may seem extravagant. All of them share one aim: to reinforce moral education for fallen souls. In the threefold division of figurative or mystic senses, one is explicitly labeled "morality." The label means that this sense refers directly to the future *mores* of the Christian people. Yet, each of the three figurative senses teaches moral meanings in some larger sense. While the parts of the tabernacle or temple offer a map of the world, they refer more urgently to the spiritual stages marked by the revelation of Old and New Laws (2-1.102.4 ad4). The stages of the Old Law are figured in the rules for oblations (102.6 ad5). The holidays of Israel foretell the coming deeds of redemption and evangelization (102.4 ad10).

Some sets of figures are ordered to specific steps in moral education. At grandest scale, changes in external worship correspond to human progress in the interior worship of God (2-1.103.3 corp). At smaller scale, there are some difficulties to be resolved about the timing of the transition from the old sacraments to the new, from worship counted as Jewish to worship recognizably Christian. During the time of Jesus's preaching, before his passion, the law and the gospel "ran at once" (103.3 ad2). So Jesus practiced and commanded some of the old observances. From the moment of his passion forward, however, the new ceremonial dispensation took effect and prohibited the old (103.4). So if the apostles appear to observe Jewish law after the resurrection, that must be only an appearance.

The old ceremonial precepts are ignored when the new sacraments arrive because worship is a profession of faith. "All ceremonies are so many protestations of faith, which is the inward worship of God. But someone can protest this inward faith both in deeds and in words" (2-1.103.4 corp). Before the Old Law was revealed, some were led by a "prophetic spirit," by "divine instinct," to devise worship that both expressed their inward devotion and even signified the mystery of the Christ who would come (103.1 corp). Once the Old Law was revealed, its rites saved some because they were anticipatory declarations of faith (2-1.103.2 corp). To continue the practice of any such rites after Christ's passion would be to dwell still in anticipation. If Christ has indeed come, then the tense of faith in a mediator has changed (103.4 corp). It is no longer future. It is present.

The New Law

A reader who reaches the *Summa*'s questions on the New Law in textual order may notice first that they are so brief. Thomas devotes four times as many articles to the Old Law as to the New (a ratio of 46:12), and the two longest of those earlier articles are as long as all of the questions on this culminating law put together. While many of the articles on the Old Law provide detailed interpretations of scriptural texts, the only exegetical dispute about the New Law concerns whether the Sermon on the Mount is a sufficient guide to interior acts (2-1.108.3).

One reason for Thomas's brevity has to do with the functions of the two halves of the moral part of the *Summa*. The detailed representation of Christian living is not meant to be provided in the discussion of Gospel as law. It will come in the long analyses of virtues that make up the *secunda secundae*. A more important reason for brevity lies in the very character of the New Law: it is not primarily written. Like Christ himself, it refuses writing for more intimate instruction. The "whole power" (*tota virtus*) of this law consists of "the grace of the Holy Spirit, which is given by faith in Christ. The new law is principally the grace of the Holy Spirit that is given by Christ to the faithful" (2-1.106.1 corp). The New Testament's precepts and counsels are at best dispositions to receiving grace or guides to its right use. The "ordinances for human feeling and human acts" contained in the "documents of faith" have no power as rules to justify. The letter of the Gospel would kill unless faith healed inwardly (2-1.106.2 corp). Thomas knows, of course, that Christ's moral teaching has content. Some of the content clarifies the Old Law; some intensifies it; some adds new counsel (2-1.107.2 corp). Still, what distinguishes the New Law is a gift of grace that issues in exterior acts by impulse or incitation (*ex instinctu*).[20] When the Gospel prescribes actions, it is either suggesting dispositions to grace or predicting consequences that will flow from it (2-1.108.1 corp).

The New Law completes natural law by restoring its inward character. Neither the natural law nor the Gospel is primarily written. Each is an inward sharing of a direction toward happiness. In the present human condition, the natural law participates in the human teleology darkly, uncertainly, inarticulately. The New Law, which is the grace brought by Christ, participates in the teleology luminously and confidently. Neither natural law nor New Law resides in a set of propositions. In the stages of divine pedagogy, written law is a way to reach unwritten law. God reveals written law only in order to remind humans of its unwritten origin and to bring humans to its unwritten end.

So far as the law of grace is the condition of the *Summa*'s intended reader, it suggests again the complex chronology of moral learning. The reader is supposed to have received the final law already as grace. She can benefit from the detailed recapitulation of all the stages of law, including the precepts of natural law. Again, the reader is presumed to have passed beyond the rites of the Old Law into the sacraments of the New, and yet the reader is given an enormously detailed exposition of Israelite rites. Some of this recapitulation might be explained as preparation for future preachers or teachers of theology. That explanation requires another: Why do preachers and teachers need to return to these topics at all? What is the role of historical recapitulation in the present moral education of Christians?

The structure of the *Summa* responds to those questions by suggesting that recapitulation is embellished recitation. The stages on law's ways are stages of speaking in aid of graced action that will require less speech. The New Law has already been given in all its brevity. Human learners still need to approach it again and again through much longer speeches. Wherever a reader finds herself in salvation history, she may use all its earlier stages as repeatable preparation. The history of divine pedagogy in law obviously prepares for the divine pedagogy of incarnation. Thomas's careful attention to the details of Israelite ritual evidently foreshadows his advocacy of sacraments as extensions through time of the scenes of incarnate instruction. His interest in the details of temple architecture prepare the reader to learn from a God who trusts manifestation over abstraction when it comes to forming embodied speakers who have fallen into sin. The Old Law is remembered in Christian scriptures and scriptural theology because it prepares souls still.

CHAPTER 9

The Gifts of the Spirit

In the questions on the motions of the human will or the stages of law and grace, a reader encounters structurally prominent portions of the *Summa*'s moral teaching. These questions serve as bookends for the *prima secundae*. The structural significance becomes more apparent when a reader comes to these sections fresh from a reading of Thomas on incarnation and sacraments. The preoccupations of that third part also bring into relief other sections of the second. Among these are the scattered questions on the gifts of the Holy Spirit. Dispersed as they are across the treatment of virtues in the *secunda secundae*, the gifts might seem to have no place whatever. In fact, their very dispersion makes them a sort of refrain—and so a regular reminder that the virtues are not the entirety of moral education.[1]

A modern reader of the *Summa* can be tempted to regard the gifts of the Holy Spirit as a merely obligatory topic—a relic of authoritative moral schemes past. If the list of gifts goes back to Isaiah 11, it has weight for medieval Christian theologians through authoritative adaptations, especially in Gregory the Great's *Moral Readings of Job*.[2] Does Thomas talk about the gifts only because he is expected to talk about them?

Thomas shows himself quite willing to discard traditional moral schemes from the *Summa* when he finds them unnecessary or misleading. The obvious example would be the variously arranged lists of seven deadly sins: A standard pattern for much of moral theology before Thomas, they disappear as an organizing principle from the *Summa*. He neither discards nor ignores the traditional topic of the gifts of the Holy Spirit. Instead, he returns to it punctually along his new itinerary.

Before assigning the gifts a regular place, Thomas argues for their necessity in any adequate account of human action. In *Summa* 2-1, he considers the gifts at the end of the treatment of virtues in general before turning to errors, vices, and sins (2-1.68). Thomas knows that older sources treat virtues and gifts interchangeably, but he writes about them at the end of a century of increasing terminological precision. Indeed, he summarizes that progress (2-1.68.1 corp).[3] With his predecessors, Thomas takes the difference between virtues and gifts as given: many virtues do not appear on the list of seven gifts and at least one item on that list—namely fear—does not appear to be a positive moral attribute at all. So there must be some difference between virtues and gifts.

A reader can understand the difference, Thomas says, by attending to "the manner of Scriptural speech." After all, Isaiah refers to these seven as "spirits." The prophet must refer to divine inspiration, which would distinguish the gifts from humanly acquired virtues. Thomas has already established that there are infused virtues: The theological virtues are always infused, the moral virtues sometimes (1-2.63.3). What distinguishes a gift from an infused virtue? They differ in function and, more precisely, the kind of help each gives to human action. The gifts are infused by God to make a human being "quickly movable by divine inspiration" (2-1.68.1 corp). They make it easier to move in response to divine *instinctus* (2-1.68.1 ad3, ad4).

The word *instinctus* is even more important here than it was in characterizing the New Law. I doubt that a single English word can render it. Certainly it cannot be rendered by our modern "instinct." In classical authors known to Thomas, the word means both incitement and inspiration. Ancient passages speak of divine *instinctus*, impulses owed to the gods. So it is in Thomas, though the inspiring divinity has changed. If Thomas speaks frequently of natural *instinctus*, he does not regard all *instinctus* as natural. Much less is it "hard-wired" by biology. Even in animals, Thomas likens some instincts to the virtue of providence: God provides them with a premonition of the future that God foreknows.[4] Describing human beings, Thomas speaks less often of natural *instinctus* than of other kinds.

Instinct can be divine or diabolical.[5] There is an *instinctus* of grace but also of prophecy.[6] Finally, most significantly for the gifts, there is the *instinctus* of the Holy Spirit.[7] In these passages, *instinctus* is sometimes described as internal or interior; in other instances, it is attributed to the agency of an external mover. For example, God (but not only God) may produce an *instinctus* from within the human being. Given this range of meaning, I will translate *instinctus* neutrally as incitement.

The Holy Spirit bestows gifts to remedy an insufficiency in the "incitement of reason." Where human reason does not suffice to move toward the end, human beings need inward help in responding to the Holy Spirit as an external mover (2-1.68.2 corp). The notion of incitement suggests Thomas's main analogy for the operation of the gifts. Just as moral virtues habituate human appetites to answer human reason promptly, so the gifts attune a human being's powers for responding to divine direction.[8] Note the implication: The whole human being is like an appetite in relation to the direction of God, who takes the place of reason. Any adequate account of human action toward the highest end should include God both as final cause and as moving cause inciting inwardly. (Recall the presence of God at the beginning of the motions of the human will.) Thomas himself supplies the conclusive metaphor: Moved in this way, human beings are so many "organs" (*organa*) of the Holy Spirit (2-1.68.4 ad1). They are the Spirit's instruments and so must be united to the Spirit as any instrument is to the artisan who wields it (2-1.68.4 ad3). Human beings are united to the Spirit by the infused theological virtues of faith, hope, and charity, which regulate the gifts (2-1.68.8 corp).

Intellectual Gifts and Knowledge of Morals

These are the main elements in Thomas's preliminary account of the gifts of the Holy Spirit. Like every account in *Summa* 2-1, this analysis is not meant to be complete. Moreover, it separates elements that are combined for action. A reader's next step is to understand how the gifts fit into the pedagogical simplification that yields the structure of the second section. In the prologue to the *secunda secundae*, Thomas has proposed two simplifying principles. First, he will unite in a single cluster of questions one main virtue, its parts, the corresponding gifts, the opposed vices, and the attached affirmative or negative precepts. Second, he will trace all moral virtues back to the three theological and four cardinal virtues while distributing the intellectual virtues under other headings.

Recall some of Thomas's rationale for the second simplification:

Of the intellectual virtues, one is prudence, which is contained and
counted within the cardinal virtues; art (*ars*) does not pertain to moral
knowledge (*scientia moralis*) . . . ; the other three intellectual virtues,
namely wisdom, insight (*intellectus*), and knowledge (*scientia*), share
even their names with certain gifts of the Holy Spirit, so that they will
be considered when considering the gifts corresponding to the virtues.
(2-1 pro)

A reader should be surprised. This rationale for distributing the intellectual virtues reverses Thomas's first rule of simplification. There Thomas
subordinated everything to the virtues. Here he puts a whole class of virtues under the gifts. It is not a minor class: The intellectual virtues that he
now subordinates are central to the philosophical ethics on which Thomas
relies, especially Aristotle's *Nicomachean Ethics*. They are also central to the
enterprise of the *Summa* itself, as this very passage attests.

The reader's surprise may grow when she notices that *scientia* appears
twice in the rationale for simplification. It figures first as the name for the
knowledge Thomas offers in the middle of *Summa*. The term then names,
second, an intellectual virtue that Thomas is eliding with the eponymous
gift of the Holy Spirit. The obvious question: How is the *scientia* offered
on these very pages related to the Spirit's gift of *scientia*? Or how far does
the *Summa*'s own teaching of moral lessons presuppose a gift in the writer
or the reader?

The question is not easy. It is tempting to dodge it by claiming that
Thomas must be using the term *scientia* equivocally. One meaning of the
term must apply to the contents of the *Summa* while another applies to
the gift of the Holy Spirit. But there is no textual evidence for that dodge.
Nor would it fit with the structural innovation Thomas is describing in
this prologue. If *scientia* as applied to morals is simply an equivocal term,
then Thomas would seem obliged to explain its various meanings separately—and precisely *not* to treat the intellectual virtue under the gift of
the Holy Spirit.

The impulse to separate philosophical and theological meanings of
scientia is contradicted more obviously by the *Summa*'s structure of moral
teaching: Thomas does not construct the definition of virtue from Aristotle. He starts rather with Augustine by way of Peter Lombard. His definition applies in the first instance to infused virtue, not acquired: "virtue
is a good quality of mind, by which one rightly lives, which no one uses
badly, which God works in us without us" (2-1.55.4 ad1). The definition
is constructed for the theological virtues and the infused moral virtues—

indeed, even for the gifts, speaking generally. It becomes a definition for acquired virtue only by subtracting the last clause or *particula*, as Thomas calls it (2-1.55.4 corp).

Why does Thomas defend the fuller definition in place of a more constricted one? A theologian should be more concerned with infused virtues than acquired ones—and not as a matter of professional taste. A theologian knows that the only adequate way to understand the teleological coherence of human action is to start from a view that includes the full range of divine helps. A theologian defines *infused* virtue and then specifies acquired virtue by a kind of subtraction. To begin from a definition that emphasizes human acquisition would exclude the most important helps that humans need in order to move coherently toward their end.

Are the four moral virtues used to organize this part of the *Summa*—the virtues of prudence, justice, fortitude, temperance—infused or acquired? The safest answer would be to say both. Thomas sometimes speaks of features that could belong to either the acquired or infused virtue, as he speaks of resemblances between acquired and infused. Certainly the correct answer cannot be that the four organizing cardinal virtues of the *secunda secundae* are only acquired virtues. Thomas sometime subdivides virtues into elements that presuppose participation in Christian life (like many aspects of *religio* or its acts, 2-2.81–87). Again, Thomas opposes to the organizing moral virtues vices that he analyzes as mortal sins. He correlates the virtues with precepts of divine law and explicitly infused moral elements—including the gifts. For the structural logic of the *Summa* to work, the four moral virtues that organize its most specific moral teaching cannot be understood only as humanly acquired virtues.

I stress the point because it helps to explain the relation of infused *scientia* to acquired *scientia*. Acquired *scientia* does belong, according to Thomas, to a separate species from infused *scientia* because it has a different definition. Still the difference is one of subtraction or diminution. Humanly acquired *scientia* is the more constricted or impoverished *scientia*. That is one reason why the Holy Spirit gives intellectual gifts.

I can show the relation with a bit more detail for the three intellectual gifts, *intellectus*, *scientia*, and *sapientia*. (I translate them, when necessary and with misgivings, as insight, knowledge, and wisdom.) Thomas uses a sort of template to discuss all of the gifts.[9] He applies it to these three. He begins by asking how each is related to the corresponding intellectual virtue as described chiefly by Aristotle (2-2.8.1 arg1, 9.1 arg1, 45.1 arg2). Thomas provides two linked answers. He first stresses that the gifts are concerned with a new range of ends or objects. Humans need infused insight because they have an end beyond nature, namely "supernatural blessedness" (2-2.8.1 ad1). Thomas often uses metaphors of increased height to explain a gift's relation to the acquired intellectual virtue. The Spirit's insight is added atop naturally acquired insight into principles and conclusions (*superadditio*, e.g., 2-2.8.1 ad2). Thomas also relies on metaphors of intensification, which point to his second answer. Human insight seeks "intimate cognition" of the intelligible hidden behind sensed qualities, words, resemblances or figures. The "supernatural light" brought by the Spirit's gift helps in each case (2-2.8.1 corp). The intellectual gifts enable the human mind to participate in divine modes of knowing (2-2.9.1 ad1, *participativa similitudo*). Participation diffuses new power: The intellectual gifts enable human beings to overcome some limits of their sense-based and time-bound discursiveness.[10] They bring not only a new range of objects, then, but also a new quality of apprehension.

The ways that gifts intensify acquired or infused virtues stands out in the gift of fortitude. It extends the underlying virtue to new dangers: "the human soul is moved further by the Holy Spirit" (2-2.139.1 corp). Still the same images and arguments are applied to the intellectual virtues. With infused insight, the human mind can "reach further to higher things" (2-2.8.1 ad1). Infused knowledge gives certainty to judgments about human affairs and, indeed, all created things (2-2.9.2 corp, 9.3 ad3). So, too, the gift of wisdom is able to do more than humanly acquired wisdom (2-2.45.3 ad1). Treating wisdom, Thomas adds details to the description of how an intellectual gift supplements or alters the underlying virtue: The gift brings a "connaturality" with the things about which wisdom is to judge. Thomas had said much earlier that the human intellect is connatural with bodily things in time (1.13.1 ad3). The gift of wisdom endows it with a new "connaturality."

The term challenges both translation and paraphrase. Elsewhere in the *Summa*, Thomas associates connaturality with many synonyms: inclination, aptitude, complaisance or agreeableness, union, and mutual adjustment or suitability.[11] He likens connaturality to a "natural love" when he uses it to describe what it is that moves an appetite toward its end. A heavy body falling, a human being delighting in sexual pleasure—these both show something about connaturality (2-1.26.1 corp, 2-2.153.4 corp). So does any operation of appetite and especially any act of love. Love always implies connaturality with what is loved. That is why Thomas concludes that the gift of wisdom is related not only to intellect but also to charity. That is also why, I suspect, he uses what may be an autobiographical example: "A person who has learned moral knowledge judges rightly by the inquiry of reason about what belongs to chastity, but the person who has the habit of chastity judges them rightly by a certain connaturality to them" (2-2.45.2 corp). He quotes Ps-Dionysius praising someone who both learns about divine things and experiences them.[12] Thomas adds that the connaturality or "compassion" of infused wisdom is produced by charity, sealing the point with a quotation from Paul: "anyone joined to God is one spirit [with God]" (1 Cor 6:17). Interestingly, the Pauline context is once again erotic. Paul is contrasting union with God to coupling with prostitutes.

Human wisdom comes by study, infused wisdom by divine gift. The gift extends wisdom to new objects or cases. It also transforms wisdom's quality throughout, making it at once clearer, surer, and more resonant with other human faculties, including affect.[13] The quality of the infused gift is in some sense the quality of the most mature virtue. It is what humans labor to acquire. Thomas argues that the essence of the gifts persists in heaven: "they perfect the human mind to follow the motion of the Holy Spirit" and so will remain most intensely, most perfectly when the human mind reaches completion (2-1.68.6 corp).

With these explanations, the question can be put again: Are the intellectual gifts of the Spirit required by one who would write the second part of the *Summa*? It is hard to see how the answer could be no. But a reader need not speculate. Twice in the questions on the gifts, Thomas distinguishes the effects of intellectual gifts from the special graces given for a particular vocation—such as being a teacher of theology. So he says that infused *scientia* or *sapientia* disposes all of the faithful living in grace to follow the incitement of the Holy Spirit in understanding divine or human things and so in knowing what to believe.[14] A further grace is required to understand how to teach that faith to others or to refute its critics. It might be tempting to read this distinction as one between the writer of the *Summa* and its readers, except that all of its readers should go on to become writers of theology or preachers of it. The more important thing is that Thomas here presupposes the intellectual gifts when considering the freely given grace of teaching morals. Writing the *Summa* presupposes both.

The Practice of Theory, or, The Gifts as Theology

The gifts of the Holy Spirit alter the scope and quality of human understanding. They bring divine incitements to action. They activate and apply the virtues. The gifts move, as it were, in the space between seeing what is to be done and doing it. Meditating on the gifts, Thomas faces a question that runs through the whole *Summa*. It concerns the kind of knowledge that theology can offer about human action. It is articulated as the relation of theory to practice.

Thomas asks of each intellectual gift whether it is speculative or practical. He puts the question first about insight (*intellectus*, 2-2.8.3). Is this gift only speculative? No, Thomas replies, because it embraces everything that falls under faith. Good actions are encompassed by the gift of insight so far as they are ruled by the higher truths disclosed to faith. The question appears next in treating the gift of knowledge (*scientia*, 2-2.9.3). Thomas argues that the Spirit gives knowledge as ordered to the certainty of faith. Faith is principally speculative, because it concerns the first truth. The first truth is also the last human end. So, while the gift of knowledge is primarily speculative, teaching what one ought to believe, it is secondarily practical, teaching what one ought to do. Thomas raises the question a third time about wisdom (*sapientia*). Wisdom too, he answers, is both speculative and practical. It begins in the contemplation of divine things, and is then directed to act according to them—with an action that is sweet and restful (2-2.45.3 ad3). Through these parallel arguments, each intellectual gift is shown to connect theory to practice.

The connection has important implications for the kind of teaching Thomas offers in the *Summa*. The gifts not only explain the causes or sources of theology, they show something important about its manner of knowing. Theology too must be somehow theoretical and practical. This implication seems to be resisted by other passages, especially a laconic article in the very first question of the first part (1.1.4). The article is often read as a simple endorsement of Aristotle. Thomas applies the Aristotelian distinction of theoretical and practical knowing, so this reading holds, to conclude immediately that theology is theoretical. Of course, that is not what the article says. In fact it makes a comparative, analogical judgment on theology's hybrid character—a character much like that of the gifts. The article also gestures toward a complex genealogy of sources and their efforts to describe the enacted effects of learning or teaching theology. The later discussion of the gifts can encourage a more resonant reading of that programmatic article in the *Summa*'s opening. Here is how the rereading might go.

The fourth article is the shortest in *Summa* 1.1. It is one step of a dialectical comparison between theology and some expectations about Aristotelian knowledge current around the middle of the thirteenth century. Some of the articles in the first question argue that theology is knowledge (1.1.2–3, 7–8). Other articles, including the fourth, stress differences between theology and prevailing conceptions about *scientia* (1.1.4–6, 9–10). Only two authorities are cited in the arguments of the fourth article. They are a small sample of those Thomas had invoked on this topic for his *Sentences*-commentary.[15] The authorities in the *Summa* do make clear that the practical is chiefly characterized as moral (the citation to James, the reference to law). Thomas argues with them that the unifying formality of theology crosses the boundaries of philosophical discourses. (This is in fact the main lesson of 1.1.4–6.) While philosophical bodies of knowledge are divided into practical and theoretical, holy teaching (*sacra doctrina*) comprises both.[16] In this way, it imitates divine knowledge, which knows both itself and the things it makes. Even so, Thomas continues without transition, holy teaching is *more* speculative than practical because it is more concerned with divine than human things.[17] Sacred doctrine considers human things insofar as they are ordered to the beatific vision of God. Yet, Thomas has already established that the formal unity of theology depends on seeing all things in the divine light (1.1.3). Theology wants to see God; it must then regard God as the end of every rational striving. Any study of God that failed to be both speculative and practical would not be theology. It would be something more like the philosopher's incomplete metaphysics.

What is the point, then, of Thomas's insisting (say, against his teacher, Albert) that theology is *more* speculative than practical? The point is in part a terminological one, a stricter application of a pertinent schema of Aristotelian language.[18] Thomas also means to exclude the view that the moral virtues, taken in themselves, could be the end of human life or that their study could be the highest knowledge. He means, more grandly, to teach the necessary dependence of human practice on an acquaintance with its speculative end. The priority of the speculative must be preserved because the end of human life is principally a loving contemplation. Still, that priority does not exclude the practical. It enables practice, because human knowledge of God is knowledge of the human end. Knowledge of God is teleological in every significant sense. Thus, this short article of the *Summa* cannot be read as supporting the view that theology is composed of discrete parts, some speculative, others practical, with only wispy connections between them. The formal unity of theology—the vision of God as at once most knowable and most desirable—makes the connection of those parts more important than their distinction.

This claim of unity is harder for contemporary readers to hear than it would have been for Thomas's first readers. Our uses of the words "theory" and "practice" carry specific and relatively recent cultural prejudices.

Especially in Christian theology, theoretical or doctrinal "information" is now located at a great distance from practical or pastoral "skills." It should go without saying that in Thomas theory is not indexed information and practice is not a skill set. It should go without saying, but perhaps it cannot. A contemporary reader of the *Summa* may need to make a longer circuit through other views of theory and practice—indeed, may need to learn at greater length how the words sound for Thomas.

One way to learn this language is to read into the authors that shape Thomas's understanding of the relations of theory to practice. He learns about them not only from Aristotle or his commentators but also from a host of other authorities. There is, for example, a textual tradition devoted to dividing and arranging the liberal arts. Boethius authorizes what will become, through Cassiodorus and Isidore, a standard division of the practical into governance of the individual, the home, and the city.[19] The division is amplified and progressively supplemented in twelfth-century compendia of learning. Hugh of St. Victor's *Didascalicon*, for example, tends to identify practical philosophy with ethics understood broadly, and so assigns it a role in repairing human nature.[20] In Dominic Gundissalinus's *On Division*, the stress falls again on the indispensability of practical philosophy for happiness.[21] A different sense of the distinction develops in Galenic medicine. It is recalled for the Latin West in such texts as Constantine the African's *Pantegni* and, slightly later, in a passage from Avicenna's *Canon* well known to Thomas.[22] Yet other ways of relating theory to practice arose in monastic writers. In John Cassian, for example, the practical or active life is what later spiritual vocabularies will call the purgative way—the knowledge of vices and their remedies, of the virtues as cures. Without the practical, Cassian insists, no one can understand the theory that is offered by a full understanding of the Scriptures.[23] These terminological lines branch out in many directions—to the *Summas* of virtues and vices, for example, but also to commentaries on Aristotle's *Nicomachean Ethics*.[24]

A contemporary reader could also learn from other texts by Thomas how he uses the words—and how he reads them in Aristotle. His reading is capacious. Consider, for example, his explanation of Aristotle's intention at the start of his literal exposition of the *Nicomachean Ethics*. Aristotle has shown that there are goods or ends; he must show next that human beings should learn about them. Thomas comments that the learning will take shape either as a speculative or as practical. He means here by "practical knowledge" a principle of operation that is labeled a virtue and likened to an art—indeed, an architectonic art.[25] Thomas explains presently that an art can be "architectonic" in two senses: either it commands an inferior art or it applies another to its own end.[26] In the first sense, politics commands all arts and bodies of knowledge, both practical and speculative. It does not compel certain conclusions; it does regulate study and practice within a city. Even speculative knowledge falls under morals insofar as it is a human activity; it, too, stands within the citizen education considered by politics. In the second sense of "architectonic," politics rules over and so uses only the practical bodies of knowledge, such as strategy, economics, and rhetoric.[27] Thomas ends his discussion of Aristotle's intention in the *Ethics* by recalling that politics has architectonic primacy only over the active realm, the realm of human things, and not the whole cosmos, for which divine knowledge is needed.

This passage from Thomas's prologue to the *Ethics* illustrates at least three senses of "practical." First, the practical is the moral, the study of the human good, including the goods of speculation. Then, second, the practical is concerned with merely human things, with the realm of human control. Finally, the practical is whatever applied knowledge serves statesmanship. Of these senses, the first is the most striking, since it encodes the mutual relations of practical and theoretical. "[Speculative] acts so far as they are voluntary pertain to moral matter, and are ordered to the end of human life."[28] While the ground of speculative truths lies beyond human willing, the human activity of speculation is of course subject to human choice—and so matter for morals. Moral philosophy comprises the practice of philosophy—and moral theology the practice of theology.

Other textual genealogies could be traced. For example, the topic appears regularly in a group of Parisian texts dating to the decade before Thomas began his writing at large scale—that is, between about 1245 and 1255. In them the question, whether theology is practical or theoretical, is fixed as a feature of any consideration of theology as *scientia*. These texts recall others, of course, going back to the beginning of the thirteenth century, in which reasons are offered for the disputative study of theological authorities. Those texts point, in their turn, to prefaces or introductions to Peter Lombard's *Sentences* that asked of it what Thomas asked of Aristotle's *Ethics*—namely, what is the pedagogical intention in this book?[29] But it is time to draw the conclusion. Thomas does not accept the terminology or the technical conclusions of immediate predecessors such as Odo, Albert, and Bonaventure. They tend either to assign theology to practice or to refuse the theoretical/practical dichotomy.[30] Still, his verbal differences with them ought not to be exaggerated. His repeated inquiry into the gifts as practical and speculative is a reminder of generations of discussion about the teaching and writing of theology—in relation to philosophy, in relation to the Christian Scriptures. Discussing the gifts, Thomas insists more clearly than he does at the beginning of the *Summa* on the complex effects of theological pedagogy. He reminds his readers of the indispensable role of affective persuasion to practice in the theory of theology. He thus uses the teaching on the gifts to supply a richer account of theology itself. They are required for learning or teaching theology. They also portray the hybrid character of theological knowing.

Pedagogies of Fear and Love

The most unusual of the Spirit's gifts is fear of God. It is unusual structurally, because it requires a series of topics not applied to the other gifts. It is unusual substantively: it does not seem to be a good thing at all. So, before Thomas can raise his usual queries about it, he has to find whatever in it might make it a good gift from a loving God.

Thomas faces a number of traditional schemes for dividing up fear. Peter Lombard names four varieties, John Damascene six.[31] Thomas chooses to defend and to deploy the fourfold list, in part because it has been fixed in theological traditions, in part because it allows him to make the essential distinction his argument requires. The Lombard names the kinds of fear as worldly, servile, initial, and filial. Human or worldly fear operates entirely within the horizon of human threats and rewards. Servile fear is the more expansive or diffuse fear of punishment, including by God. Filial fear is the fear of being blamed by someone loved or respected—such as God. Initial fear is a sort of transitional middle between servile and filial. Thomas is intent upon distinguishing the four fears because they require different moral judgments. He also wants to register the mixture of motives in them, since changes in that mixture are stages of progress toward God.

Progress is the goal of the gift of fear. It is also Thomas's criterion for analyzing it. The kinds of fear interest Thomas only to the extent that they might turn human beings toward God (2-2.19.2 corp). Worldly fear can turn away from God—say, when the fear of some suffering or loss leads one to forsake Christian living. At other times, fear of evil things can push a human being to cling to God. The threat of divine punishment can drive servile fear toward God. The prospect of blame can drive filial fear in the same direction. A mixture of the two animates initial fear.

Thomas is most interested, as an analyst and exponent of moral formation, in transforming servile fear into filial. He is careful to distinguish two types within it (2-2.19.4). The first type of servile fear is so attached to certain goods that it sees contrary punishment as the greatest possible evil. That sort of fear is radically opposed to love. More promisingly, the second type of servile fear flees punishment without regarding it as the greatest evil, because it recognizes that its end lies in God. This servile fear can exist alongside charity. If Thomas still wants to distinguish this second type from filial fear (2-2.19.5), he also wants to show how it can be purified by charity (2-2.19.6).

As far as any servile fear is like self-love, it stands to love as self-interest does. Not all self-love is excluded by charity. A person may love herself in God, for God's sake. She may love some things because of their special relation to her without excluding God as her highest end. She may also fear separation from God with a pure fear (*timor castus*), even while she also fears divine punishment as punishment, without succumbing to the conviction that avoiding pain is the highest end of human life. While this last fear resembles the servile in its aversion to pain, it is able to exist alongside charity—though only for a time. As charity grows, fear of punishment must diminish, because love drives it out (2-2.19.10). The substance of servile fear—the remnant of risky fear—is entirely excluded in glory (2-2.19.11). The same progressive education is shown in Thomas's account of filial fear. Filial fear grows alongside charity to be perfected in the life to come (19.10–11). The pedagogical role of the so-called initial fear is clear even in its name. It describes the "state of beginners" (*status incipientium*), in whom the first stirrings of charity mix fear of punishment with the beginnings of reverence for God (2-2.19.8 corp).

Thomas presents the pedagogy of fear under love most clearly when he considers the scriptural saying that fear is the beginning of wisdom. The article he devotes to the saying is a sort of summary of his discussion of all the gifts. He begins by noting that wisdom is understood differently by "the philosophers" and "by us" (2-2.19.7 corp, *a philosophis, a nobis*). Here "us" means not Thomas in the royal we or even Christian theologians, but Christians simply. "Our life is ordered and directed to divine fulfillment (*fruitio*) according to a certain participation of divine nature, which is by grace." Hence, "we" do not consider wisdom only as cognitive, in the manner of philosophers; wisdom for the Christian is "directive of human life, which is directed not only according to human reasons, but also according to divine reasons." Christian wisdom takes as its first principles the articles of faith. They are its beginning in its essence. Yet, with regard to its effect, the beginning of Christian wisdom can be said to be fear. Servile fear disposes to wisdom when the fear of punishment drives human beings from sin. Chaste or filial fear is the first effect of wisdom. It leads one to revere God and so to be subject to God. In this sense, scriptural fear of God is like the root of the tree of the divine wisdom (2-2.19.7 ad2).

Far from being the outlier, fear reveals something about the pedagogy accomplished in all of the gifts. This is Christian pedagogy simply, the pedagogy of "our life." The gifts are a way of talking about ongoing divine help in the soul's education. "Our" need for them carries forward the revision in the notion of virtue that Thomas began in defining virtue as infused. Consider the gift of counsel. Counsel corresponds to the key Aristotelian virtue of prudence. Introducing this gift, Thomas argues that it is needed as supplement to the virtue of prudence, whether acquired or infused, since that virtue can never close the gap between general considerations and particular circumstances. Only the providential knowledge of individual contingencies can show what is to be done in a given case (2-2.52.1 ad1). This explains a qualification that Thomas had introduced when arguing that the virtue of prudence must have knowledge of particulars (2-2.47.1 ad2, 47.3 corp). It shows exactly where Thomas draws the limits around Aristotelian *eubulia*, a virtue that all agree is required for the operation of prudence. In the presentation of the gift of counsel, the reader learns that prudence must be underwritten by ongoing divine instruction in order to fulfill its function.[32] This holds beyond the present life: The gift of *consilium* continues in beatitude both as regards choice of action and general dependence on divine teaching (2-2.52.3 corp). The gifts—like infused virtues—are not given once for all. They are an ongoing disposition of the soul to the operation of the Holy Spirit. They are, in other words, an ongoing moral education.

In contrast to law, their education is not described in verbal or even visual terms. It operates as an incitement to fluid motion, as accomplished ease. It appears as promptness of response. All of the gifts, but especially those that correspond to intellectual virtues, operate in the space between theory and practice. They produce quick action. The presence of fear among the gifts only underscores the immediacy. The gifts lead a human being to respond with the nondiscursive immediacy of a passion—like what we call the instinct of flight. Only the gifts are given not for flight but for the pursuit of God. They are the instant response of love.

Without repeating Thomas's metaphors of motion and intensity, it is hard to paraphrase his account of the gifts. Still it might be that a contemporary theology would want to turn to the language of affect and even sensibility. Recast in that way, the gifts can be understood as the opposite of the hardness of heart that required the suffering of an incarnate God. Fallen human minds were anything but quickly responsive to the incitements of the Spirit. They had to be reached by gruesome spectacle. The Spirit's provision of gifts completes the education of the passion while also serving as a quiet reminder of its necessity.

CHAPTER 10

Vocations and *Viae*

The "moral part" of the *Summa* begins with Thomas's revision of what Greek philosophers knew as the *synkrisis*, the persuasive comparison of promises about happiness. It ends with his thorough recasting of the ancient pattern in view of the vocations of grace. The moral part concludes by reminding readers about the limits on fulfillment in this life even as it urges them toward forms of life that will lead to the fullness beyond.

A reader should keep that structure of persuasion in view when turning to the last sequence of questions in the *secunda secundae*. Otherwise, it may seem an anticlimax—or else disappear from view altogether. On its surface, this last section treats virtues that pertain to kinds or groups of individuals distinguished by calling (2-2.171 pro). It is by no means an appendix to the main treatment of seven virtues. It is the section that finally assembles virtues into morally instructive ways of life. Treating these special virtues, Thomas can consider both the highest pitch of certain operations in the present life and, more important, the patterns for living that are likeliest to respond to divine grace. This concluding section is both Thomas's response to Aristotle's ambivalent praise of contemplation at the end of the *Ethics* and his version of the *Politics* as the study of regimes in which virtue is best learned. In both ways, it prepares for the teaching of an incarnate God and his regime of sacraments.

Thomas divides the special virtues into graces freely given, ways of life, and offices or states. The first division considers prophecy and gifts of speech. The second compares active and contemplative lives. The third considers states of perfection, namely, the episcopacy and the religious life. Notice the order. It might seem appropriate to place the extraordinary gifts of prophecy at the very end—as a final description of human nature elevated beyond itself in anticipation of the life to come. Thomas chooses instead to end by comparing lives and describing states of "perfection" or complete formation. His comparisons and descriptions become exhortations. He exhorts the reader to take up a way of life that will hasten her movement toward beatitude. Performing this exhortation, he confronts for a final time in the *Summa*'s moral part the relation of choice to grace, of education to vocation.

In some Islamic and Jewish texts known to Thomas, the topic of prophecy served as the limit case for human intellectual activity in the present life. That is one reason why Thomas is so quick to take "prophecy" as a general name for all freely given graces that enable cognition beyond ordinary limits (2-2.171 pro). For him, as for some of his predecessors, prophecy means grasping and then teaching truth "that exists far away" (*procul existens*).[1] Thomas even recalls a fanciful etymology that derives the Latin *prophetia* from the Greek *phanos*, in the particular sense of making apparent what would be hidden by remoteness.

Prophecy's principal act is understanding. Expression in speech or verification by miracles comes afterward (2-2.171.1 corp). Prophecy is said to cover or comprehend at least one of the intellectual gifts: Wisdom falls under prophecy, but so do truths of faith, discernment or testing of spirits, and directing human actions (2-2.171 pro). Indeed, prophecy can sometimes seem to be a sort of master category in a specifically Christian treatment of the intellectual powers, the culmination of intellectual virtue under grace. Yet, it is not a virtue. It is only a fleeting anticipation of divine knowledge. It does not produce the beatific vision in the present life. The minds of *viatores* remain in *via*. There is no way to reach the end of the journey this side of death. So even prophecy must be read into the moral pedagogy that is human history.

That is why the *Summa* turns from prophecy to contemplation and vocation. Giving the present limits on human cognition, how is the reader to understand the place and value of contemplation in human life? And how is she to find a way of life that might allow her to pursue the full vision of God with some confidence? These concluding questions of the *Summa*'s moral part are often read as if they were no more than a self-interested apology for the Dominican way of life. That reading understates Thomas's vocational hope. To write for Dominicans is not to write for an exception in moral life; it is to write for deliberate moral formation. Dominican life is moral life by metonymy. The reader of the *Summa* would do better to take Thomas at his word. He argues for a mixed life of contemplation and action because he regards Christian communities pursuing such a life as the best schools for a comprehensive moral education—that is, for learning how to respond in the present to grace that leads to the future.

Even in this paraphrase, the underlying paradox stands out. How does one choose a *vocation*? Or what is it to exhort readers to undertake what is after all grace?

Prophecy, Cognition, and Speech

Prophecy names all the freely given graces that fortify or exalt human cognition in the present life. Thomas has before him an abundance of scriptural evidence—a long line of holy figures. There are many prophets he could consider, in both the Old Testament and the New, and much detail about their lives. Instead, Thomas also recalls the use made of prophecy in various Islamic and Jewish authors, notably Avicenna, Averroes, and Maimonides. With them, Thomas wants to understand what prophecy can show about the operation of the human mind at the limits of the present life. He wants to make sense of scriptural cases; he also wants a general account that will classify levels of prophecy by the means of their operation.

The question of degrees begins with a negative conclusion: prophecy is not the vision of the essence of God given to the blessed (2-2.171.2 corp). Conversely, none of the blessed can prophesy (2-2.174.5). Prophecy is a transitory illumination, not a steady disposition or habit. Thomas uses a teacher's analogy: Prophets are like students who do not know the principles of a body of knowledge, and so have to be taught, again and again, about single cases falling under it.[2] At its lower levels, prophecy can seem much less like a clear vision of something than like an incitement (*instinctus* again) moving one to an action (2-2.171.5 corp, 173.3 corp). Indeed, prophecy in its central meanings implies some obscurity in the truth known or some distance from it (2-2.174.2 ad3). The highest prophecy is seen without images, just as the brightest students can understand without examples. Still, most human beings most of the time have to be led to understanding by sensible examples (2-2.174.2 corp). So too with prophets, who do not escape the circumstances of incarnate knowing.

Prophecy is not an advanced application of human science. It is a special showing (*manifestatio*) by means of divine light. The light may show things that could otherwise be known by human experience or reasoning, or things beyond any human knowledge, or even things not yet knowable to any created intellect (such as future contingents). What makes all of these count as prophecy is the analogous operation of divine light (2-2.171.3 ad3). Corollaries follow. No preexisting natural disposition is required to be a prophet, since God can create the required disposition along with the transient illumination (2-2.172.3 corp). Nor does reception of the prophetic insight require preexisting grace, infusion, or charity (2-2.172.4 corp). It does not even require settled moral goodness, though an unsettled soul is liable to receive divine illumination poorly. Since prophecy does not arise by natural exercise or cultivation, it does not depend on any of the usual moral circumstances. Prophecy is thus contrasted with ordinary moral education. Still, Thomas understands the function of prophecy as teaching. If its cause seems to violate the circumstances of human learning, its purpose is to help others learn.

The divine illumination offers Thomas—as it offered his predecessors—a chance to think about the maximum infusion of divine light possible in the present life. While living a human life, the prophet cannot see the essence of God. Whatever is seen is seen in certain likenesses that are lit up by divine light (2-2.173.1 corp). More technically, Thomas distinguishes four elements of illumination: the influx of intelligible light, the sending (*immissio*) of intelligible species, the impress (*impressio*) or arrangement (*ordinatio*) of imaginative forms, and the expression (*expressio*) of sensible forms (2-2.173.1 corp). The first element, the light, works in various ways on the other three following the rhythm of all human understanding, namely representation leading to judgment (2-2.173.2 corp). Sometimes the prophet "sees" through external senses, sometimes by imaginary forms, sometimes by intelligible species impressed directly on the mind. The light can be given for the sake of interpreting what others report or what the prophet experiences by ordinary means or even as a guide to actions. More interesting, perhaps, than the exact typology is the steady emphasis on the function of various sorts of images across human understanding, natural and supernatural. In prophecy, too, embodied minds rely on images.

Thomas does not regard prophecy as only a sort of laboratory for cognitive models. Nor is it just another occasion for reinforcing his original lesson about the limits on human fulfillment in the present life. Prophecy is a grace, given for uplifting the individual and the community. The grace empowers at least two scenes of instruction. The first is in prophetic illumination itself: "a certain cognition impressed on the mind of the prophet by divine revelation in the manner of a certain teaching" (*per modum cuiusdam doctrinae*, 2-2.171.6 corp). Such teaching is typically given to the prophet so that it may be taught in turn to others in a second scene: "secondly [prophecy] consists in speech, by which the prophets announce to others what they have known in having been divinely taught" (*divinitus edocti*, 2-2.171.1 corp). Prophecy is a sequence of teachings. If its higher grades rely less and less on activating the senses or staging episodes for imagination, prophecy most properly speaking still relies on some sort of image. Even when God impresses something directly on a prophet's mind without images—and so exceeds the ordinary meaning of the term—Thomas still describes the event as a sort of showing or manifesting. "The end of prophecy is *showing* some truth existing above humankind" (2-2.174.2 corp, emphasis added). Since prophecy is typically given to be passed on, Thomas divides it both rhetorically and cognitively. For example, he notes prophecy of warning, predestination, and foreknowing (2-2.174.1 corp). This is only one division among the many that he inherits. Part of his labor in these questions is to find some way of harmonizing or at least charitably construing the competing precedents.

The gift of speech is added to the consideration of prophecy because of teaching. The gift accomplishes two rather different things. The first is a "grace of languages" that allows someone to preach in unlearned languages or to interpret them when others use them. Thomas has in mind both Pentecost and the episodes of glossolalia in the early churches. He is quite clear that these striking gifts are less valuable than prophecy itself, which they serve as instruments (2-2.176.2 corp). Prophecy ranks higher because it is more useful to the upbuilding of the Christian community. This claim brings Thomas to the other meaning of the grace of languages: It is a grace that enables a speaker (or a writer) to instruct the intellect, to move the passions, and so to persuade listeners (2-2.177.1 corp). The three verbs Thomas uses are *instruere*, *movere*, and *flectare*. They recall but also revise a famous Ciceronian triplet mentioned by an objection. According to Cicero, the goal of rhetoric is to teach, to delight, and to move, that is, *docere*, *delectare*, *flectare*.[3] On its second meaning, the grace of languages is an infused art of rhetoric.

Contemporary readers who reach this passage in the *Summa* are often interested in what Thomas says next—namely, that women are never given such graces for public teaching. The argument is hardly original. It is also evidently circular in the way that the ideology of patriarchy can often be. If most women that Thomas knew were not "perfected in wisdom" (2-2.177.2 corp), that might have had something to do with their being barred from study. I do note that Thomas's arguments apply only to public teaching. He prohibits to women neither private teaching nor prophecy. Beyond that, I do not think that his conclusion merits defense. Still, Thomas's error, however damaging it has been in the hands of church administrators, should not obliterate the truth that he offers on either side of it. He links teaching to prophecy because he understands prophecy as teaching. God gives extraordinary graces to prophets. God also gives graces to teachers. Included among them is the rhetorician's gift of effective speech. In the next questions, Thomas turns that gift to a recognizably rhetorical end—namely, persuading his readers to enter into a way of life from which they can learn how to live.

The Union of Contemplation and Action

Thomas does not start the persuasion to contemplative life with a bland definition. He tries instead to build up a picture from several sides. He wants his readers to see contemplation not as an achievement but as an activity recognized in operation. He begins by asking whether contemplation is purely intellectual. He remembers, of course, the texts of ancient philosophy for which contemplation was the seal of separation from the body and all bodily passions. Classical writers spoke of *ataraxia* or impassiveness as the most desirable stage. Thomas takes the opposite view. If it is true that contemplation is deeply an activity of the mind, it is also true that the passions play a decisive role in drawing the mind to contemplation. This is the reading Thomas gives of an authority from Gregory: "the contemplative life is holding fast with one's whole mind to the love of God and neighbor, and inheriting the sole desire for the Ruler."[4] The love of God, the passionate desire for God, sets the heart on fire with the intention of seeing God's beauty. This is the source of contemplative life.

The desire to see God is so much the source that one ought not to confuse contemplative life with moral life or the moral virtues. The two have different ends. The virtues that Thomas describes so carefully in *Summa* 2-2 can of course be dispositions to contemplation. They foster contemplation by shaping character and quieting the soul's tumults. Still they are no more than aids to the single unifying act of contemplation, which is the vision of truth. The traditions that Thomas inherits divide this single act and distribute it over a complex hierarchy, just as traditional moral analysis breaks down the virtues into complex schemata. Richard of St. Victor, for instance, set forth six stages of contemplation. What does Thomas say to Richard's elaborate hierarchy or to similar patterns in Bonaventure or Bernard? He insists that multiplying steps of approach to God should not distract from the end—which is knowledge of God.

Having persuaded the reader to keep the end in view, Thomas must warn her again not to be premature in claiming to reach it. Full vision of God is not attainable in this life (2-2.180.5). It is not attainable because humans live at present as a spirit in a body—not accidentally or halfway, but really and naturally. The visions and mystical raptures recorded in the spiritual traditions cannot be cases of seeing God's essence. They must be imaginative experiences wrought by grace in embodied rational souls—or else moments in which the soul is somehow separated from the body, stretched between this life and the next, as perhaps happened during the Apostle Paul's rapture. But neither Paul in rapture nor Benedict in exalted vision could actually contemplate God's essence as it is while still living in a mortal body (2-2.180.5 corp and ad3). They could not see without dying.

Within the present life, Thomas does allow a certain sequence of steps in contemplation (2-2.180.6). He models three steps after a geometrical image from Ps-Dionysius. Dionysius describes the three motions of spirit as circular, straight, and oblique. Thomas interprets these to name the activity of the soul dwelling on God, the activity of the soul rising to God from corporeal things, and the activity of the soul receiving angelic illuminations and becoming more like the angels in its understanding. The circle, the straight line, and the oblique line are appropriate metaphors because they remind a reader that the activity of contemplation is not finished in this life. It is an activity that cannot be completed short of death. Indeed, it is intrinsically an eternal activity, both in itself and so far as the human can share in it (2-2.180.8). The activity will carry human beings through death into the immediate contemplation of God's essence.

What is the human reader to do in the meanwhile? Thomas replies with an argument that has something of testimony about it, something of the heartfelt report of a practitioner. He argues that there is nothing better to do than contemplation because there is nothing more delightful. The delight is twofold: one arising from the object of contemplation, the other from the exercise of contemplative capacity. The power to contemplate is the deepest human power. It is the only activity that fulfills the soul's capacities, concentrates them. Activity in conformity with what a thing is—that defines delight. Contemplation delights as well because of its object. It sees the most desired lover. It fulfills the passions just as fully as it does the intellect. Or, more strictly, it joins intellect to passion through the highest object of each.

Writing at such a pitch, and perhaps remembering again the end of Aristotle's *Ethics*, Thomas recognizes that contemplative life may seem unattainable because too divorced from practical needs. So he puts a frame around his picture of contemplation. It is a description of a context that opens the possibility of contemplation within human life.

Understanding the lived relation of contemplation to action requires the right distinction between principle and application. In principle, the life of contemplation is superior to the life of action, for at least eight different reasons (2-2.182.1). (Thomas draws them from Aristotle and then amplifies them.) The principle, laid out in this way, gives priority to contemplation, which is, Thomas adds, the great liberation of the human soul (2-2.182.1 ad2). Moreover, since it is better to love God than one's neighbors, it must be better to lead a contemplative life than an active one (2-2.182.2). So far, the general principle.

Thomas then makes the qualifying application. In some cases, he says, someone may be so filled with the divine love that she is willing, for God's sake, to be separated from God for a time in order to do something pleasing to God. In such cases, where contemplation flows out into action, action is more meritorious than contemplation. Thomas makes a similar exception when he considers whether the active life can impede the contemplative. The obvious answer is an emphatic yes. Thomas observes, not without humor, that it is very difficult to do two things at once. Still, there is another and subtler way in which activity can aid contemplation: Active life can help bring the soul into proper order. It can help someone to learn virtues, to form character, to break down vices. Life in the world becomes a school for contemplation by being a school for the disposing virtues that are contemplation's usual prerequisites (2-2.182.3). If actions in the world steal time from contemplation, their effect can still be to improve the soul's capacity for contemplation. In individual lives, then, it is better to begin with the active life and only then to approach contemplation (2-2.182.4).

Thomas has made three qualifications or exceptions to the priority of contemplation: in favor of works done from excess of love, in favor of learning virtues from action, in favor of learning action before contemplation.

Together they suggest his response to any dichotomy of action and contemplation. Thomas makes the response explicit in the discussion of the
religious life. The topic being disputed is whether contemplative religious
life is preferable to active religious life (2-2.188.6). In principle, Thomas
first reasons, contemplation is better than action, so a contemplative religious life ought to be better than an active one. But as he proceeds in
the determination, he applies the principle against the dichotomy. There
are really two kinds of action: action that flows from the fullness of contemplation and action that does not. The first kind is seen in teaching and
preaching, in the contemplative's giving back to God the results of contemplation through community. This sort of action is better than contemplation without action. It is better to illuminate another, Thomas writes,
than simply to receive light without giving it off again. It is better to hand
on contemplation than simply to savor it.

Offices and States

For Thomas, a state of life (*status* again) is a permanent undertaking that re-
shapes a person by reconfiguring her obligations and liberties (2-2.183.1).
Differences of state in the church are connected with the degrees of charity,
with the spiritual division into beginners, the proficient, and the perfect or
complete (*incipientes, proficientes, perfecti,* 2-2.183.4). "*Incipientes*" now carries a definite meaning for spiritual formation, one that a reader might well
take back to the *Summa*'s prologue. The states of perfection are undertakings to obligations that teach the perfection of Christian life in charity
(2-2.184.1). Charity is the universal precept for all Christians, the counsels
of perfection only instruments for attaining it (2-2.184.3). Of course, not
everyone who undertakes to use the instruments does use them, and some
use them who do not publically undertake to do so (2-2.184.4). Then, too,
the outward states of perfection are but reflections of the inward liberties
and obligations to charity judged by God. Still, these public undertakings
remain powerful helps in human moral education. The religious life offers
itself as effective education in the best human life (2-2.186.1–2).

The state of religion is a certain learning or exercise for coming into
human completion (2-2.186.2). It is like medical therapy or schooling
(2-2.186.2 ad1). The three basic counsels of Christian religious life are
justified by reference to the needs of education in charity that leads to
God. So, too, the variety of religious rules: They represent the variety of
ways to learn love (2-2.188.1). Each of these arguments builds toward a

persuasive appeal. It is revealed only in the very last question of the moral part. Thomas is not describing religious life as an elective education. He is proposing religious life as a response to the desire for beatitude. Do you want to learn how to enact the coherent human life described in the *secunda pars?* Take up a way of life that is a school for charity.

The last question of the moral part seems to me one of the most affecting in the entire *Summa.* I do not mean that Thomas piques the reader's curiosity by indiscreet disclosure. I mean that he insists almost recklessly on the imperative of moral formation. He begins by arguing that someone does not have to be proficient in the precepts before undertaking to practice the counsels. Grace can supply what is lacking. So, too, the benefit of the doubt ought always be given to any obligation to try religious life—whether because of a vow or an oblation, even against parental wishes or when one is a priest. A reader can hear Thomas the oblate at Monte Cassino and the captive of his family. She can be reminded just how effectively the Dominicans recruited new members from the universities. Still the argument is no special pleading, no unprincipled defense of Dominican prerogatives. Thomas argues for a trial of the religious life because he considers "Christian religion" (in this resonant sense) the most promising regime of education—the curriculum in which one is most likely to be taught how to attain God.

The last two articles of the *Summa*'s moral part place the prospect of religious life squarely before the reader. Persuading someone to enter the religious life is not illicit, Thomas insists. Indeed, it is a great good (2-2.189.9). The claims of religious life are so strong, Thomas adds, that it is not wrong to enter religious life *without* extensive counseling and protracted deliberation (2-2.189.10). Because Christian religion is something certainly from God, because it offers so sure a way to learn charity, Thomas urges all due haste in embracing it.

Thomas ends his reply to the last objection by citing Matthew and Gregory on Job (2-2.189.10 ad3). Matthew teaches that religion is the light yoke of Christ. Gregory asks: How would God burden us when it is God who teaches us to avoid every care-bringing desire, who advises us to escape the laborious duties of this world? Thomas adds: "Whoever takes on the easy yoke binds himself to reflect the divine fullness and the eternal rest of souls." Thomas then prays: "Let him who promised this to us also lead us to it—our Lord Jesus Christ, who is God above all things, God, blessed through the ages." There is a similar doxology at the end of the *prima pars,* but not a petition. I take the petition as a final sign of the directness with which Thomas asks for an urgent response to the *Summa*'s moral teaching. The petition recapitulates the image of Christ as the way to God with which Thomas began this middle part of the *Summa*.

The prayer makes clear that the reader's response, if it comes, will not come only from the reader. Christ must lead. Christ must answer with and in the reader—the same Christ whose moral teaching will be made manifest across the last part of the *Summa*, in incarnation, narrated life, and remembered sacraments. That Christ has of course already accompanied the reader through the *Summa*'s middle, now concluded.

CONCLUSION

The Good of Reading

In the prologue to the *Summa*, Thomas Aquinas makes an implicit promise to his reader. Criticizing the pedagogical faults of other texts, he undertakes not to waste her time. The promise is significant in a book of moral formation. Formation studies human time before shaping it. Formation also requires time, consumes it. If Thomas had not made his promise, his book would still raise questions about time for an alert reader. Has the reader spent her time well in reading the *Summa* or in learning to read it better?

The *Summa* makes claims on its readers' lives. For some, the claims are exerted over decades and shape a "career." Already there is a slip. Thomas did not write the book to provide employment for exegetes assigned to it. His book claims more than the labor of interpretation. It proposes a larger formation—or, more exactly, it wants to help as it can with divine formation. What, then, does the *Summa* suppose to be the relation between moral shaping and learning how to read better?

Some of the last century's best readers of Thomas—Marie-Dominique Chenu, Henri de Lubac, Yves Congar—paid special attention to the historical steps Thomas took when writing it. They also believed that reading a book like the *Summa* could change the present if only you could take right steps into it. Alongside other advocates of "the new theology" or "*ressourcement*," they were eager to recover the original meaning of texts like the *Summa* because that meaning still compelled them. As Henri Bouillard once explained, the shared hope was to "draw Christian doctrine from its sources, to find in it the truth of our life."[1] Their kind of historical reading wagered that some contemporary readers could still be changed by it.

How? Or which ways of reading the *Summa* over months or years or decades enable it to become life changing? These are instances of a much larger question: How are souls saved by studying Christian texts? According to Thomas in the *Summa*, that larger question has no sure answer in the present life. Recall his argument that the best a reader can do at present when judging her own state of grace is to conjecture (2-1.112.5). She ought to hold even her conjectures lightly.

If I can sometimes distinguish progress from regress in my memories of reading the *Summa*, I cannot know with certainty whether my progress in interpretation has contributed to progress in virtue. While I may judge that I have discovered more of the purposes in Thomas's text, the text itself counsels agnosticism about whether I have made unqualified progress toward its highest purpose. The *Summa* wants to help however it can in God's drawing human souls back to God. About my present place in that return, it is not the time to judge.

The question of what all this reading of the *Summa* has done to me is one that I cannot now answer. It may still be important that I reach the point of asking it. The question registers the effects of having taken the *Summa* seriously. It may also recall Thomas's fundamental convictions that the most urgent moral pedagogy for embodied souls is through incarnations, sacraments, and "incorporation" into churchly community. A reading of the *Summa* that remains within the text is an incomplete reading of the *Summa*.

So my question needs to be reversed. Instead of asking how the *Summa* might have changed me over the decades, I should ask how my reading of it has encouraged other changes. The scene of instruction in the *Summa* is minimalist both in composition and in purpose. (I could also say that structure and style are purpose in it.) Thomas makes himself most useful to beginners in theology by sustaining belated anticipation—by pointing backward to incarnation (revealed, repeated) and forward to life with God in transformed flesh. The *Summa* clears the way it describes. Its reading changes lives by pointing them to other powers for change.

Minimalism is not reduction. Thomas opens a way through multiple theological languages while appreciating their beauties and correcting their excesses. He thus provides an antidote to the perennial demand for simplistic certainty. A work famous for spawning doctrinal controversies may have most to teach us about the limits of doctrinal demonstration. The *Summa* should be studied most seriously not for its "robust realism" or its "philosophic Aristotelianism" or even its "virtue ethics." It has most to offer as a steadfast challenge to our craving for slogans.

Bouillard, introducing a history of Thomas on grace and conversion, pleads that a historical reading can claim at least as much "fidelity" as the systems of official Thomism. By book's end, he is ready to say more. In contrast to Scholastic manuals and even specialized theological argument, "a historical study reveals . . . how far theology is linked to time, to the becoming of the human spirit." Bouillard concludes: "the history of theology makes us see the permanence of divine truth, at the same time that it reveals to us what is contingent in the notions and the systems in which we receive it."[2]

I began by confessing that my education in reading the *Summa* had been an education in working through distorted relations to the text. The details of the confession were my own, but the point about reading is hardly original. A reader who continues with a text over time becomes a better reader of it by stages. She lives the doubled time of rereading. The doubling is familiar from philosophical and religious memoir—say, from Augustine's *Confessions*. There is Augustine the narrator and then Augustine the protagonist of the narrated events. The two occupy one name or one body but at different ages. The older Augustine, the narrator, not only talks about the younger Augustine, he also talks after him, from the retrospect of a point nearer the end. The plot of the *Confessions* is, of course, how the younger Augustine becomes the older Augustine. The book narrates a sentimental reeducation.

Augustine himself converts memoir into exegesis. The *Confessions* is a book about learning how to read the Christian Scriptures. It ends by inscribing the story of a life into its latest reading of that governing text. Augustine gives a picture of every education over years in reading a strong Christian book. A reader is always correcting her younger self. She is always trying to read even the corrections back into the persisting, the encompassing book—and then beyond it to God. Compared to life with God, the Scriptures too are a provisional pedagogy.

The study of a single work in the "history of theology" may let us see the contingency of our own readings of it. We are educated even so.

The distorted relations to the *Summa* that I have wanted to contest in this book share a refusal to enter into Thomas's pedagogy. So I hardly want this book to foster another distortion: an idolatry of the text as a life-consuming end in itself. The *Summa* gestures toward a pedagogy beyond itself—indeed, beyond any text. Learning to read the *Summa* better is learning when to let go of it in order to follow its moral trajectory, its *via*. Thomas adjudicates inherited languages in hopes of rectifying misleading speech about human life as motion toward God. He does not want a reader to stop with speaking about God. Indeed, the structure of his book supposes that practice in learning to speak by learning to read will prepare for learning other lessons.

If things go well, a reader's relation to the text of the *Summa* over many readings will prepare for relations to other moral teaching. A reader who can learn from a moral book about how to live better is a reader who can learn morals simply. As Augustine knew, and Thomas after him, habits of reading moral texts over time are like a little mirror of the reader's moral dispositions.

A chronicle of misreadings might seem melancholy. It is also a chronicle of a persistent challenge posed by a text.

I began by suggesting to a contemporary reader a device for reactivating some at least of the *Summa*'s pedagogy. Begin with the third part, I said, with the incarnation, the life of Christ, the sacraments. Only then return to the middle or moral part of Thomas's great work. Perhaps I was too timid. The main problem for contemporary readers may not be Thomas's profession of God's embodied pedagogy for fallen humanity. We may be held back by more general assumptions—about the kind of work he has written or the kind of knowledge that theology might be.

When the writers of the *ressourcement* proposed to read the *Summa* "historically," they meant to strip away the Neoscholastic interpretations that had been pasted over it during centuries. They also imagined that a reflectively historical reading would be more attentive to Thomas's text in its relations with human lives within history. "Historical" reading meant for them reading that could change history. Does it still? How many readers now invest historiography with hopes for recording some lives in order to change others?

I have no interest in protecting the *Summa* behind museum glass in order to display it as a relic or a curiosity. I want instead to see how the *Summa*'s manner of teaching might still work. For my purposes, many standard models of 'historical' reconstruction are not in fact useful—especially so far as they assume unbridgeable distance and demand dispassionate objectivity. So my proposal to read backward was both a confirmation and an undoing of history writing.

Perhaps historicism is no longer the threat to reading it was during my youth. Perhaps history, too, has been engulfed by the label "information." What remains outside of information? If we were to begin again, my less timid counsel for the contemporary reader would be to take up the *Summa* under the conventions for reading literature. She might well understand more by reading the *Summa* as a very odd novel or epic poem than by stepping back from it to talk objectively about its contexts—or by chopping it up into bits small enough to squeeze through the sieve of some prevailing definitions for ethics, philosophy, or theology. Reading the work as literature, she would not only activate a wider range of appropriate skills, she would also permit herself the possibility of being moved by the text. Being moved is, in Thomas, the presupposition of being formed.

The most significant historical changes in the reading of the *Summa* have been produced by fashions in genre dictated by competing ideals of knowledge. (In another context, it would be important to add that many of the ideals were in turn the fantasies of power.) These changes demanded that the *Summa* be what it was not: an encyclopedia of orthodoxy or a compendium of demonstrations or a code of regulations. Thomas's book conforms to the expectations of none of those genres. In fact, it did not succeed in creating a genre of other works like it, despite provoking hundreds of commentaries. Like an angel, the *Summa* may be the single instance of its species.

Acknowledging this history of misrecognition, a writer on the *Summa* might either despair or else decide to misrecognize boldly—deliberately. I have done that in my final proposal about literature. I do not think that the *Summa* fits into one or another of the genres we pile together confusedly under the label "literature." I do think that the *Summa* is more like some works in that pile than many works we call "ethics" or "moral theology." What is more to my point, the habits a reader typically brings to literature are more likely to yield integral meanings of the *Summa* than the habits of analytic philosophy of religion or dogmatic theology in the legal mode.

One virtue we bring to literary works is the practice of rereading as if for the first time. That habit responds to the impulses that led Thomas to invent the form of the *Summa* and then to continue within it up to the moment when he stopped writing altogether.

ACKNOWLEDGMENTS

Though sketches of some of these pages go back to the early 1990s, the occasion for composing a first draft was given during 2011–2012 by a Luce Fellowship from the Association of Theological Schools. I am very grateful both for the writing-time and for the collegiality of the other fellows in my year.

When I began to describe the book as an exercise in reading the *Summa* backward (quite an elevator pitch), Helen Tartar did not blink an eye. She said on the spot that Fordham University Press would be interested in the project. Helen did not live to see the finished book. I thank Richard Morrison and Thomas Lay for their unwavering support after such a bitter loss.

The longest gratitude is due to generations of students who listened to me talk about Thomas across forty years. I thank them for their questions and observations. I apologize for the blunders and the longueurs. This book is the best sense I can make of what Thomas wrote. The rest is up to you.

Among my students, I single out especially Peng Yin, who read and re-read the final drafts of this manuscript with generous attention. He saved me from many mistakes. I clung too tenaciously to the ones that remain.

1. Lacordaire, *Mémoire*, 125.

2. See also the astute remarks on "timeliness" in Pieper, *Silence of St. Thomas*, especially 75–79.

3. For some examples of this early misreading, see Jordan, *Rewritten Theology*, 8–10.

4. Here and throughout the book, I use feminine pronouns for the imagined reader of the *Summa*. I first adopted this rule to remind myself and my readers that Christian theology should never have been restricted to men—either in its concerns or in its authorized speakers. It then occurred to me that I was also following the ancient usage by which the Christian soul is gendered as feminine.

5. I read the articles as collected by David Burrell in Lonergan, *Verbum*.

6. Lonergan, letter of May 11, 1973.

7. Lonergan, *Method in Theology*, especially chapter 7.

INTRODUCTION. THE *SUMMA*'S ORIGINS: THREE FABLES AND A CANDID COUNTERPROPOSAL

1. Choosing this topic, Thomas reprises several of his earlier prologues, notably *Contra Gent.* lib.1 cap.1 and *Lect. Sent.* pro (Boyle and Boyle 73–74). For my conventions in citing works by Thomas Aquinas, see the first section of the Works Cited. Unless otherwise indicated, all parenthetical citations are to the *Summa*. In some portions of this chapter, I reprise arguments I have made in Jordan, "Structure."

2. The phrase "what belongs to the Christian religion" (1 pro) also helps resolve an old debate about the relation in the *Summa* between the terms "holy teaching" (*sacra doctrina*) and "theology" (*theologia*). These terms are not simple synonyms; they have different histories and so different associations or uses. Still, both terms must apply to what Thomas writes in the *Summa* or else there is no point in invoking them to justify its undertaking. The two are connected through the rich sense of "Christian religion." For a review of the

debate about the relation of the terms, see Oliva, "Quelques éléments de la *doctrina theologiae*."

3. See the prologue to the Dominican constitutions of 1228: "the observance of canonical religion (*in observantia canonice religionis*)" (Thomas, *De oudste Constituties*, 311; compare Tugwell, *Early Dominicans*, 456). The phrase is taken from the Praemonstratensian constitutions that served as model for the Dominicans. I return to the rhetorical context of the constitutions at the end of this chapter.

4. The crucial word here is "useless." Thomas does of course introduce topics of his own in the *Summa* just as he had in his earlier writing. Indeed the hagiographer, William of Tocco, makes the young Thomas renowned in part for proposing new topics of debate. See William of Tocco *Historia* cap.15 (Le Brun-Gouanvic 122 ll. 19–20).

5. Other notions in the prologue may carry technical meanings that are liable to escape contemporary readers. For example, Thomas gestures in it to the three main activities of the medieval teacher of theology: *lectio* (as *expositio*), *disputatio, repetitio* (see Boland, *St. Thomas Aquinas*, 89–90).

6. I use the word "minimalism" as a deliberately anachronistic analogy. I am thinking not so much of painting or sculpture as of music. The *Summa* achieves its distinctive stylistic effects by stylized repetition of core motifs.

7. See Boyle, *Setting of the Summa theologiae*, 8–12; Torrell, *Initiation*, 207–211; Mulchahey, *"First the Bow is Bent in Study . . . ,"* 278–306.

8. The uniqueness of theology as a teaching that offers both truth and blessedness is also the main point of the prologue with which Thomas began his review of Lombard's *Sentences* at the school in Rome. See *Lect. Sent.* pro (Boyle and Boyle, 73–74).

9. Thomas *Super Boet. De Trin.* pro n.4.

10. Thomas *Super Dion. De div. nom.* pro.

11. It is good to remember that this overly familiar title may well not be Thomas's own. Early testimonies refer to the work under a large range of alternate titles. For an early survey, see Walz, "De genuino titulo *Summae theologiae*."

12. A reader can notice this especially when Thomas is commenting a text, whether of Aristotle or the Christian Scriptures. See, for example, the phrase *"summa solutionis"* at *Scriptum Sent.* lib.1 dist.24 q.1 pro, *Sent. Metaph.* lib.12 lect.12 n.11, *Sent. De gen.* lib.1 lect.15 n.3 and n.6. Compare *"quasi in summa epilogando,"* *Super Ioan.* cap.1 lect.2.

13. Thomas *Super Dion. De div. nom.* cap.2 lect.1 (*"ut in summa dicatur"*), cap.2 lect.5 (*"comprehendit in summa"*), cap.11 lect.4 (*"ut in summa omnia colligamus"*). Compare the notion of gathering together *"summatim"* in *Scriptum*

Sent. lib.2 dist.24 q.3 pro, *Sent. Phys.* lib.4 lect.12 n.7, *Super Ier.* cap.23 lect.6, and especially *De art. fid.* pro (*"oporteret totius theologiae comprehendere summatim difficultates"*).

14. Thomas *Scriptum Sent.* lib.4 dist.6 q.2 art.2 qc.1 ad1 (with regard to the Bible), lib.4 dist.7 q.1 art.3 qc.2 (confirmation as confession of faith), *Super Epp. Pauli: ad Hebraeos* cap.11 lect.1 [*reportatio vulgata*] (the articles of faith), *In orat. dom.* art.7 (the Lord's Prayer).

15. Thomas likens a *summa* to a chapter-summary in *Scriptum Sent.* lib.4 dist.8 q.1 art.2 qc.2 ad4: "having as in a chapter and summa (*in capitulo et summa*) all that the other sacraments contain singly." When interpreting Aristotle's *Metaphysics*, he glosses *capitulatim* as "comprehended in a certain compendium (*quodam compendio*)" (*Sent. Metaph.* lib.5 lect.3 n.8; compare *Sent. Phys.* lib.2 lect.6 n.1). Reading Paul, Thomas explains that *capitulum* itself means "a brief collection (*complexio*) containing many things . . . since, just as the head (*caput*) virtually and as if in summary (*quasi summarie*) contains everything that is in the body, in just this way the chapter heading contains everything that is to be said" (*Super Epp. Pauli: ad Hebraeos* cap.8 lect.1). With something like this sense, the eighteenth-century historian of philosophy William Enfield translates *Summa theologiae* as "Heads of Theology" (Enfield, *History of Philosophy*, 2:374).

16. Thomas *Sent. De anima* lib.1 cap.1 n.6. For looser associations of *summa* with brevity, *Compend. theol.* lib.1 cap.1, *Super Matt.* cap.11 lect.1 [*reportatio Leodegarii*].

17. Thomas *Super Epp. Pauli: ad Hebraeos* lib.1 lect.2 [*reportatio vulgata*] (*"non statim proponit ei summa"*), speaking of Paul's manner of writing.

18. Thomas explains that Ps-Dionysius would have not taken up the task of writing except that his mentor, Hierotheus, wrote only "in general and in *summa*" (*Super Dion. De div. nom.* cap.3). Again, according to Thomas, Basil reads the opening of Genesis as referring *"summatim"* to what it will later unfold as the work of seven days (*De potentia* q.4 art.1 ad15).

19. For what I have called the protreptic persuasion of the *Contra Gentiles*, see Jordan, *Rewritten Theology*, 89–115.

20. For example, the prologue to *Summa theol.* 2-1.22 announces that the goodness or badness of the passions will be treated before their comparison. The actual order in 2-1.24–25 is reversed. Again, the prologue to 2-2.39 gives the order of consideration as schism, altercation, sedition, and war. In the event, the order is schism (39), war (40), altercation (41), and sedition (42).

21. So the unannounced question on divine happiness (1.26) follows the announced question on divine power (1.25; compare the schema in 1.14 pro). Again, the enumeration of a second effect of divine governance (1.105 pro)

is not projected in the introduction of the consideration of the effects (1.104 pro).

22. Even if Thomas meant to write the *Summa* as an unbroken chain of deductions, he would presumably have done so according to his understanding of deduction rather than one of ours. Logic also has a history. Contemporary readings that want to stress the *Summa*'s rigor often begin by rendering its arguments into current logical forms that bear little relation to Thomas's remarks on definition and demonstration.

23. Chenu, "La plan," reprised in his *Introduction à l'étude*, 255–276. For reactions to Chenu through 1998, see Johnstone, "The Debate on the Structure." For a more recent critique of Chenu, see te Velde, *Aquinas on God*, 11–18. For critical elaborations of Chenu, see O'Meara, *Thomas Aquinas Theologian*, 56–64, and Torrell, *Aquinas's Summa*, 17–62, especially 27–29.

24. Thomas, *Super Sent.* lib.1 dist.2 pro: "So in the first part he determines concerning divine things according to their *exitus* from the beginning [or principle]; in the second according to the *reditus* to the end . . . "

25. *Exitus* by itself is not a technical term for Thomas. If it sometimes refers in the *Summa* to the procession of creatures from God (e.g., 1.90.3 arg2), it is applied more often in other contexts—say, to Trinitarian processions or active operations or local motions. The *exitus/reditus* couplet (in its nominal or verbal forms) appears only four times outside quotations in the *Summa* and never with regard to the procession and return of creatures (see 1.14.2 arg1, 2-2.39.3 corp, 2-2.189.4 arg2, 3.55.2 ad2; for the couplet in quotations, 1.114.5 corp, 3.40.1 ad3).

26. In Chapters 4 and 5, I argue that there is something like the pattern of *exitus* and *reditus* behind the details of textual progress. What I call the *Summa*'s scene of instruction is constituted by an interplay of belatedness and anticipation. Still, Thomas's pattern is pedagogical, not cosmic.

27. As Peter Candler has shown, Thomas refers to the pedagogical motion of the *Summa* not only with a network of metaphors (of which *via* is the most obvious) but with terms like *ducere/ductio*, leading, or the more precise (and Ps-Dionysian) *manuductio*, leading by hand. See, for example, *Summa theol.* 1.88.2 arg1, 2-2.82.3 ad2, 2-1.96.5 ad2, and Candler, *Theology, Rhetoric, Manuduction*, especially 100–102, 129, 132, 137–138.

28. For a brief survey of the use of questions across fields, see Lawn, *Rise and Decline*, 3–44.

29. Thomas was already using this abbreviated form of the *quaestio* in his Roman *Lectura* on the *Sentences*. While most of the chapters of the *Contra Gentiles* are not written as disputes, they certainly illustrate the abbreviation of arguments grouped in tight sequence.

30. There is more to be said about the pedagogy of the dispute and its use of authorities. I try to say it in Chapters 4 and 5.

31. This is part of the meaning of "*articulus*" as Thomas defines it in *Summa theol.* 2-2.1.6.

32. Readers who doubt the point should compare the varieties of textual division in the *Summa of Theology* with those in the Franciscan *Summa 'of Brother Alexander'* or even Thomas's own *Scriptum* on the *Sentences*.

33. It follows that no part of the *Summa* was intended to be a separable *philosophy* of human nature—despite the efforts of many generations to extract or erect one. For a recent example in English, which is candid about its methodological disagreements with Thomas, see Pasnau, *Thomas Aquinas on Human Nature*, especially 10–16. My own view is that Thomas never intends to write just as a philosopher, since he held that Christians were called to knowledge beyond philosophy. On this point, I endorse the views of Victor Preller in "Water into Wine," especially at 262.

34. It is in this sense that Thomas's *sacra doctrina* and so the *Summa* itself can be called "deeply christoform" (Ryan, *Formation in Holiness*, 114). For additional mentions of Christ as the beginning of the *Summa*, see Ryan again, 113–116.

35. Let me mention only two famous passages in the documents Thomas would have learned as a young Dominican. The first is (again) the opening of the prologue to the Dominican constitutions of 1228: "Since we are enjoined by the precept of the rule to have one heart and one soul in the Lord, so it is right that since we live under a single rule and by the vow of one profession, we should be found to be uniform in the observance of canonical religion" (Thomas, *De oudste Constituties*, 311; compare Tugwell, *Early Dominicans*, 456). Life *in* Christ is the foundation of the rule. The second passage is the peroration that closes Jordan of Saxony's encyclical letter of 1233: "But you who are not [yet] this, give yourself to work, pursue effort, so that you may grow towards salvation in the one who deigned to call you to this grace in which you stand, to make you perfect, not to make you tepid—our good and pious savior, the Son of God, Jesus Christ" (Kaeppeli, "B. Iordani de Saxonia litterae encyclicae," 185; compare Tugwell, *Early Dominicans*, 124–125).

36. Barth, *Die Römerbrief (Zweite Fassung)*, 13–15. In a public conversation, Leo Strauss credits this preface with setting forth "the principles of an interpretation that is concerned exclusively with the subject matters as distinguished from historical interpretation." See Klein and Strauss, "A Giving of Accounts," 2.

37. I also realize—indeed, I gladly affirm—that a reader unpersuaded by my counterproposal may decide to read this book otherwise than in its

printed order. In that case, I would counsel starting with the middle section, then moving to the last section, and only then returning to the first section.

38. A single year's production of scholarly commentary on Thomas requires several years to read, many more to digest inwardly. It is, in the strictest sense, impossible for a reader to keep up with such production. In this book I do not even try. I mention only items that have been important to my reading, whether positively or negatively. Many other works will be passed over because their projects or results are not even "commensurable" with mine—because they begin from utterly different assumptions. I also remain eager to correct the myopia of English-speaking scholarship. There is no reason to assume that the *recent* crop of works on Thomas *in English* will be more helpful than older works or those in other languages. Indeed, there is every reason to suspect that recent works in English will tend to reinforce our prejudices as readers rather than correcting them. I confess that I too have contributed to the annual quota of Thomistic scholarship over several decades. In what follows, I will refer to those earlier writings where they seem to offer fuller help on a point under discussion. I will *not* recall every point where I might have said something similar—or different.

39. In what follows, I say relatively little about the first part of the *Summa*. That is because I am trying to undo the habits of recent periods in which certain sections of that part seemed the entirety of the *Summa*. My intention here is to provide annotated instructions for reading the moral teaching of the *Summa*, which is its center.

PART I. SACRAMENTS, GOSPEL, INCARNATION

1. Prümmer, *Fontes vitae*, 377 (canonization process at Naples, no. 79); compare William of Tocco *Historia* cap.47 (Brun-Gouanvic 181). For a collation of sources on the event and its sequel, see Torrell, *Initiation*, 424–425. William also records the legend that Thomas dictated a brief exposition of the Song of Songs during his days at the Cistercian abbey of Fossanova (cap. 57 [Brun-Gouanvic 196]). No copy of this text has been found.

2. John of Damascus, *De fide orthodoxa*, cap.86 nn.4–17 (Buytaert 309–318).

1. INCARNATION AS INSTRUCTION

1. Foucault, *Les mots et les choses*, 32.

2. See, for example, Thomas *Contra gent.* lib.1 cap.9.

3. The classical *locus* for the two kinds of *copia* is Quintilian, *Institutio oratoria* 10.1.

4. This crucial series of arguments for the incarnation might remind a medieval reader of the compact schemata used for composing moral sermons.

It might also recall the medieval arts of memory and their relation to moral instruction. For Thomas's role in these elaborations, see, for example, Yates, *Art of Memory*, 70–78, but also Rivers, *Preaching the Memory of Virtue and Vice*, especially 81–88.

5. I do not mean to trivialize the disagreement. In Bonaventure, the claim for an incarnation without human sin fits into a much larger pattern of argument, including a retracing of 'natural' morality to its Christic form. See, for an eloquent example, Emery, "Reading the World Rightly and Squarely," especially 212–214.

6. The phrase comes from an ancient antiphon that begins, "*O admirabile commercium!*" Since the sixth or seventh century, that text has been incorporated into many liturgies of the Christmas season. Thomas may know it as a Magnificat antiphon at the vespers for the Octave of Christmas (that is, the feast of the Circumcision). It also appears as a seasonal antiphon in the Dominican "little hours" of the Virgin. For the dating, see Herz, *Sacrum Commercium*, 25–32. Compare the liturgical citation in *Summa theol.* 3.2.11 arg3. Replying, Thomas does not deny the citation. He explains its sense.

7. The passage in question is Lombard *Sententiae* lib.3 dist.6 cap.2. A great deal of scholarly work has gone into naming the opinions that Thomas criticizes here. I suggest that leaving them anonymous better conforms to the *Summa*'s pedagogical design. There is no need for the reader to learn the recent names. Indeed, there may be a risk of contention or some other vice opposed to charity.

8. Augustine *De Trinitate* lib.14 cap.8 (Mountain 50A:436, line 11). The phrase appears famously in Bernard of Clairvaux (*Sermones super Cantica Canticorum* sermo 27 n.10 [Leclercq 1:189]). Much of the contemporary discussion of the phrase in Thomas has gotten tangled in the debate over the natural desire for God. For an older study from the middle of that debate, see Langevin, "*Capax Dei.*"

9. I consider some complications of reading Thomas on image "aesthetically" in Jordan, "Thomas Aquinas, Sacramental Scenes."

10. According to the search functions of the *Index Thomisticus*, 400 of the *Summa*'s 587 mentions of "*imago*" or its inflected forms fall in the *prima pars*.

11. For the notion of image in Trinitarian contexts, see especially Thomas *Summa theol.* 1.34–35 and 1.45 with Merriell, *To the Image of the Trinity*, 153–235. For angels and human beings as images of God, see especially 1.56, 1.59, and (most extensively) 1.93.

12. For remarks on idolatry, see especially Thomas *Summa theol.* 2-2.94.1. For worship of images of Christ, see 3.25.3–4.

13. No Christian theology is required to reject Gentile fables about the gods. Even a pagan philosopher can laugh at them—as Aristotle did (*Summa theol.* 1.97.4 arg3).

14. Thomas probably takes the phrase from Peter Lombard *Sententiae* lib.4 dist.13 cap.2.

2. SEEING GOSPEL STORIES

1. See Chenu, *Introduction à l'étude*, 268–272; McGinn, *Thomas Aquinas's Summa theologiae*, 107 ("a clear division between the theoretical . . . and the historical"). See the criticisms by Boyle, "The Twofold Division."

2. Chenu, "La théologie au XIIIe siècle," 67–68.

3. Lubac, *Exégèse médiévale*, Seconde Partie: II, 301. Thomas is credited with the terminological clarification of locating metaphor within the letter or *littera* of the text, thus distinguishing it from the spiritual senses (compare 290).

4. For example, Augustine, *De doctrina Christiana*, 2.6.7, where Augustine confesses puzzlement at his own delight in an image of the teeth in Song of Songs 4:2, 6:6.

5. Thomas *Super Ps.* pro, "*hic liber [materiam] generalem habet totius theologiae.*"

6. Thomas *Super Iob* pro.

7. The exposition of Isaiah is now dated to Thomas's time with Albert in Cologne—so before his writing on the *Sentences* or his inception as regent master in Paris. See Torrell, *Initiation*, 40–52, and the summary in the catalogue by Emery, 493. Torrell rightly insists on the interest of the exposition's marginal notes, which suggest ways in which it could be preached. My point is just that that the "pastoral" or "homiletic" character of Isaiah is clear enough in the main exposition.

8. Thomas *Super Is.* pro n.1: *auctor, modus, materia.*

9. In this passage, Thomas twice uses *venustas* for beauty. The word is unusual for him. Outside this text and a few quotations, it occurs only twice: *De verit.* q.22 art.11 ad2 and *Contra impugn.* pars 3 cap.1 corp (paraphrasing Basil).

10. Compare Thomas's use in sermons of the pattern of Christ's fourfold advent: in the flesh, in the human mind, at the death of the just, in the general judgment. See *Ecce rex tuus* (Leonine 44/1:58a, lines 32–36).

11. Consider as examples *Summa theol.* 3.40.3 ad3, 3.41.1 corp (with its topical schema), 3.43.4 ad1 (where the quotations are particularly extensive).

12. On the importance of Eastern Christian sources for *Summa* 3, see L.-J. Bataillon, "Saint Thomas et les Pères."

13. The Ottawa and Blackfriars editions trace the motto to a text printed in *PL* 184:778A. This is an *Instructio sacerdotis* sometimes attributed to Bernard of Clairvaux. But that text is not a verbal match. It reads "*ut omnis sua actio esset tua lectio, et omnis sua vita esset tua doctrina.*" Blackfriars adds a citation to *PL* 217:411D, where a similar variation occurs in a sermon ascribed to Innocent III ("*omnis Christi actio, Christiani sit lectio*"). A better guess for Thomas's source would be Peter Lombard's commentary on the psalms (*PL* 191:295A, "*Christus enim cujus actio nostra est instructio*"). More important than identifying an exact "source" is to recognize that the motto has a wide circulation in homiletic contexts. See, for example, William of Auvergne, *Sermones de tempore* (Morezoni 230A:53 line 6).

14. Thomas *Scriptum Sent.* lib.3 dist.17 q.1 art.3 qc.1 corp; lib.4 dist.1 q.2 art.5 qc.3 arg1, dist.2 q.2 art.3 qc.1 arg2 and ad2, dist.4 q.3 art.1 qc.2 arg1, dist.9 q.1 art.5 qc.1 sc1, dist.13 q.1 art.2 qc.4 arg1, dist.15 q.4 art.2 qc.2 sc2, dist.18 q.1 art.3 qc.4 arg3.

15. Thomas will say the same thing with other words. He will quote Ambrose: "his example informs us about the precepts of virtue" (3.40.1 ad3, after Ambrose, *Expos. in Luc.* 5 [Adriaen 150 lines 461–462]). Or a text he thinks is Augustine: "the savior did (*gessit salvator*) all things in proper places and times" (3.46.9 corp and 46.10 sc, after *Quaestiones ex novo testamento* n.55 [PL 35:2252]). Thomas will make mottos of his own, as when he pairs teaching and action: "Christ did and taught the same things" (3.40.4 arg2; compare 3.41.2 corp, Christ doing a mystery).

16. I will return to this notion in Part 2 when describing the belatedness of the *Summa*'s scene of instruction.

17. It is the scriptural story that matters to the *Summa*, not whatever legends about Jesus that sprang up around it. For example, Thomas dismisses claims by the *Liber de infantia salvatoris* that Jesus performed miracles when a child by quoting Damascene: "these are fictions and falsehoods" (3.43.3 arg1, ad1). By contrast, he establishes certain facts about Jesus's life by simple reference to "the authority of evangelical Scriptures" (3.45.4 sc).

18. Bunyan, *Pilgrim's Progress*, 28–36.

19. Peter Lombard *Sententiae* lib.3 dist.3 cap.2 (= cap.8 in the sequential numeration), "*Quod autem sacra Virgo ex tunc ab omni peccato exstiterit.*"

20. See, notably, "Alexander of Hales" *Summa theologica* lib.3 inq.1 tract.2 q.2 memb.2-3 (CSB 4:111–126).

21. Respectively, Thomas *Summa theol.* 27.3 ad1 and 28.4 corp.

22. The mediation of revelation through a hierarchy of human instruction is dear to Thomas. It is the topic of his inaugural sermon as a doctor of theology, the *breve principium* written around the verse, *Rigans montes* (Ps 103:13).

23. For example, the "figuring" of Christ's power to judge and the defeat of the devil in 3.362 ad3; the prefiguring of the preaching to the gentiles and the Jews, 3.36.6 corp; and so on.

24. Tanizaki, *In Praise of Shadows*, 13–14, 19–20.

25. For the synonymy, see Thomas *Summa theol.* 2-2.23.1 ad1, 2-1.35.5 sc. Compare the emphasis on the self-communication of the good God as the source of the incarnation in 3.1.1 corp: *"se aliis communicet," "se creaturae communicet."*

26. Thomas *Summa theol.* 3.46.4 corp, after Augustine *In Ioannis evangelium tractatus* tract.119 par.2 (Willems 36:658 lines 4–5).

27. The principle is reiterated with an explicit back-reference in the discussion of Christ's resurrection (3.56.1 ad2).

28. For the primacy of divine love as motive and lesson, see also 3.46.4 ad1 (the fire of charity).

29. The phrase "truth answers to figure" (*veritas respondet figurae*) or some variation on it appears a number of times in the *Summa*'s questions on the passion, beginning with 3.46.4 ad1. See also 3.46.10 arg2 and ad2. Of course, the principle is qualified by application, as most principles in Thomas are. So he will remind his readers that truth need not correspond to figure in every detail, since it also exceeds the figure (3.48.3 ad1).

30. The moral accent can be heard whenever Thomas begins to gather typological arguments in these questions. Consider, as just one example, the explanations of the choice of Jerusalem as site (3.46.10 ad1).

31. See, for example, *Summa theol.* 2-1.102.3 ad8 ("for the forming [*ad informationem*] of human life," that is, of a life more human than bestial); 102.6 ad1 ("to prohibit cruelty and excessive pleasure [*voluptas*] and fortitude for sinning").

32. For example, *Summa theol.* 2-2.32.2 ad3, 108.4 ad1, and so on. In other passages, *severitas* is contrasted with laxity (2-2.120.1 arg1 and ad1) and with clemency or meekness (2-2.157.2 arg1, ad1, ad2). The latter contrast leads Thomas to explain the relation of severity to justice.

3. SACRAMENTAL BODIES

1. Thomas arranges topics that his close predecessors and contemporaries had grown accustomed to inserting at the beginning of the treatment of sacraments. See the introductory comments in Albert the Great *Sent.* lib.4 dist.1 art.1 (Borgnet *Opera* 29:4): *"Incidunt autem quaestiones ante Litteram quatuor."*

2. Peter Lombard *Sententiae* lib.4 dist.1 cap.1 n.1.

3. There is an interesting story to be told about the fortune of medical metaphors in sacramental theology, especially when used by someone (like

Albert) with a considerable knowledge medicine. With other readers, Chauvet judges the subordination of medical analogies one of Thomas's achievements in the *Summa* (see Chauvet, *Symbol and Sacrament*, 11–12 with note 4).

4. See especially Thomas *Scriptum Sent.* lib.4 dist.1 q.1 art.2 qc.2.

5. The bigger puzzle in Thomas's argument against prelapsarian sacraments concerns marriage. Thomas is quite clear that any marriages among human beings before sin would not have been sacramental. They would have concerned only the "*officium naturae,*" the natural use of procreation (3.61.2 ad3). This is one sign of a larger ambivalence in Thomas's remarks on the line between natural and divine laws with regard to marriage.

6. Augustine *De civitate Dei* lib.10 cap.5, as in Peter Lombard *Sententiae* lib.4 dist.1 cap.2 (CSB 2:232).

7. Thomas *Expos. Pery.* lib.1 lect.2, 4–5.

8. Thomas *De verit.* q.9 art.4 arg4.

9. Thomas *De verit.* q.9 art.4 ad4.

10. Thomas *Summa theol.* 3.60.1 sc, after Augustine *De civitate Dei* lib.10 cap.5; 3.60.6 arg1, after Augustine *Contra Faustum* lib.19 cap.16 (Zycha 25:513, line 7); 3.61.1 sc, after Augustine *Contra Faustum* lib.19 cap.11 (Zycha 25:510, line 1). Supporting these emphases on visibility is the definition of sign as perceptible: "beyond the species that [a sign] presses on the senses, it makes something else come into cognition" (*Summa theol.* 3.60.4 corp). The definition is taken from Augustine *De doctrina Christiana* lib.2 cap.1 n.1 (Green 57, no. 1).

11. For example, Lonergan once objected strongly to taking at face value Thomas's images of causal flow in the sacraments (review of Iglesias, 612 and throughout).

12. In his *Scriptum* on Peter Lombard, Thomas acknowledges the doctrine's recent elaboration. He there surveys the consensus of "all the moderns" (*omnes moderni*, *Super Sent.* lib.4 d.4 q.1 a.1 corp). *Moderni* refers to writers known to him as contemporaries or immediate predecessors.

13. For the attribution to Ps-Dionysius, see Bonaventure *Super libros Sententiarum* lib.4 dist.6 pars.1 art.1 (CSB 4:137).

14. Some of the earlier uses are unclear. For example, Peter Lombard argues against rebaptizing those already baptized by heretics so long as it was done "following the character of Christ" ("*servo charactere Christo,*" *Sententiae* lib.4 dist.6 cap.2 n.3 [CSB 2:269]). By "character" here the Lombard might refer to the baptismal formula, but he could mean just as well the moral imprint of Christ.

15. Gy, "La documentation sacramentaire," 429, suggests that Thomas took from this verse the decisive connection between sacramental character and Christ's priesthood.

16. Thomas *Summa theol.* 3.22.2 corp: "and thus everything that is exhibited to God so that the human spirit is carried towards God can be called 'sacrifice.'"

PART II. WRITING SCENES OF MORAL INSTRUCTION

1. I here return to an argument that I made first in "Missing Scenes."

4. SCENES OF INSTRUCTION

1. The popularization of the notion of a "Thomistic synthesis" goes back to the nineteenth century. Though it appears earlier, it was promoted by Maurice De Wulf, for whom "synthesis" is interchangeable with "system" (see, for example, *Histoire de la philosophie médiévale*, 247–248). The "Scholastic synthesis" is one protagonist in de Wulf's historiography, especially when he wants to characterize Thomas (*Histoire*, 259–290). Of course, De Wulf speaks of all kinds of syntheses, in philosophy and theology, across the centuries from antiquity to modernity. The discovery of "systems" in medieval philosophy goes back through Victor Cousin to Enlightenment historiography of philosophy. It was popularized by Enfield's Englishing of Jacob Brucker's *Historia Critica Philosophiae*. So, for example, Enfield speaks of the "monstrous forms" of the "system" of Scholastic philosophy (*History of Philosophy*, 2:390).

2. With "spiritual exercises," I recall both Hadot, *Exercices spirituels*, and Foucault, *L'herméneutique du sujet*. With such telegraphic references, and even more with the characterizations in these paragraphs, I treat complex things too simply. I am only trying to encourage the recognition of something that has gone curiously missing from our stories about Thomas Aquinas and the history of ethics.

3. Harold Bloom uses the phrase "scene of instruction" to do several things. (See, for example, Bloom, *Map of Misreading*, 41–62.) I doubt that I learned the phrase from him; I am certain that I give it a different and simpler sense. For an earlier effort to describe scenes and to call for their restoration, see Jordan, "Missing Scenes."

4. Thomas *Catena in Matt.* cap.26 lect.13, quoting Origen.

5. See Thomas *Super Ioan.* cap.21 lect.5 on the *specialis dilectio* that Christ felt for John.

6. Thomas *De potentia* q.6 art.5 arg.6 and ad6, to which compare *Summa theol.* 1.90.1 corp, 2-2.94.1 corp, 2-2.122.2 ad2.

7. See, for examples of the image of veiling, *Sent. Metaph.* lib.1 lect.4 n.15 (in a comparison of poets and philosophers), lib.3 lect.11 n.3 ("*sub quodam tegmine fabularum*"). Compare the poets' deployment of certain "enigmas of fables" ("*aenigmatibus fabularum*," *Sent. Metaph.* lib.1 lect.4 n.15).

Integumentum was used by some of Thomas's twelfth-century predecessors to explain philosophical enjoyments of allegory. Thomas uses *tegumen* less deliberately to describe any sort of covering or protection. *Sent. Metaph.* lib.3 lect.11 n.3 is the only passage I can find in the corpus where Thomas uses the word when speaking in his own voice to describe a literary device.

8. Thomas *Super 1 Tim.* cap.4 lect.2.

9. See Thomas *Sent. de anima* lib.1 lect.12. The "poet theologians," including Orpheus, are elsewhere placed before philosophy or distinguished from it; see *Sent. Phys.* lib.2 lect.2, *Sent. Metaph.* lib.12 lect.6 and 12, *Sent. Meteor.* lib.2 lect.1. On the "fables" of both Pythagoreans and poets, *Scriptum Sent.* lib.2 dist.6 q.1 art.3 ad5, *Contra Gent.* lib.2 cap.44 n.7 (paraphrasing Aristotle), *Sent. De anima* lib.1 lect.8 n.25. On Homer as "fabulator," *Sent. Meteor.* lib.1 cap.16 n.2; on fable as proper to poets, *Sent. Metaph.* lib.1 lect.3 n.4.

10. On the contrast between poetry and philosophy, see again Thomas *Sent. Metaph.* lib.1 lect.3–4 generally and 15.

11. Thomas *Sent. Metaph.* lib.3 lect.11 n.3 (only author knows), *Sent. De caelo* lib.2 lect.1 n.8.

12. On the fables of the Manicheans, Thomas *Summa theol.* 2-2.25.5 corp; of heretics generally, *Contra gent.* lib.3 chap.27 n.11, *Super 1 Tim.* lib.1 lect.2.

13. Thomas *Sent. Metaph.* lib.3 lect.11 n.6.

14. Thomas *Sent. De caelo* lib.1 lect.21. *Coordinalia* and *auditionalia* do not occur elsewhere in Thomas's corpus. He takes them from Moerbeke's translation of Simplicius's commentary on *De caelo*.

15. Thomas *Sent. Phys.* lib.1 lect.1 n.4: "*naturali auditu, quia per modum doctrinae ad audientes traditus fuit.*"

16. Thomas *Sent. De caelo* lib.1 lect.22, which reports the disagreement between Simplicius and Alexander. On Plato's use of parable and fable, compare *Super Metaph.* lib.7 lect.11 n.18.

17. Thomas *Super Dion. De div. nom.* pro; *Sent. De anima* lib.1 lect.8.

18. Thomas endorses the theological notion of condescension (*condescensio*). It is traditionally applied to passages of the Scriptures in which literally false locutions must be understood as concessions to the weakness of the first readers. So, for example, the account of creation in Genesis 1 appears to contain scientific and philosophical errors, but they are excused as divine condescension to the cosmological ignorance of the ancient Israelites. (On Genesis, see Thomas *Summa theol.* 1.68.3 corp, 1.70.1 ad3. For the *condescensio* of the Scriptures generally, see *Super Dion. De div. nom.* lib.1 lect.2.) *Condescensio* figures not just in the Scriptures: every careful teacher employs it. A skilled teacher does not deliver the whole of an art at once, "but slowly, condescend-

ing to [the student's] capacity" (*Summa theol.* 2.2-1.7 ad 2). Again, Aristotle practices *condescensio* when he accepts false views for the sake of dialectical progress (*Sent. De sensu* lib.1 lect.5).

19. Readers of Thomas may dispute about his intentions with regard to philosophy, but they cannot dispute so easily about his use of the word "philosopher," *philosophus*. He never applies the word to himself, and he applies it only accidentally (I think) to others he knows to be Christians. See Jordan, *Rewritten Theology*, 63–64, and more generally Chenu, "Les 'Philosophes.'"

20. In the *Summa*, recall especially 1.1.9 arg1-2 and ad1-2. For an earlier version of the argument, see *Scriptum Sent.* lib.1 dist.1. q.5 arg3 and ad3. In the *Scriptum*, the parabolic mode of theology is equated with the metaphorical and symbolic (lib.1 pro q.1 art.5 corp).

21. Here Thomas gathers the traditional considerations canvassed more fully in *Catena in Matt.* cap.13 lect.2.

22. Compare Thomas *Super Psalm.* ps.48 n.2. Earlier in the *Summa*, Thomas had argued that Christ's use of parables was in no way intended to deceive the crowds (1.111.3 ad4).

23. Thomas *Super Ioan.* cap.12 lect.6.

24. I do not mean to exaggerate Thomas's choice among genres. The teaching traditions within which he wrote occluded certain forms. So it might be better to borrow what de Lubac says of his relation to Aristotle: "St. Thomas received Aristotle: he did not have to choose him" (*Surnaturel*, 473). In the same way, he received genres.

25. Boland rightly emphasizes that a public dispute is a communal search for truth (e.g., Boland, *St. Thomas Aquinas*, 19–20). I do not take this as "crowdsourcing" or even as a pragmatist's trust in the way shared inquiry might approach truth over time. It is instead a reminder of the relation between theological inquiry and the community constituted by divine revelation continued in sacraments.

26. Thomas *Summa theol.* 2-2.10.7 corp.

27. Thomas *Summa theol.* 2-2.10.7 ad3, "*propter veritatem manifestandam et errores confutandos.*"

28. Thomas *Quol.* 4 q.9 art.3 corp. It is tempting to translate, "whether something is the case," but then the task would be to examine the semantic presuppositions that lurk in the puzzling phrase, "the case."

29. The examples here of authorities to be used with certain groups follow those in *Contra gent.* lib.1 cap.2 n.4.

30. Thomas *Princ.* "*Rigans*" cap.2.

31. Thomas *Contra Gent.* lib.1 cap.3 n.2. I treat these chapters and the structure of the work more fully in *Rewritten Theology*, 89–115. I note there

and repeat here my thanks to those who responded to my reading of Thomas's purposes in constructing the *Contra Gentiles*.

32. Thomas *Contra Gent.* lib.1 cap.9 nn.2–5 for this quotation and those in the rest of the paragraph.

33. This seems to be the view of Gauthier in the Leonine edition of *Sent. de anima*, Leonine *Opera omnia* 45:289*–293*.

34. Thomas *Contra Gent.* lib.1 cap.1 n.4.

35. For the image of the "root of truth" (*radix veritatis*), see *Quol.* 4 q.9 art.3 corp.

5. FROM SCENES TO AUTHORITIES

1. Like so many terms ending in -ism, "Scholasticism" was originally a polemical coinage. It was meant to mock the quibbles or foibles of the medieval schoolroom. When the term was rehabilitated for more neutral scholarly use in the nineteenth century, it still carried this historical reference. Hauréau, for example, defines Scholasticism thematically by the question of universals but chronologically as "the philosophy taught in the schools of the Middles Ages" from Alcuin to Ockham (*Histoire de la philosophie scolastique* [1872], 1:36). Objecting to extrinsic definitions, Maurice de Wulf proposes to define "Scholasticism" much more elaborately in relation to certain "fundamental doctrines" that constitute a "system" or "synthesis" across the leading authors of Western Europe (*Introduction à la philosophie néo-scolastique*, 47–57, 129–134). I favor instead Martin Grabmann's suggestion that Scholasticism be defined in terms of its methods, not least those of disputation and commentary (*Die Geschichte der Scholastischen Methode* [1909–11], 1:36–37). Even Grabmann fails sufficiently to appreciate the objection that the most satisfying definition of a sweeping generalization like "Scholasticism" still helps only a little in reading the works grouped under it. To say that more concretely: Defining "Scholasticism" meticulously does not add much to understanding the *Summa*.

2. *Tabula libri Ethicorum* is the draft of such a topical index for Aristotle's *Nicomachean Ethics* prepared by Thomas's secretaries. There is a similar index for some of Aristotle's scientific tracts among Albert's works. For both, see Torrell, *Initiation*, 334–336.

3. Gilson in a letter to Lubac: "In fact, [Thomas's] terminology is extremely free, because he never rejects an expression if it is possible to justify it *in some sense*" (Gilson and Lubac, *Lettres*, 66 [letter of June 20, 1965]).

4. I here condense readings of the three texts that I present more fully in Jordan, "Cicero, Ambrose, and Aquinas 'on Duties.'"

5. Cicero *De officiis* 1.1.1.

6. Cicero *De officiis* 1.1.1, 1.1.3, 1.45.160, 2.1.1, 3.1.1, 3.2.5, 3.33.121 (twice).

7. For example, in 1.11.37 Cicero mentions Cato's letter to his son Marcus on entering combat without having taken the requisite oath.

8. Cicero *De officiis* 1.22.78. Compare the claim that the best inheritance a father can pass down is the glory of a reputation for virtue (1.33.121).

9. Cicero *De officiis* 1.11.35 (Winterbottom 15 lines 3 and 17), "*maiores nostri*" and "*more maiorum*"; 1.13.40 (17 lines 27–28), "*a maioribus nostris constitutum*"; 1.25.86 (35 line 11), "*in nostra republica*"; and so on.

10. Among the first book's heroes, Scipio Africanus (1.18.61, 1.32.116), Cato (1.31.112), Regulus (1.13.39), and Cicero himself (1.22.77); among its villains, Marcus Crassus (1.8.25, 1.30.109), Julius Caesar (1.8.26, 1.9.43, 1.30.108), Quintus Fabius Labeo (1.10.33), Lucius Sulla (1.9.43, 1.30.109).

11. See, for example, Cicero's references to Atticus (1.28.97), Cato the Elder (1.11.36–37, 1.29.104), Ennius (1.8.26, 1.16.51, 1.18.61), and Terence (1.9.30).

12. Ambrose *De officiis ministrorum* lib.1 cap.7 n.24 (Testard 1:106).

13. For "our" writings, see Ambrose *De officiis ministrorum* lib.1 cap.9 n.29 (Testard 1:109), "*nostra legent si volent,*" contrasted with the works of philosophers, "*qui illa non legunt*"; lib.1 cap.45 n.231 (1:202), "*in nostris,*" which includes both David and Paul; lib.1 cap.28 n.133 (1:159), "*de Scripturis nostris,*" Moses and David as sources of pagan philosophy; lib.2 cap.8 n.43 (2:29), "*in nostris,*" with reference to David.

14. Respectively, Ambrose *De officiis ministrorum* lib.1 cap.35 n.175, lib.1 cap.40 n.206, lib.3 cap.1 n.5, lib.3 cap.8 n.53, lib.3 cap.17 nn.98–99, and lib.3 cap.19 n.116.

15. Ambrose *De officiis ministrorum* lib.1 cap.24 n.107 (Testard 1:147), "*pater Abraham*"; lib.3 cap.15 n.92 (2:124), "*ad nostrum Moysen.*"

16. Ambrose *De officiis ministrorum* 1.3.11 (Testard 1:100). Compare lib.1 cap.7 n.23 on Ambrose's delighted commendation of Psalm 39.

17. Ambrose *De officiis ministrorum* lib.1 cap.25 n.116 (Testard 1:151). For other remarks on *exemplum*, see lib.1 cap.30 n.154, Paul in 2 Corinthians 8:15, quoting Exodus 16.18; lib.1 cap.31 n.162, the earth's bounty; lib.2 cap.11 n.56, Joseph, Solomon, Daniel; lib.2 cap.18 n.93, Solomon; lib.3 cap.18 n.108, the Israelites crossing the Red Sea. On the power of example generally, see Ambrose *De officiis ministrorum* lib.3 cap.22 n.139; on the contrast between historical examples and the fictions of philosophical dispute, see lib.3 cap.5 nn.29, 32.

18. Ambrose *De officiis ministrorum* lib.3 cap.13 n.82 (Testard 2:121).

19. See, for example, Ambrose *De officiis ministrorum* lib.1 cap.1 n.3, the Son of God chooses the apostles; lib.1 cap.14 n.53, the Lord Jesus provides

the most satisfying witness; lib.1 cap.50 n.252, Christ is the foundation of all the virtues; lib.2 cap.2 n.5, Jesus defines happiness; lib.2 cap.30 n.154, the teaching of the apostle gives way to the teaching of the Lord himself; lib.3 cap.6 n.43, what the Lord Jesus taught in parable; lib.3 cap.11 n.75, what the Lord said to those who approached him.

20. Ambrose *De officiis ministrorum* lib.3 cap.18 n.108 (Testard 2:132–133).

21. See Thomas *Summa theol.* 2-2.58.11 arg2 and sc; 77.3 arg2 and sc; 123.5 arg2; 141.2 arg2-3; 144.1 arg3; 145.3 arg3; and 168.2, throughout.

22. Thomas *Summa theol.* 2-2.145.1 sc (Cicero), 145.2 ad1 (Cicero). Cicero and Ambrose appear elsewhere in tandem as part of a dialectical sequence. See, for example, *Summa theol.* 2-2.58.11 sc (Ambrose) and 58.12 sc (Cicero); 77.1 sc (Cicero) and 77.3 sc (Ambrose).

23. For a tabulation of references to the *Nicomachean Ethics* in *Scriptum* 1, see Jordan, *Rewritten Theology*, 78–80.

24. Thomas *Contra errores* pars prior pro, for this quotation and the others in this paragraph.

25. Thomas *Contra Gent.* lib.1 cap.9 n.4.

6. THE *SUMMA* IN (OUR) LIBRARIES

1. Here I skip over all the difficulties of "publication" in manuscript cultures. Both ancient and medieval texts are filled with complaints about unauthorized circulation of incomplete works. Earlier parts of the *Summa* seem to have been in circulation before the last parts were finished. Whether Thomas would have approved the circulation of the unfinished third part is another question. But I cannot imagine him, like Virgil, ordering its destruction. That assertion of vain authorship would contradict his humble view of Christian teaching.

2. Readers interested in such histories might begin with McGinn, *Thomas Aquinas's Summa theologiae*, 117–209 (the best in English). To construct more extended reading lists, a reader would have recourse to the bibliographies like Kennedy, *A Catalogue of Thomists*; Redmond, *Bibliography of the Philosophy in the Iberian Colonies*; Wyser, *Der Thomismus*, 5–53; and so on.

3. See, for example, the remark on "*vitia capitalia*" in *Summa theol.* 1-2.84.4 ad5, to which compare *De malo* q.8 art.1 ad1, ad6, ad8.

4. In Raymond's *Summa de casibus*, direct crimes against God are simony (1.1–3), simple unbelief (1.4), heresy (1.5), schism (1.6), or the combination of these last two in apostasy (1.7). Less direct crimes against God are breaking vows (1.8), breaking oaths and other perjuries (1.9), mendacity or adulation (1.10), divination (1.11), and disrespect for solemn feasts (1.12). Indirect crimes against God are sacrilege (1.13), crimes against church sanctuary

(1.14), refusal of tithes, first fruits, or oblations (1.15), and violations of the laws of burial.

5. For example, Ps 75.12 in Thomas *Summa theol.* 2-2.88.2 arg1 = Raymond *Summa de casibus* 1.8.2 (p. 55a); Jerome on Jeremiah, *Summa theol.* 2-2.89.3 = *Summa de casibus* 1.9.3 (p. 82b); Augustine in *De mendacio*, *Summa theol.* 2-2.89.2 = *Summa de casibus* 1.9.1 (p. 81b); 1 Kings 14.38, Jonah 1.7, and Acts 1.26 together, *Summa theol.* 2-2.95.8 arg2 = *Summa de casibus* 1.11.[3] (pp. 103b–104a).

6. For definitions of terms: "*emptio et venditio*," *Summa theol.* 2-2.100.1 ad5 = *Summa de casibus* 1.1.2 (p. 5a); "*haeresis*," *Summa theol.* 2-2.11.2 and 3 = *Summa de casibus* 1.5.1 (p. 38a–b); "*apostasia*," *Summa theol.* 2-2.12.1 = *Summa de casibus* 1.7.2 (p. 47b); "*sacrilegium*," *Summa theol.* 2-2.99.1 titulus = *Summa de casibus* 1.13.1 (p. 115a). For arguments: on the greater gravity of solemn vows, *Summa theol.* 2-2.88.7 ad1 = *Summa de casibus* 1.8.2 (p. 56a); on implied reference to authority in vows, *Summa theol.* 2-2.88.12 ad2 = *Summa de casibus* 1.8.9 (p. 67b); on justifying theft under necessity, *Summa theol.* 2-2.66.7 sc = *Summa de casibus* 2.6.10 (p. 224b); on scriptural precedent for lying, *Summa theol.* 2-2.110.3 arg3 = *Summa de casibus* 1.10.3 (p. 100b). For schemata of adjudication or punishment: the simoniac monk, *Summa theol.* 2-2.100.6 ad5 = *Summa de casibus* 1.1.4 (p. 14a–b); the punishments for sacrilege, *Summa theol.* 2-2.99.4 = *Summa de casibus* 1.13.3 (pp. 115b–116a).

7. In what follows, I return to topics I have treated in *Rewritten Theology*, especially 8–10. I hope not only to improve on the arguments there but also to revise them by contesting assumptions about how we judge reception.

8. Grabmann, "De summae divi Thomae Aquinas," 157.

9. Boyle, "The *Summa confessorum* of John of Freiburg," 257. I follow the original pagination rather than the reprinting in Boyle, *Facing History*.

10. There are some 600 surviving copies of the *Summa pisana* as against about 280 copies of *the secunda secundae*. See Boyle, "The *Summa confessorum*," 260, on the character of text, and Kaeppeli, *Scriptores ordinis praedicatorum*, 1:158–165, "Bartholomaeus de S. Concordia," item n.436, where the number of extant manuscripts is given as 602.

11. McGinn, *Thomas Aquinas's Summa theologiae*, 119, citing Mulchahey.

12. My complaint against early modern Thomism is not in the least original. It is also not particularly sharp. For example, in two letters to Henri de Lubac, Etienne Gilson refers to Cajetan's commentary on the *Summa* as the *corruptorium* or "corruptory" (Gilson and Lubac, *Lettres*, 19 [letter of July 8, 1956], 74 [letter of June 21, 1965]). Gilson is recalling a medieval Thomist joke: Thomas's early readers dubbed "the corruptory" a Franciscan compendium of Thomas's errors actually entitled the *Correctorium* or *Correctory*. The

complaint that Cajetan often rewrites the *Summa* rather than commenting on it has been made since his commentary first appeared. Only the optical illusion of a "Thomist Tradition" fuses Cajetan with his opponents.

13. Vitoria *De indis* I pro nn.2–3 (Pereña 5–7) on communal discernment; I cap.2 n.14 (Pereña 61) on divine illumination for those who follow natural law.

14. Suárez *De legibus* lib.2 cap.5 nn.14–15 and 2.6 n.10 and n.19 (Pereña and Abril 72–73, 91–92, 101–102).

15. Liberatore, *Istituzioni di etica e diritto naturale*, 260–269.

16. William of Tocco *Historia* cap.16 (Le Brun-Gouanvic 123–126).

17. Leo XIII, *Aeterni patris*, [n.17].

18. Moreover, the wayfarer hopes not in the present possession of grace but in God's omnipotent mercy (2-2.18.4 ad2).

19. For example, there is the "perception" of one's inner delight and contempt for earthly things or the lack of awareness of having sinned seriously (2-1.112.5 corp). The more important point is that the arguments Thomas uses against demonstrative certainty about one's own possession of grace would apply equally or more to other persons.

PART III. MORAL THEOLOGY ON THE WAY TO ITS END

1. Peter Lombard *Sententiae* lib.2 dist.26 (in general) and lib.2 dist.28–29 (before the Fall).

2. The division according to "heart, mouth, and deed" comes to Thomas through Peter Lombard *Sententiae* lib.2 dist.42 n.4. The division according to "weakness, ignorance, and malice" descends through *Sententiae* lib.2 dist.22 n.4. Thomas deploys both distinctions in other passages, even within the *Summa*, though he is always careful to point out that they are not classifications by genus or essential species.

7. THE GOOD THAT DRAWS THE WILL

1. Peter Lombard *Sententiae* lib.4 dist.49.

2. Thomas *Scriptum Sent.* lib.4 dist.49 q.1 art.3 qc.1–4.

3. Albert the Great *Sententiae* lib.1 dist.1 arts.9–10, 15, 23.

4. Thomas *Scriptum Sent.* lib.1 dist.1 qq.1–2.

5. Gauthier in Leonine *Opera omnia* 47:235*. Compare William of Tocco *Historia* cap.14 (Le Brun-Gouanvic 118 lines 70–72).

6. Albert the Great *Super Eth.* prol. n.4 (Cologne *Opera* 14/1:3 lines 61–80).

7. The Last Judgment would have been discussed in a section of the third part that Thomas never reached. Note the forward reference at *Summa theol.* 2-1.3.3, "as will be clear below, when treating of the resurrection."

8. This list simplifies the longer sequence in *Contra gent.* lib. 3 cap.26–44, which had combined an argument from Aristotle's *Nicomachean Ethics* lib.1 cap.7 with one from Peter Lombard's *Sententiae* lib.4 dist.49. The long and rather rambling list in *Contra gent.* is reduced to order in the *Summa*, perhaps under the influence of Augustine, *De Trinitate* 13.4: "*quidam posuerunt beatitudinem in voluptate corporis, quidam in virtute animi, quidam in aliis rebus.*" This is cited in *Summa theol.* 1-2.5.8 arg1; compare Augustine *De civ. Dei* lib.18 cap.41.

9. Thomas could certainly have learned something of the genre from Augustine's remarks on the *Hortensius* in *Confessions* 3.4.

10. Boethius *Consolatio* lib.2 prose 5–7, lib.3 prose 2.

11. Boethius *Consolatio* lib.3 prose 2 (Bieler lines 41–42).

12. Thomas *Summa theol.* 2-1.2.1 sc, 3 sc, 4 sc, 6 sc. The other four citations occur in 2-1.2.1 arg2 and 3 arg3.

13. Compare the citations of Aristotle's *Physics* in *Summa theol.* 2-1.1.1 sc, 2 sc, 4 corp, with the adjacent citations of Augustine (2-1.1.3 sc, 6 sc, 7 sc, 8 sc) and Philippians or Matthew (2-1.1.5 sc).

14. See e.g. the sermon in D'Avray, *Preaching of the Friars*, 260–271, against wealth. See also D'Avray, "Sermons to the Upper Bourgeoisie."

15. On the dating, see LE 44/1:296.

16. To take a few details: compare the association of Origen with the error of Plato (LE 44/1:300–301, lines 95–97) with *Summa* 2-1.5.4 corp; the enumeration of five goods from Boethius (LE 44/1:302–304) with 2-1.2.1–8.

17. For an example of Thomas on the preacher's moral progress from another sermon, see *Exiit qui seminat* (LE 44/1:122–124).

18. *Beata gens* LE 44/1:318, lines 97–129; compare 321, lines 280–297.

19. Thomas argues his understanding of pastoral work in a quodlibetal question, *Quol.* 1 q.7 art.2. The dating of the quodlibetal questions is speculative, but this question may well have been disputed during Easter 1269. That would place it a bit before the final composition of this part of the *Summa*. See Torrell, *Initiation*, 304–309, on the dating and the sense.

20. The number of interventions in the debate is difficult to calculate. It serves as a sobering reminder of the scale at which Thomistic controversy is conducted. Laporta provides a partial bibliography for the latter half of the nineteenth century and the first half of the twentieth (*La destinée de la nature humaine*, 22). De Lubac himself summarizes then recent Thomistic exegesis in *Surnaturel*, 449–451. Fuller bibliographic annotations on the debate before 1950 or so can be found in Colombo, "Il problema del soprannaturale" (with the bibliographic summary, 600–607); for the decade following, Colombo, "Il desiderio di vedere Dio." Still the debate has hardly subsided since the

1960s. Consider, for example and in English, Hütter, *Dust Bound for Heaven*, 129–246, and the many texts it canvasses.

21. Here as elsewhere, Thomas varies his terminology. In nearby passages, Thomas will often speak of *amor, desiderium* or *concupiscentia*, and *delectatio*, which he treats as equivalent to *gaudium* (2-1.25.2 corp & ad 2; compare 2-1.25.4 corp). Again, Thomas interchanges *complacentia* with *connaturalitas* and *coaptatio* (2-1.27.1 corp, 27.4 corp).

22. Thomas also speaks of a "natural desire" in humans to know causes or to know all things (1.12.1 corp, 1.12.8 ad 4). They share with other creatures a natural desire to continue in being (1.63.3 corp, 1.75.6 corp).

23. Thomas *De malo* q.5 art.1 ad15, art.3 corp. These texts form the main support for Laporta's argument that human nature, left to its own devices, would have a natural end other than the vision of the divine essence granted in the beatific vision (see his *La destinée de la nature humaine*, 114–115).

24. De Lubac, *Surnaturel*, 456.

25. Gilson, "Sur la problématique Thomiste de la vision béatifique," 74–75.

26. *Beata gens* LE 44/1: 317, lines 5–10.

27. In *Summa* 2-1.5.7 corp, Thomas argues that God could create beatitude and the right will required for it simultaneously in a human being. The "order of divine wisdom" judged that only God should have beatitude without moving toward it, since only God has beatitude naturally. "Since however beatitude exceeds all created nature, no creature as such (*pura creatura*) can obtain beatitude appropriately (*convenienter*) without the motion of operations, through which it tends toward it."

28. For example, Gauthier, "Saint Maxime le Confesseur," 98, collapsing *usus, consensus*, and *imperium* into *electio*; Pinckaers, "La structure de l'acte humain," 409–410, merging *consensus* into *electio, judicium practicum* into *consilium*.

29. In fact, Thomas knows this authority only through the so-called *Liber de fortuna*. See Deman, "Le 'Liber de Bona Fortuna,'" especially 38–50, with a reading edition of the pertinent passage of the original text on 39–40.

8. STAGES ON LAW'S WAY

1. See, for example, *Super Sent.* lib.2 dist.28 q.1 prol, lib.2 dist.35 q.1 art.2 corp, lib.3 dist.37 q.1 art.5 qc.1 sc2, lib.4 d.1 q.1 a.5 qc.1 ad4. For other instances in the *Summa*, see 2-1.98.6 corp (twice), 2-1.101.3 corp, 2-2.44.8 sc, 2-2.104.5 ad2, 2-2.154.2 ad1.

2. *Summa theologiae* 2-2.16 (faith), 22 (hope and the gift of fear), 44 (charity), 56 (prudence), 122 (justice), 140 (fortitude), 170 (temperance).

3. For the gradual pedagogy of precepts, see *Summa theologiae* 2-2.22.1 corp (on the sequence of kinds of preambles).

4. The quotation figured prominently in the opening questions about human blessedness. See *Summa theol.* 2-1.2.arg2, 3.2 arg2, 3.3 arg2, 4.7 arg2.

5. Here as throughout I do my best to represent Thomas's arguments without deploring or even tracing their dangerous implications. In these passages on the Old Law, for example, a reader confronts many of the images of Christian supersession. In other authors, the very same images are cited to authorize violence against Jews or other religious groups likened to them.

6. Justinian *Institutes* 1.2 prol (law of nature), 1.2.1 (law of peoples), 1.2.11 (their shared attributes).

7. Isidore *Etymologiae* lib.5 cap.4 (Lindsay line 25–line 8).

8. Gratian *Concordantia* 1.5.1 [prol] (Richter-Friedberg 1:7), 1.8.1 and 1.9.1 [prol] (Richter-Friedberg 1:12 and 1:16).

9. Gratian *Concordantia* 1.1 [prol] (Richter-Friedberg 1:1).

10. Raymond of Peñafort *Summa iuris* 1.1 (Rius Serra 1:23).

11. For the four kinds of law, see "Alexander of Hales," *Summa theologica* 3.2.1–4 (CSB 4:313–339).

12. See Crowe, *Changing Profile*, 187–191, for similar arguments. The opposite view is represented by Manser, *Das Naturrecht*, 51–61.

13. On the scope and continuity of divine pedagogy, see Levering, *Christ's Fulfillment of Torah and Temple*, 15–30.

14. Compare Chareire, *Éthique et grace*, 160 n. 1.

15. For the explicit mentions of Maimonides in these questions, *Summa theol.* 2-1.101.1 arg4; 101.3 ad3; 102.3 ad4, ad6, ad11; 102.4 sc and ad2; 102.5 ad4; 102.6 ad1, ad8.

16. For examples of the repression of disordered desire, *Summa theol.* 2-1.102.3 ad14 ("*ad excludendam omnem carnalem dulcedinem et voluptatem*"); 102.5 ad1 ("*ad debilitationem concupiscentiae in membro illo*"); 102.6 ad1 ("*fomentum luxuriae*"), ad6 ("*ad declinandam luxuriam*") ad8 ("*ad tollendam universaliter occasionem concupiscentiae*"). For examples of the correction of cruelty, 2-1.102.3 ad8 ("*ad informationem humanae vitae*," that is, of a life more human than bestial); 102.6 ad1 ("*prohiberi crudelitas et voluptas et fortitudo ad peccandum*").

17. Compare this with Thomas's decision to undertake a literal commentary on Job. Gregory the Great's *Moral Readings of Job* was a fundamental text for Thomas as for many other Christians writing on morals in Latin. There is no question of displacing Gregory's authority (*Super Job* pro, at the conclusion). Still Thomas finds it useful to reclaim the letter of the scriptural text.

18. Note also that the term almost always refers to the pagan past. In *Summa theol.* 2-1.101.2 arg2, the objector explains the simulations of theatrical representation long ago ("*olim repraesentabantur*").

19. I mean the passages in which Thomas allows for multiple readings without deciding among them. Examples of such passages can be found at *Summa theol.* 2-1.102.3 ad2 (turtle and dove), ad6 (ways of killing); 102.4 ad2 (tabernacle and temple); 102.6 ad4 (cooking of kid); 103.4 ad3 (apostolic food prohibitions). These are different from passages in which Thomas notes an exegetical disagreement and then argues around it (103.4 ad1, Jerome and Augustine).

20. I will reconsider *instinctus* in Chapter 9.

9. THE GIFTS OF THE SPIRIT

1. For an argument about the gifts as a limit on "Thomistic" ethics and politics, see Jordan, "Democratic Moral Education," some arguments from which I here expand.

2. Two passages from Gregory are particularly important for Thomas's account in the *Summa*. In *Moralia* lib.1 n.27, Gregory expounds Job 1:2, but he cites Isaiah 11:2–3. On a moral reading, Job's seven sons become the gifts of the Holy Spirit, while Job's three daughters are the theological virtues (Adriaen 143:45–46). In *Moralia* lib.2 n.49, expounding Job 1:18–19, Gregory describes the relation of the "gift" of the Holy Spirit to the cardinal virtues, but also its function as an antidote to temptation (Adriaen 143:105–108).

3. Thomas here follows the doxography of Albert the Great and Bonaventure in their expositions of Peter Lombard *Sentences* lib.3 dist.34. For modern accounts of the development, one can still begin with Lottin, "Les dons du Saint-Esprit," but should then turn to the much more recent summary by Stroud, "Thomas Aquinas' Exposition of the Gifts of the Holy Spirit," 7–68.

4. *Summa theol.* 2-1.3.6 (incomplete prudence), 2-1.40.3 ad1 (premonition).

5. For divine *instinctus* (or "of God"), see *Summa theol.* 2-1.68.1 corp and ad2-4, 68.2 corp, 103.1 corp; 2-2.67.1 ad1, 97.2 ad3, and 171.5 corp.

6. For the *instinctus gratiae*, *Summa theol.* 2-1.108.1 corp and ad2, 3.69.5 corp. For prophetic *instinctus*, 2-2.87.1 ad3, 171.5 corp (the lowest in genus of prophecy), 173.4 corp, and 174.3 corp.

7. *Summa theol.* 2-1.68.2 corp and ad2-3, 68.3 corp, 68.4 corp, 68.5 ad1; 2-2.19.12 corp, 83.13 ad1, 122.4 corp, 147.5 ad3, 185.2 ad3; 3.25.3 ad4, 29.1 ad1, 36.5 corp and ad2.

8. The analogy to the moral virtue is announced in 2-1.68.3 corp, then repeated in 68.4 corp, 68.5 corp, 68.7 corp (as enthymeme), and 68.8 corp (by juxtaposition).

9. The template appears clearly in the juxtaposition of the questions on *intellectus*, *scientia*, and *sapientia* (2-2.8 and 9 and 45). The most common topics are: Is it a gift? Is it speculative or practical? How is it related to the beatitudes or the fruits? (The first and last of these are the basic topics, appearing in the discussions of every gift.) The next most common topics concern the relation of the gift to grace, which is often raised as an issue of how widely distributed it is. The greatest deviation from the template is seen in the question on *timor*, which requires a complex division of kinds of fear.

10. Here it is interesting to recall Thomas's reiterated arguments about the appropriateness of God's revealing truths that could also be known by philosophy. Right at the beginning of the *Summa*, for example, Thomas argues that God reveals philosophical conclusions because even though some human beings might reach them by reason alone, they do so only after a long time and with an admixture of error. That is not enough assurance for salvation. If human beings are to reach God "more appropriately and certainly," they need revelation even of philosophical conclusions (1.1.1 corp). Thomas reiterates the argument near the beginning of the *secunda secundae*, enumerating the deficiencies of acquired *scientia*—the last of which is its lack of certainty (2-2.2.4 corp). For other iterations of the argument, see *Super Boet. De Trin.* q.3 art.1 corp, *De verit.* q.14 art.10 corp, *Contra gent.* lib.1 cap.4.

11. Thomas *Summa theol.* 2-1.23.4 corp (*inclinatio, aptitudo*), 2-1.27.1 corp (*complacentia*), 2-1.32.3 ad3 (*unio*), 2-1.27.4 corp (*coaptatio*).

12. The reference is to Ps-Dionysius, *Divine Names* 2.9 (PG 3:648).

13. Compare the schema in *Summa theol.* 1.64.1, where the gift of wisdom is identified strictly as an affective cognition of truth producing the love of God.

14. Thomas *Summa theol.* 2-1.68.5 ad1, 2-2.9.1 ad2, 2-2.45.5 corp and ad1.

15. Compare Thomas *Scriptum Sent.* lib.1 pro q.1 art.3 qc.1. The text from *Metaphysics* 2.1 is identical. There are different passages from James (2:26, 1:22), but they express exactly the same idea. For the *Summa*'s use of James 1:22, recall Albert's commentary on the *Sentences* lib.1 dist.1 A:pro art.4 sc4, quoting James 1:25 (Borgnet 25:18).

16. Thomas rephrases this conclusion in *Summa* 1.1.5 corp as "*ad aliquid speculativa, ad aliquid practica.*" Compare his *Scriptum Sent.* lib.1 pro q.1 art.3 qc.1 corp, "*quantum ad quid practica est et etiam speculativa.*"

17. Compare *Scriptum Sent.* lib.1 pro q.1 art.3 qc.1 sc.2, though there the argument refers to "*Angelos et alias creaturas, quae non sunt ab opere nostro.*"

18. I agree with Kluxen that Thomas faults his predecessors for a misunderstanding of the practical but disagree on how that misunderstanding affects the substance of the positions. See Kluxen, "Metaphysik und praktische Vernunft," 83.

19. Boethius *In Isagogem Porphyrii commentorum editio primo* lib.1 cap.3 (Brandt 8 lines 1–2, 9 lines 13–32); Cassiodorus *Institutiones* lib.2 cap.3 n.7 (Mynors 112 lines 1–6); Isidore *Etymologiae* lib.2 cap.4 n.16 (Lindsay lines 3–8).

20. Hugh of St.-Victor *Didascalicon* lib.1 cap.5 (Buttimer 12); compare lib.1 cap.11 (Buttimer 22 line 8), lib.2 cap.1 (24 lines 22–24), lib.3 cap.1 (48 line 7).

21. Dominicus Gundissalinus *De divisione philosophiae* prol. (Fidora and Werner 52–86, especially 64–70).

22. Constantinus Africanus *Pantegni theor.* lib.1 cap.1 (Basel 4), but compare the prologue in Erfurt Amplon. MS Q184 f.1r, as in Schum, *Exempla codicum Amplonianorum*, 6 and plate 9; Avicenna *Canon* lib.1 fen.1 doct.1 (Venice [1507] f. 1ra).

23. Cassian *Conlationes* conl.14 cap.2 (Petschenig 399 lines 4–8).

24. For the discussion of practical and theoretical in such commentaries, see Wieland, *Ethica—Scientia practica*, 105–118.

25. Thomas *Sent. Eth.* lib.1 lect.2.

26. Thomas *Sent. Eth.* lib.1 lect.2.

27. Ibid.

28. Ibid.

29. For examples of these earlier texts on the Lombard, Hugh of St. Cher's *Scriptum super Sententias* (Stegmüller 1:43–46) and an anonymous abridgment of it (Stegmüller 1:104); Roland of Cremona, as in Sileo, *Teoria della scienza*, 69. Sileo provides many more illustrative texts.

30. See as examples Odo *Quaest. theol.* (Sileo 2:51, lines 42–51); Albert the Great *Sent.* lib.1 dist.1A art.4-5 (Borgnet 25:18–20); Bonaventure *In Sent.* lib.1 prol q.3 (CSB 1:12).

31. Peter Lombard *Sententiae* lib.3 dist.34 cap.4; John Damascene *De fide orthodoxa* cap.29 (Buytaert 121–122).

32. In 2-2.52.1 ad1, Thomas interchanges *prudentia* and *eubulia*. This abbreviates a number of earlier arguments. At 1-2.57.6, Thomas had introduced *eubulia* as the good or right counsel that is a necessary part of prudence. In 2-2.51.1-2, he had argued that *eubulia* is indeed a virtue and one closely ordered to prudence, even if distinct from it. Compare *Sent. Eth.* lib.6 lect.8.

10. VOCATIONS AND *VIAE*

1. The phrase is repeated across these questions. See *Summa theol.*
2-2.171.1 corp, 171.3 corp, 172.5 corp, 173.1 corp, 174.5 corp.

2. As a reader should expect, there are striking analogies between prophecy and theology, which is compared to a science subalternated to the vision of the blessed (1.1.2 corp).

3. Cicero *De oratore* 2.115 (*probare, conciliare, movere*), with 2.128 (*conciliare, docere, concitare*); compare Augustine *De doctrina Christiana* lib.4 cap.12 n.27 (Green 228, no. 74). The same triplet is recalled through Augustine at *Contra impugn.* pars 3 cap.5 corp, where it is applied to the task of the churchly teacher.

4. Thomas *Summa theol.* 2-2.180.1 sc, from Gregory the Great *Homiliae in Hiezechihelem* lib.2 hom.2 (Adriaen line 191).

CONCLUSION: THE GOOD OF READING

1. So de Lubac remembers an anniversary speech by Bouillard. See Lubac, *Mémoire*, 29.

2. Bouillard, *Grace et conversion*, 16 (fidelity), 211 (linked to time), 219 (permanence of divine truth).

WORKS BY THOMAS AQUINAS

There is no single best edition for the works of Thomas Aquinas. What is worse, no edition has ever succeeded in imposing a standardized system of citation (like the Stephanus numbers for Plato or the Bekker numbers for Aristotle). Once finished, the edition of the complete works commissioned by Pope Leo XIII, the "Leonine" *Opera omnia* (Rome and then elsewhere, 1882–), will be a superb and comprehensive text. Yet the Leonine is likely to remain unfinished for a long time and in at least two senses. First, not all of Thomas's works have been edited for the series. Second, those work published before 1950 already need to be revised.

The best "edition" of the complete works now available is the one maintained online as the Corpus Thomisticum at corpusthomisticum.org. The Corpus had its origin in the machine-readable texts that Roberto Busa prepared for his computer-generated lexical analysis and concordance, the *Index Thomisticus* (Stuttgart, 1974–). Busa used in each case what he regarded as the best available edition, including a number of Leonine texts. For the Corpus Thomisticum, Enrique Alarcón reviewed Busa's texts and in some cases improved on them. So while the texts of the Corpus Thomisticum are obviously not in themselves critical editions, they do report the results of a number of such editions. They do so in readily accessible form and with precise textual divisions. Indeed, it is worth remembering that before Alarcón and his colleagues made these texts available online, most readers interested in Thomas's Latin consulted it in a ragtag collection of different editions, especially those published by the Turin house of Marietti throughout the twentieth century. The Marietti editions often reproduce texts taken from earlier printed versions of Thomas, the "vulgate Thomas." The vulgate versions were also used for editions of the *opera omnia* published in Parma by Fiaccadori (1852–73) and in Paris by Vivès (1871–80).

I cite Thomas's works by their medieval textual divisions as they appear in the Corpus Thomisticum. Most of my citations are to Thomas's

Summa. In that work, the textual divisions are both fixed and minute, so I am able to cite them parenthetically. I typically give the number of the part, the question, the article, and the textual unit within the article, using the following abbreviations:

2-1	*prima secundae* (first part of the second Part)
2-2	*secunda secundae* (second part of the second Part)
ad	reply to a (numbered) *argumentum*
arg	*argumentum* (usually "objection" in English)
corp	*corpus* (body) or *responsio* (response) of an article
pro	*proemium* or *prologus*, preface or prologue
sc	*sed contra*

So, for example, "2-2.4.5 arg3" refers to *Summa theologiae*, *secunda secundae*, question 4 article 5 "objection" 3.

Citations are a bit more complicated for Thomas's other works. In them, the medieval textual divisions can be more cumbersome. Since the kinds of textual division vary from work to work, it is easy for a reader to lose track of what the strings of numbers mean. To avoid confusion, I label the kind of textual division using the abbreviations already listed and some others:

art	*articulus*, "article"
cap	*capitulum*, "chapter"
lect	*lectio*, "reading," a standard excerpt in a text being commented
lib	*liber*, "book," typically the largest textual division
n	number, a section division inserted by a modern editor
q	*quaestio*, "question"
qc	*quaestiuncula*, "little question," usually a subsection of an article

Since textual divisions can sometimes vary from edition to edition, it is important to remember that I follow those in the Corpus Thomisticum. I also follow this system of expanded citation for other medieval works and for early Christian works on which Thomas relies. I revert to the more compact system of decimal notation for classical works.

I give below my abbreviations for all of the works of Thomas that I cite. Each abbreviation is followed by the work's title just as it appears in Gilles Emery's summary catalogue (in Torrell, *Initiation*, 483–525). There are sometimes small differences between the title in Emery's catalogue and the one on the main list of works in the Corpus Thomisticum. The Corpus also sometimes disagrees with itself about the exact title for a given work.

For the most important texts, or for texts that do not appear in the Corpus, I also list below the critical edition I have consulted when it was necessary to consider variant readings or to investigate more precisely Thomas's sources.

Individual Works by Thomas Aquinas

Beata gens = *Sermo in festo omnium Sanctorum "Beata gens . . . ." Multis modis sancta mater Ecclesia . . .* I follow the text in the Leonine *Opera omnia* 44/1 (2014).

Beati qui habitant = *Sermo de omnibus Sanctis "Beati qui habitant . . . " Unam esse societatem Dei . . . .* I follow the text in the Leonine *Opera omnia* 44/1 (2014).

Catena = *Glossa continua super Evangelia (Catena aurea)*

Compend. theol. = *Compendium theologiae seu brevis compilatio theologiae ad fratrum Raynaldum*

Contra err. Graec. = *Contra errores Graecorum*

Contra gent. = *Summa contra Gentiles.* Critical edition: *Liber de veritate catholicae Fidei contra errores infidelium seu Summa contra Gentiles*, vols. 2–3, ed. P. Marc, C. Pera, P. Caramello (Turin and Rome: Marietti, 1961).

Contra impugn. = *Contra impugnantes Dei cultum et religionem*

Contra retrah. = *Contra retrahentes*

De art. fid. = *De articulis fidei et ecclesiae sacramentis ad archiepiscopum Panormitanum*

De malo = *Quaestiones disputatae De malo*

De potentia = *Quaestiones disputatae De potentia*

De rat. fidei = *De rationibus fidei ad Cantorem Antiochenum*

De reg. = *De regno ad regem Cypri*

De spir. creat. = *Quaestiones disputatae De spiritualibus creaturis*

De verit. = *Quaestiones disputatae de ueritate*

De virt. = *Quaestiones disputatae De virtutibus*

Ecce rex tuus = *Sermo in prima dominica adventus dominis "Ecce rex tuus . . ." Multa sunt mirabilia.* I follow the text in the Leonine *Opera omnia* 44/1 (2014).

Expos. Pery. = *Expositio Libri Peryermenias*

In orat. dom. = *In orationem dominicam*

In symb. apost. = *In Symbolum Apostolorum*

Lect. Sent. = *Lectura super libros Sententiarum.* This text is not in the Corpus Thomisticum. I follow the critical edition: *Lectura romana in primum Sententiarum Petri Lombardi*, ed. Leonard E. Boyle and John F. Boyle (Toronto: PIMS, 2006).

Princ. "Rigans" = *Principium "Rigans montes . . ." (recensio vulgata)*

Quol. = *Quaestiones de quolibet*

Scriptum Sent. = *Scriptum super libros Sententiarum.* Critical editions: for the prologue, A. Oliva, *Les débuts de l'enseignement de Thomas d'Aquin et sa conception de la "Sacra Doctrina": Édition du prologue de son* Commentaire des Sentences *de Pierre Lombard.* (Paris: J. Vrin, 2006), 303–340. For the main body of the text through 4.22, P. Mandonnet and A. Moos, eds., *Scriptum super libros Sententiarum magistri Petri Lombardi episcopi Parisiensis* (Paris: P. Lethielleux, Parisiis, 1929–47).

Sent. De anima = *Sentencia Libri De anima*

Sent. De caelo = *Sententia super librum De caelo et mundo*

Sent. De gen. = *Sententia super libros De generatione et corruptione*

Sent. De sensu = *Sentencia Libri De sensu et sensato*

Sent. Ethic. = *Sententia Libri Ethicorum*

Sent. Metaph. = *Sententia super Metaphysicam*

Sent. Meteor. = *Sententia super Meteora*

Sent. Phys. = *Sententia super Physicam*

Sent. Politic. = *Sententia Libri Politicorum*

Summa theol. = *Summa theologiae.* For both variant readings and sources, I collate the edition in the Leonine *Opera omnia* 4–12 (1888–1906) with *S. Thomae de Aquino Ordinis Praedicatorum Summa Theologiae,* ed. Institut d'Études médiévales d'Ottawa, rev. ed. (Ottawa: Commissio Piana, 1953).

Super Boet. De Trin. = *Super Boetium De Trinitate*

Super De causis = *Super Librum De causis*

Super Dion. De div. nom. = *Super librum Dionysii De divinis nominibus*

Super Epp. Pauli = *Expositio et Lectura super Epistolas Pauli Apostoli*

Super Ier. = *Super Ieremiam*

Super Iob = *Expositio super Iob ad litteram*

Super Is. = *Expositio super Isaiam ad litteram*

Super Ioan. = *Lectura super Ioannem*

Super Matt. = *Lectura super Matthaeum*

Super Ps. = *Postilla super Psalmos*

Super Threnos = *Super Threnos*

Tabula = *Tabula Libri Ethicorum*

OTHER WORKS

Albert the Great. *Commentarii in I–IV Sententiarum.* In his *Opera omnia,* edited by Auguste Borgnet, vols. 25–30. Paris: Vivès, 1890–99.

———. *Super Ethica: Commentum et quaestiones.* Edited by Wilhelm Kübel, in the Cologne *Opera Omnia,* vol. 14 part 1. Munster: Aschendorff, 1987.

"Alexander of Hales." *Summae Theologiae pars quarta.* Venice: Franciscus Franciscius, 1575.

————. *Summa theologica*. Edited by members of the Collegium S. Bonaventurae. Quaracchi: Collegium S. Bonaventurae, 1924–30.

Ambrose. *De officiis ministrorum*. Edited by Maurice Testard as *Saint Ambroise: Les Devoirs*. Paris: "Les Belles Lettres," 1984.

————. *Expositio secundum Lucam*. Edited by Marcus Adriaen. CCSL 14. Turnhout: Brepols, 1957.

Augustine. *Contra Faustum*. Edited by Josephus Zycha. Vienna: F. Tempsky, 1891.

————. *De civitate Dei*. Edited by Bernardus Dombart and Alphonsus Kalb. CCSL 47–48. Turnhout: Brepols, 1955.

————. *De doctrina Christiana*. Edited by R. P. H. Green. Oxford and New York: Clarendon Press, 1995.

————. *De Trinitate*. Edited by W. J. Mountain. CCL 50–50A. Turnhout: Brepols, 1968.

————. *In Iohannis evangelium tractatus CXXIV*. Edited by Radbodus Willems. CCL 36. Turnhout: Brepols, 1954.

————. *Quaestiones ex novo testamento*. Migne PL 35.

Avicenna [Ibn Sina]. *Canon medicinae*. In *Liber Canonis*. Venice, 1507; reprint, Hildesheim: Georg Olms, 1964.

Barth, Karl. *Die Römerbrief (Zweite Fassung) 1922*. Edited by C. van der Kooi and K. Tolstaja. Zurich: Theologischer Verlag, 2010.

Bataillon, L.-J. "Saint Thomas et les Pères: De la *Catena* à la *Tertia Pars*." In *Ordo sapientiae et amoris: Image et message de saint Thomas d'Aquin à travers les récentes études historiques, herméneutiques et doctrinales: Hommage au professeur Jean-Pierre Torrell OP à l'occasion de son 65e anniversaire*, ed. Carlos-Josaphat Pinto de Oliveira, 15–36. Fribourg: Eds. Universitaires, 1993.

Bernard of Clairvaux. *Sermones super Cantica Canticorum*. Edited by Jean Leclercq, Charles H. Talbot, and Henri M. Rochais. Rome: Editiones Cistercienses, 1957–58.

———— (pseudo). *Instructio sacerdotum*. In Migne *PL* 184.

Bloom, Harold. *Map of Misreading*. New York: Oxford University Press, 1975.

Boethius. *In Isagogen Porphyrii commentorum editio primo*. Edited by Samuel Brandt. CSEL 48. Vienna: F. Tempsky, 1906.

————. *Philosophiae consolatio*. Edited by Ludwig Bieler. CCSL 94. Turnhout: Brepols, 1957.

Boland, Vivian. *St. Thomas Aquinas*. Continuum Library of Educational Thought 1. London and New York: Continuum, 2007.

Bonaventure. *Commentaria in quattuor libros Sententiarum*. Edited by members of the Collegium S. Bonaventurae in his *Opera omnia*, vols. 1–4. Quaracchi: Collegium S. Bonaventurae, 1882–89.

Bouillard, Henri. *Conversion et grace chez S. Thomas d'Aquin.* Paris: Aubier/ Montaigne, 1944.

Boyle, John F. "The Twofold Division of St. Thomas's Christology in the Tertia Pars." *Thomist* 60 (1996): 439–447.

Boyle, Leonard E. *Facing History: A Different Thomas Aquinas.* Louvain-la-Neuve: Fédération Internationale des Instituts d'Études Médiévales, 2000.

———. *The Setting of the Summa theologiae of Saint Thomas.* Toronto: PIMS, 1982.

———. "The *Summa confessorum* of John of Freiburg and the Popularization of the Moral Teaching of St. Thomas and of Some of His Contemporaries." In *Saint Thomas Aquinas, 1274–1974: Commemorative Studies,* 2:245–68. Toronto: PIMS, 1974.

Bunyan, John. *Pilgrim's Progress, Grace Abounding, and A Relation of His Imprisonment.* Edited by Edmund Venables. Oxford: Clarendon Press, 1879.

Candler, Peter M. *Theology, Rhetoric, Manuduction, or Reading Scripture Together on the Path to God.* Grand Rapids, Mich.: Wm. B. Eerdmans, 2006.

Cassian. *Conlationes patrum XXIV.* Edited by Michael Petschenig with supplementary material by Gottfried Kreuz. Vienna: Verlag der Österreichischen Akademie der Wissenschaften, 2004.

Cassiodorus. *Institutiones.* Edited by R. A. B. Mynors. Oxford, Clarendon Press, 1961.

Chareire, Isabelle. *Éthique et grace: Contribution à une anthropologie chrétienne.* Paris: Éditions du Cerf, 1998.

Chauvet, Louis-Marie. *Symbol and Sacrament: A Sacramental Reinterpretation of Christian Existence.* Translated by Patrick Madigan and Madeleine Beaumont. Collegeville, Minn.: Liturgical Press, 1995.

Chenu, Marie-Dominique. *Introduction à l'étude de saint Thomas d'Aquinas.* Montreal: Institut d'études médiévales, 1954.

———. "La plan de la *Somme théologique* de Saint Thomas." *Revue Thomiste* 47 (1939): 93–107.

———. "La théologie au XIIIe siècle." *AHDLMA* 2 (1927): 31–72.

———. *La théologie comme science au XIIIe siècle.* 3d ed., Paris: J. Vrin, 1953.

———. "Les 'Philosophes' dans la philosophie chrétienne médiévale," *Revue des sciences philosophiques et théologiques* 26 (1937): 27–40.

Cicero. *De officiis.* Edited by Michael Winterbottom. Oxford: Clarendon Press, 1994.

———. *De oratore.* Edited by Kazimierz F. Kumaniecki. Stuttgart: B. G. Teubner, 1969.

Colombo, Giuseppe. "Il desiderio di vedere Dio: Dieci anni di studi tomisti: 1957–1967." *Scuola cattolica* 99: *Supplemento bibliografico* (1971): 3–60.

———. "Il problema del sopranaturale negli ultimi cinquant'anni." In *Problemi e orientamenti di teologia dommatica*, 2:545–607. Milan: C. Marzorati, 1957.

Constantinus Africanus. *Pantegni theorica.* Text as in Erfurt, Wissenschatliche Bibliothek der Stadt, MS Amplon. Q. 184.

Crowe, Michael Bertram. *The Changing Profile of the Natural Law.* The Hague: M. Nijhoff, 1977.

D'Avray, D. L. *The Preaching of the Friars: Sermons Diffused from Paris before 1300.* Oxford: Clarendon Press, 1985.

———. "Sermons to the Upper Bourgeoisie by a Thirteenth-Century Franciscan." In *The Church in Town and Countryside*, edited by Derek Baker, 187–199. Oxford: Published for the Ecclesiastical History Society by B. Blackwell, 1979.

Deman, T. "Le 'Liber de Bona Fortuna' dans la théologie de S. Thomas d'Aquin." *Revue des sciences philosophiques et théologiques* 17 (1928): 38–58.

Dominicus Gundissalinus. *De divisione philosophiae = Über die Einteilung der Philosophie: Lateinisch—Deutsch.* Edited by Alexander Fidora and Dorothee Werner. Freiburg and Basel: Herder, 2007.

Emery, Gilles. "Bref catalogue des oeuvres de saint Thomas." In Torrell, *Initiation*, 483–525 (see under Torrell).

Emery, Kent, Jr. "Reading the World Rightly and Squarely: Bonaventure's Doctrine of the Cardinal Virtues." *Traditio* 39 (1983): 183–218.

Enfield, William. *The History of Philosophy, from the Earliest Times to the Beginning of the Present Century; Drawn up from Brucker Historia Critica Philosophiae.* London: printed for J. Johnson, 1791.

Foucault, Michel. *L'herméneutique du sujet: Cours au Collège de France, 1981–1982.* Edited by Frédéric Gros under the direction of François Ewald and Alessandro Fontana. Paris: Gallimard/Seuil, 2001.

———. *Les mots et les choses.* Paris: Gallimard, 1966.

Gauthier, R. A. "Saint Maxime le Confesseur et la psychologie de l'acte humain." *Recherces de théologie ancienne et médiévale* 21 (1954): 51–100.

Gilson, Etienne. "Sur la problématique thomiste de la vision béatifique." In his *Autour de saint Thomas*, 59–88. Preface by Jean-François Courtine. Paris: J. Vrin, 1983. The essay was originally published in *AHDMLA* 31 (1964): 67–88.

Gilson, Etienne, and Henri de Lubac. *Lettres de M. Etienne Gilson addresées au P. Henri de Lubac et commentées par celui-ci.* Paris: Éditions du Cerf, 1986.

Grabmann, Martin. "De summae divi Thomae Aquinatis theologicae studio in Ordine fratrum Praedicatorum iam saec. XIII et XIV vigente." In *Miscellanea Dominicana in memoriam VII anni saecularis ab obitu S. Patris Dominici (1221–1921)*, 151–161. Rome: F. Ferrari, 1923.

————. *Die Geschichte der Scholastischen Methode*. Freiburg: Herder, 1909–11.

Gratian. *Decretum, sive Concordantia discordantium canonum*. In *Corpus Juris Canonici*. Edited by E. L. Richter and E. Friedberg. Leipzig: B. Tauchnitz, 1879–81.

Gregory the Great. *Homiliae in Hiezechihelem prophetam*. Edited by Marc Adriaen. CCSL 142. Turnhout: Brepols, 1971.

————. *Moralia in Job*. Edited by Marc Adriaen. CCSL 143–143B. Turnhout: Brepols, 1979–85.

Gy, Pierre-Marie. "La documentation sacramentaire de Thomas d'Aquin: Quelle connaissance S. Thomas a-t-il de la tradition ancienne et de la patristique?" *Revue des sciences philosophiques et théologiques* 80 (1996): 425–431.

Hadot, Pierre. *Exercises spirituels et philosophie antique*. Preface by Arnold I. Davidson. Revised edition. Paris: Albin Michel, 2002.

Hauréau, Barthélemy. *Histoire de la philosophie scolastique*. Paris: Durand et Pedone-Lauriel, 1872.

Herz, Martin F. *Sacrum commercium: Eine begriffsgeschichtliche Studie zur Theologie der Römischen Liturgiesprache*. Munich: K. Zink, 1958.

Hugh of St. Cher. *Scriptum super Sententias*. Edited by Friedrich Stegmüller. *Analecta Upsaliensia*. Lund: Lundequistska bokhandeln, 1953.

Hugh of St. Victor. *Didascalicon de studio legendi*. Edited by Charles Henry Buttimer. Washington, D.C.: Catholic University Press, 1939.

Hütter, Reinhold. *Dust Bound for Heaven: Explorations in the Theology of Thomas Aquinas*. Grand Rapids, Mich.: Wm. B. Eerdmans, 2012.

Innocent III (pseudo). Sermon. In Migne *PL* 217.

Isidore. *Etymologiae*. Edited by W. M. Lindsay. Oxford: Clarendon Press, 1911.

John of Damascus. *De fide orthodoxa: Versions of Burgundio and Cerbanus*. Edited by Eligius M. Buytaert. St. Bonaventure, N.Y.: Franciscan Institute, 1955.

Johnstone, Brian. "The Debate on the Structure of the *Summa Theologiae*." In *Aquinas as Authority*, ed. Paul van Geerst, Harm Goris, and Carlo Leget, 187–200. Leuven: Peters, 2002.

Jordan, Mark D. "Cicero, Ambrose, and Aquinas 'on Duties' or The Limits of Genre in Morals." *Journal of Religious Ethics* 33, no. 3 (2005): 485–502.

————. "Democratic Moral Education and the Gifts of the Holy Spirit." *Journal of Religious Ethics* 44, no. 2 (2016): 246–259.

————. "Missing Scenes." *Harvard Divinity Bulletin* 38, nos. 3–4 (Summer/Autumn 2010): 58–67.

————. *Rewritten Theology: Aquinas after His Readers*. Oxford: Blackwell, 2006.

———. "Sacramental Characters." *Studies in Christian Ethics* 19, no. 3 (2006): 323–338.

———. "Structure." In *Cambridge Companion to the* Summa theologiae *of Thomas Aquinas*, edited by Philip McCosker and Denys Turner, 34–47. Cambridge: Cambridge University Press, 2016.

———. "Thomas Aquinas, Sacramental Scenes, and the 'Aesthetics' of Incarnation." In *Image and Incarnation: The Early Modern Doctrine of the Pictorial Image*, edited by Walter Melion and Lee Palmer Wandel, 161–172. Leiden: E. J. Brill, 2015.

Justinian. *Institutiones*. Edited by Paul Krüger. In *Corpus iuris civilis*, vol. 1. Berlin: Weidmann, 1893.

Kaeppeli, Thomas. "B. Iordani de Saxonia litterae encyclicae (1233)." *Archivum Fratrum Praedicatorum* 22 (1952): 177–185

———. *Scriptores ordinis praedicatorum medii aevi*. Rome: S. Sabina, 1970–93.

———. "Una raccolta di prediche attribuite a S. Tommaso d'Aquino," *Archivum Fratrum Praedicatorum* 13 (1943): 72–94.

Kennedy, Leonard A. *A Catalogue of Thomists, 1270–1900*. Houston: Center for Thomistic Studies/University of St. Thomas, 1987.

Klein, Jacob, and Leo Strauss. "A Giving of Accounts." *The College* [St. John's College, Annapolis and Santa Fe] 22, no. 1 (April 1970): 1–5.

Kluxen, Wolfgang. "Metaphysik und praktische Vernunft." In L. Oeing-Hanhoff, ed., *Thomas von Aquin 1274/1974*, 73–96. Munich: Koösel, 1974.

Lacordaire, Henri-Dominique. *Mémoire pour le rétablissement en France de l'ordre des frères prêcheurs*. Paris: Debécourt, 1839.

Langevin, Gilles. *"Capax Dei": La créature intellectuelle et l'intimité de Dieu*. Bruges and Paris: Desclée de Brouwer, 1966.

Laporta, Jorge. *La destinée de la nature humaine selon Thomas d'Aquin*. Paris: J. Vrin, 1965.

Lawn, Brian. *The Rise and Decline of the Scholastic 'Quaestio Disputata,' with Special Emphasis on Its Uses in the Teaching of Medicine and Science*. Leiden and New York: E. J. Brill, 1993.

Leo XIII. Encyclical letter *Aeterni patris* [August 4, 1879]. *Acta Sanctae Sedis* vol. 12, edited by Iosephus Pennachi and Victorius Piazzesi, 97–115. Rome: Typographia Polyglotta, 1894. The paragraph numbering, not found in the original, is taken from the online version at the Vatican's website.

Levering, Matthew W. *Christ's Fulfillment of Torah and Temple: Salvation According to Thomas Aquinas*. Notre Dame: University of Notre Dame Press, 2002.

Liberatore, Matteo. *Istituzioni di etica e diritto naturale*. Rome: Ufficio della Civiltá cattolica, 1865.

Lonergan, Bernard J. F. Letter of May 11, 1973, to Mark D. Jordan.

———. *Method in Theology*. London: Darton, Longman, and Todd, 1973.

———. Review of E. Iglesias, *De Deo in operatione naturae vel voluntatis operante. Theological Studies* 7 (1946): 602–613.

———. *Verbum: Word and Idea in Aquinas*. Edited by David B. Burrell. Notre Dame, Indiana: University of Notre Dame Press, 1967.

Lottin, Odon. "Les dons du Saint-Esprit chez les théologiens depuis Pierre Lombard jusqu'au saint Thomas d'Aquin." *Recherches de théologie ancienne et médiévale* 1 (1929): 41–61.

Lubac, Henri de. *Exégèse médiévale: les quatres sens de l'écriture*. Paris: Aubier, 1959–64.

———. *Mémoire sur l'occasion de mes écrits*. Namur: Culture et vérité, 1992.

———. *Surnaturel: Études historiques*. Paris: Aubier, 1946.

Manser, Gallus. *Das Naturrecht in thomistischer Beleuchtung*. Fribourg: Paulusdruckerei, 1944.

McGinn, Bernard. *Thomas Aquinas's Summa theologiae: A Biography*. Princeton: Princeton University Press, 2014.

Merriell, D. Juvenal. *To the Image of the Trinity: A Study in the Development of Aquinas' Teaching*. Toronto: PIMS, 1990.

Mulchahey, M. Michèle. *"First the Bow is Bent in Study . . .": Dominican Education before 1350*. Toronto: PIMS, 1998.

Oliva, Adriano. "Quelques éléments de la *doctrina theologiae* selon Thomas d'Aquin." In *What Is "Theology" in the Middle Ages?* ed. Mikolaj Olszewski, 167–193. Munster: Aschendorff, 2007.

O'Meara, Thomas Franklin. *Thomas Aquinas Theologian*. Notre Dame and London: University of Notre Dame Press, 1997.

Pasnau, Robert. *Thomas Aquinas on Human Nature: A Philosophical Study of Summa theologiae Ia 75–89*. Cambridge: Cambridge University Press, 2002.

Peter Lombard. *Commentarius in Psalmos*. In Migne *PL* 191.

———. *Sententiae in IV libris distinctae*. 3rd ed., Grottaferrata: CSB, 1971–81.

Pieper, Josef. *Philosophia negativa: Zwei Versuche über Thomas von Aquin*. Munich: Kösel-Verlag, 1953.

Pinckaers, Servais. "La structure de l'acte humain suivant saint Thomas." *Revue thomiste* 55 (1955): 393–412.

Preller, Victor. "Water into Wine." In *Grammar and Grace: Reformulations of Aquinas and Wittgenstein*, edited by Jeffrey Stout and Robert MacSwain, 253–267. London: SCM Press, 2004.

Prümmer, Dominicus M. *Fontes vitae S. Thomae Aquinatis notis historicis et criticis illustrati*. Toulouse: Privat, Bibliopolam, 1911.

Quintilian. *Institutio oratoria*. Edited by Ludwig Radermacher and revised by Vinzenz Buchheit. Leipzig: Teubner, 1971.

Raymund of Peñafort. *Summa de casibus*. From his *Summa . . . de poenitentia, et matrimonio, cum glossis*. Rome, 1603. Reprinted Farnborough: Gregg Press, 1967.

———. *Summa iuris*. Edited by José Rius Serra in Raymund. *Opera omnia*, vol. 1. Barcelona: Universidad de Barcelona, Facultad de Derecho, 1945.

Redmond, Walter Bernard. *Bibliography of the Philosophy in the Iberian Colonies of America*. The Hague: M. Nijhoff, 1972.

Rivers, Kimberly A. *Preaching the Memory of Virtue and Vice: Memory, Images, and Preaching in the Late Middle Ages*. Turnhout: Brepols 2010.

Ryan, Fáinche. *Formation in Holiness: Thomas Aquinas on Sacra doctrina*. Leuven and Dudley, Mass.: Peeters, 2007.

Schum, Wilhelm. *Exempla codicum Amplonianorum Erfurtensium saeculi IX–XV*. Berlin: Weidmann, 1882.

Sileo, Leonardo. *Teoria della scienza teologica: Quaestio de scientia theologiae di Odo Rigaldi e altri testi inediti (1230–1250)*. Rome: Pontificium Athenaeum Antonianum, 1984.

Stroud, James W. "Thomas Aquinas' Exposition of the Gifts of the Holy Spirit: Developments in His Thought and Rival Interpretations." Ph.D. dissertation, Catholic University of America, 2012.

Suárez, Francisco. *De legibus (II 1–2): De lege naturali*. Edited by Luciano Pereña, V. Abril, *et al*. Corpus Hispanorum de Pace 13. Madrid: CSIC / Instituto Francisco de Vitoria, 1974.

Tanizaki, Junichiro. *In Praise of Shadows*. Translated by Thomas J. Harper and Edward C. Seidensticker. Sedgwick, Me.: Leete's Island Press, 1977.

Thomas, Antoninus Hendrik. *De oudste constituties van de Dominicanen: Voorgeschiedenis, tekst, bronne, onstaan en ontwikkeling (1215–1217)*. Bibliothèque de la Revue d'histoire Ecclésiastique vol. 42. Leuven: Universiteitsbibliotheek/Universitaire Uitgaven, 1965.

Torrell, Jean-Pierre. *Aquinas's Summa: Background, Structure, and Reception*. Translated by Benedict M. Guevin. Washington, D.C.: Catholic University of America Press, 2005.

———. *Initiation à saint Thomas d'Aquin: Sa personne at son œuvre*. Paris: Cerf and Fribourg: Éditions Universitaires de Fribourg, 1993.

Tugwell, Simon, ed. *Early Dominicans: Selected Writings*. New York, Ramsey; Toronto: Paulist Press, 1982.

Velde, Rudi A. te. *Aquinas on God: The 'Divine Science' of the Summa Theologiae*. Aldershot and Burlington: Ashgate, 2006.

Vitoria, Francisco de. *Relectio de indis, o libertad de los indios*. Edited by Luciano Pereña and José Manuel Pérez Prendes. Corpus Hispanorum de Pace 5. Madrid: CSIC, 1967.

Walz, Angelus. "De genuino titulo *Summae theologiae*." *Angelicum* 18 (1941): 142–151.

Wieland, Georg. *Ethica, scientia practica: Die Anfänge der philosophischen Ethik im 13. Jahrhundert*. Munster: Aschendorff, 1981.

William of Auvergne. *Sermones de tempore*. Edited by Franco Morenzoni. Corpus Christianorum Continuatio Mediaevalis 230A. Turnhout: Brepols, 2011.

William of Tocco. *Historia S. Thomae de Aquino*. In *Ystoria sancti Thome de Aquino de Guillaume de Tocco (1323)*, edited by Claire Le Brun-Gouanvic. Toronto: PIMS, 1996.

Wulf, Maurice de. *Histoire de la philosophie médiévale précédée d'un aperçu sur la philosophie ancienne*. Louvain: Institut supérieur de Philosophie; Paris: Félix Alcan; Brussells: Oscar Schepens, 1900.

———. *Introduction à la philosophie néo-scolastique*. Louvain: Institut supérieur de Philosophie, and Paris: Félix Alcan, 1904.

Wyser, Paul. *Der Thomismus*. Berne: A. Francke, 1951.

Yates, Frances. *The Art of Memory*. Chicago: University of Chicago Press, 1966.

CPSIA information can be obtained
at www.ICGtesting.com
Printed in the USA
JSHW051951200122
22135JS00002B/151